FLYBY

THE INTERPLANETARY ODYSSEY OF VOYAGER 2

Books by JOEL DAVIS

FLYBY: The Interplanetary Odyssey
of Voyager 2   1987
ENDORPHINS: New Waves in
Brain Chemistry   1984

FLYBY

THE INTERPLANETARY ODYSSEY OF VOYAGER 2

JOEL DAVIS

ATHENEUM

NEW YORK

1987

Uranus and Miranda composite on front jacket
(*Photograph courtesy of NASA/JPL*)

Excerpts from *Rings: Discoveries from Galileo to Voyager* by James Elliot and Richard Kerr, published by the Massachusetts Institute of Technology, copyright © 1984 by the Massachusetts Institute of Technology, are used with permission.

Davis, Joel, ———
Flyby : the interplanetary odyssey of Voyager 2.
1. Project Voyager. I. Title.
TL789.8.U6V52463 1987   919.9′204   86-47944
ISBN 0-689-11657-8

Published simultaneously in Canada by
Collier Macmillan Canada, Inc.
Composition by Maryland Linotype Composition Company,
Baltimore, Maryland
Manufactured by Haddon Craftsmen, Scranton, Pennsylvania
Designed by Cathryn S. Aison

FIRST EDITION

This one is for my grandmother, Augusta Farkas,
who saw it all from the Wright Brothers on;
and for Dr. Charles Stembridge,
who didn't quite make it,
but still had the best seat of all.

ACKNOWLEDGMENTS

This is the part of the book that most readers skip. It just seems so boring to read a long list of names. However I humbly request that readers do take the few minutes needed to read these acknowledgments. For I owe many men and women a debt that I will never be able to fully repay; it is simply impossible to write a book of this kind without the help of hundreds of other people. There is no room here to acknowledge all of them, and I hope that those not mentioned, either here or in the text, will understand that I've not forgotten their kindness and assistance. However, I would like to single out some by name:

On Project Voyager: first, my thanks to Project Manager Richard P. Laeser, Mission Planning Office Manager Charles Kohlhase, Flight Engineering Office Manager Bill McLaughlin, assistant project scientist Ellis Miner, and Peter Doms, chief of the Science Investigations Support team, for taking time to read and comment on early drafts of different chapters. Any errors of fact are mine, not theirs. Also: Dave Bliss, Robert

Brooks, Jr., Robert Hamilton Brown, Anne Bunker, Robert Cesarone, Mick Connolly, Pieter de Vries, Dan Finnerty, Doug Griffith, Rudy Hanel, Candice Hansen, Anne Harch, Linda Horn, Torrence Johnson, Arthur L. Lane, Sue Linick, Howard Marderness, Ray Morris, Bob Nelson, Bob Poynter, Paul Schulte, Brad Smith, Larry Soderblom, Rich Springer, Edward Stone, Len Tyler, Brad Wallis, Jim Warwick, Randii Wessen, Donna Wolff, Susan Yewell, and Carolyn Young.

Also, at the Jet Propulsion Laboratory: Dr. Lew Allen, Director; Mr. Frank Collela, Manager, JPL Public Affairs; Mr. Frank Bristow, Manager, Public Information; Allan Wood, PIO Senior Representative; and Public Information Specialists Mary Beth Murrill, Henry Fuhrmann, and Frank O'Donnell.

This book took a year to research and write, and it involved many months spent away from home and friends. For various help and kindnesses I thank Father Kerry Beaulieu; my parents, Gerald and Toni Davis; Judy Flinders; my agent, Russell Galen; Sister Patricia Glen, SP; Father Jim Jorgenson; Andy and Carolyn Lanyi; the librarians at the Washington State Library, Olympia, and the Astronomy/Physics Library at the University of Washington, Seattle; Sister Mary Giles Mailhot, OSB; Sister Mary Ruth, IHM; the parish of St. Bede's Catholic Church in La Canada; the community of St. Michael's Catholic Church in Olympia; and Joy Yancey.

And then there's Marie . . . who gamely put up with my frequent absences, bad moods, and compulsive writing sprees, drove me to and from the airport more times than was humanly acceptable, and read every word of every draft of this book. Greater love hath no woman.

Finally, thanks to the One who makes it all real.

—Joel Davis
Olympia, Washington,
January 24, 1987

CONTENTS

Introduction THE GOOD DEED OF VOYAGER 2
by *Isaac Asimov* xiii
Chapter 1 BEFORE VOYAGER 3
Chapter 2 THE PERILS OF VOYAGER 2 30
Chapter 3 NEW WORLDS 52
Chapter 4 THE "QUIET CRUISE" 83
Chapter 5 THE PERILS OF MARK IV-A 105
Chapter 6 CLOSING IN 128
Chapter 7 FAR ENCOUNTER 148
Chapter 8 FLYBY 176
Chapter 9 ENDINGS AND RETURNS 207

ILLUSTRATIONS

FOLLOWING PAGE 144

Voyager model *(Photograph courtesy of NASA/JPL)*

Voyager Control Room *(Photograph courtesy of NASA/JPL)*

Principal scientists and managers for the Voyager 2 mission to Uranus *(Photograph courtesy of NASA/JPL)*

Peter Doms and Dan Finnerty *(Photograph by Joel Davis)*

Bill McLaughlin *(Photograph by Joel Davis)*

Bobby Brooks *(Photograph by Joel Davis)*

Candy Hansen *(Photograph by Joel Davis)*

Charles Kohlhase *(Photograph by Joel Davis)*

Saturn on TV monitor *(Photograph by Joel Davis)*

Len Tyler *(Photograph courtesy of NASA/JPL)*

Edward Stone *(Photograph courtesy of NASA/JPL)*

Press room *(Photograph courtesy of NASA/JPL)*

Jupiter's Great Red Spot *(Photograph courtesy of NASA/JPL)*

Io *(Photograph courtesy of NASA/JPL)*

Saturn *(Photograph courtesy of NASA/JPL)*

Saturn's rings *(Photograph courtesy of NASA/JPL)*

Voyager 2's path through the Uranus system
(Computer Graphics courtesy of James Blinn, NASA/JPL)

Uranus *(Photograph courtesy of NASA/JPL)*

Cloud movement on Uranus *(Photograph courtesy of NASA/JPL)*

Uranus's epsilon ring *(Photograph courtesy of NASA/JPL)*

Uranus's ring's *(Photograph courtesy of NASA/JPL)*

Family portrait of Uranus's major moons
(Photograph courtesy of NASA/JPL)

Two shepherd satellites *(Photograph courtesy of NASA/JPL)*

1985U1 *(Photograph courtesy of NASA/JPL)*

Miranda *(Photograph courtesy of NASA/JPL)*

Miranda's Grand Canyon *(Photograph courtesy of NASA/JPL)*

Miranda's chevron *(Photograph courtesy of NASA/JPL)*

Miranda's fault scarp *(Photograph courtesy of NASA/JPL)*

Ariel *(Photograph courtesy of NASA/JPL)*

Umbriel *(Photograph courtesy of NASA/JPL)*

Titania *(Photograph courtesy of NASA/JPL)*

Oberon *(Photograph courtesy of NASA/JPL)*

Goodbye Uranus *(Photograph courtesy of NASA/JPL)*

Voyager 2's Neptune encounter
(Painting courtesy of NASA/JPL)

Introduction
THE GOOD DEED OF VOYAGER 2

by *Isaac Asimov*

Voyager 2 is the most successful unmanned plane-tary probe ever sent out. There have been many others: those that landed on Venus, scanned Mercury, and mapped both planets (the first by radar rather than light); those that mapped Mars in detail, to say nothing of landing on Mars and testing its soil chemically; and those that preceded Voyager 2 in passing through the asteroid belt and beyond in order to sail into the vast void in which the outer planets circle.

None, however, did quite as spectacular a job as Voyager 2. In a flight of nine years, the Voyager 2 probe managed to skim by both Jupiter and Saturn and then move on to Uranus, where it made observations of a giant world so far from Earth that the ancients didn't know it existed. It gleams in the sky just barely brightly enough to be seen as a very dim star.

And Voyager 2 is not yet done. For several years, it will continue to forge through space until it passes Neptune, the farthest major planet we know. (Pluto is farther most of the time, but it is an icy little pipsqueak, smaller than our Moon.)

Its long flight has been full of adventure, of narrow squeaks, of seeming disasters somehow averted or righted. Joel Davis tells the full story, in all its drama and excitement, in the book you are holding.

But Voyager 2 has also done something that no one could possibly have foretold or foreseen.

Let us backtrack. History is full of natural disasters, many of them beyond any possibility of human control. There are endless tales of floods and storms, earthquakes and volcanic eruptions, droughts and pestilence, every one bringing endless suffering. There are human-sponsored disasters, too, such as wars. Those of us who are past middle age can remember World War II, the most disastrous ever fought, and we all dread the possibility of a war that might easily end the human race.

Even those achievements which we can be proudest of take their toll. No great bridge, no great skyscraper, no great tunnel has been built, without a cost in human life. The automobile, which no one would dream of giving up, kills 50,000 people a year in the United States alone. We are inured to deaths in air disasters, in mines, in factories, from chemical poisons and radioactive leakage.

It follows, then, that few of us can really expect the exploration of space to be disaster-free. We *know* it will cost lives, and it has. The United States lost three astronauts on the ground in a space-capsule fire in 1967. The Soviet Union lost three astronauts when a leak developed as they were getting ready to return to the atmosphere.

What makes disasters in space exploration different, however, is that the whole world is watching. In December 1985, a plane crashed in Newfoundland and killed over 250 soldiers. No one watched the crash. The report came after the fact, making it just another news item—like many others. The nation took the blow, shook its head, and, except for the immediate families of those lost, went about its business.

A little over a month later, however, on January 28, 1986, the *Challenger* space shuttle was launched with a crew of seven. In front of millions of eyes, a minute and a half after take-off, it turned into a fireball. Those millions realized they had watched seven lives snuffed out. To make it worse, one of the seven was a teacher, the first "ordinary" person chosen to go into space.

Few tragedies have ever shaken the United States —and, indeed, the world—as much as that *witnessed* disaster. Not even the assassination of an American president jolted so many into a state of shock from which they recovered with such difficulty.

We all know the aftermath for the American space program: the self-flagellation of "What did we do wrong?"; the determination to make everything ten times as safe before we move again; the repeated postponement of everything.

It seems difficult to imagine how the situation could have been worse. But suppose that Voyager 2 had not just passed Uranus at the time. Suppose that the results, spectacular and exciting, weren't coming in.

By the sheerest chance, we had one of the great *successes* of the space program playing before our eyes, just as the *Challenger* disaster struck. Don't get me wrong. Nothing that Voyager 2 could have done, or discovered, could possibly have given us back those seven heroic lives. It couldn't have given us back our lost confidence or made up for the shock and horror of it all.

But Voyager 2 did show us, just when we needed it most, that space exploration can provide success as well as disaster. *That* was the good deed that no one had foreseen. Without the example of Voyager 2, the *Challenger* disaster might have plunged us so incredibly deep into disillusion and depression as to have foreclosed our space effort forever—or at least for so long that we would have left space exploration to the Soviet Union, to western Europe, to Japan.

As it is, Voyager 2 provided just that unexpected push that may make it possible for us to recover in time.

We must realize that all progress toward great goals requires us to overcome the obstacles that inevitably stand in the way. The highways to success have never been smooth. They are paved with heartbreak.

But we must not give up. Disasters will come again, but successes like that of Voyager 2 will also come again.

FLYBY

*THE INTERPLANETARY ODYSSEY OF
VOYAGER 2*

Chapter 1
BEFORE VOYAGER

He was a refugee, music teacher, telescope maker, workaholic, and superstar scientist of the late eighteenth and early nineteenth centuries.

He was Friedrich Wilhelm Herschel, later William Herschel, still later Sir William Herschel.

Though he was not the first person to see the planet Uranus, he was the first person to see it and recognize it as a celestial object not previously known. For that reason he is rightly called the discoverer of the seventh planet in the solar system.

It was a discovery that rocked science.

Herschel delivered the final blow to the universe of the ancient Romans, Greeks, and Babylonians, a universe with five planets, a sun, and a central earth circled by a moon, all surrounded by a celestial sphere dotted with stars. Copernicus, Galileo, Kepler, Newton, and Halley had destroyed most of that worldview. In the "new" solar system, the sun lay at the center of the solar system. Jupiter had four moons of its own. Earth (with its

3

moon) was just one of six planets circling the sun in elliptical paths. Gravity was an invisible force of attraction which held the planets to their paths around the sun. Comets were not strange stars which made solitary journeys past Earth but were inhabitants of the solar system, bound to the sun by gravity. Some of them, such as the comet now called Halley's, sped past Earth on regular paths.

One ancient truth, though, still remained untouched. There were only five planets (not counting Earth) in the cosmos: Mercury, Venus, Mars, Jupiter, and finally Saturn, nearly half a billion kilometers from the sun. In all of human history, no other planet had been discovered.

On the night of March 13, 1781, William Herschel doubled the diameter of the known solar system.

Friedrich Herschel was born in 1738 in Hanover, Germany, son of a gardener turned musician. He followed in his father's footsteps and studied violin and oboe. At some point in his youth he acquired an interest in natural philosophy and the work of Kepler, Leibniz, and Newton. In 1757, Herschel left Germany when French troops occupied Hanover. The Seven Years War had begun in Europe the year before. France and England were in conflict both on the Continent and in the New World across the Atlantic. The young musician departed for England.

London was crawling with musicians, and Herschel, nineteen years old, poor, with Hanover-accented English, knew he had little chance in that metropolitan madhouse. The prospects in the suburbs, though, were somewhat better, and he managed to make a living in the towns northeast of London. He performed in public concerts and private recitals, taught music to middle-class families, composed, and conducted.

The next nine years were not hugely profitable, perhaps, but were comfortable enough. He anglicized his name to William, grew proficient in the language (though he never lost the Hanover accent), and kept very busy. In 1766 he received an intriguing offer. The staff of the Octagon Chapel in Bath wanted him to be their organist. The appointment was something of a coup for Herschel. The Octagon Chapel was a rather fashionable place in a city that had become a popular resort for the *nouveaux riches* of London society. Bath had grown from a dirty provincial town of 2,000 inhabitants in the late 1600s to a flourishing city of 34,000 by the time Herschel settled in. The whole place had been largely rebuilt, excavation of the Roman baths for which the city was named had begun, the theater was popular, and the local citizens went to considerable effort to prove they were no longer country bumpkins.

Bath was a perfect place for Herschel. The city was large enough to provide him steady work as a musician, and his annual income rose accordingly. Within a few years he was making more than £400 a year from his teaching and playing. He was becoming a respected and prosperous gentleman.

Herschel did not live alone. By now his sister Caroline, twelve years younger than he, had joined him in Bath as she pursued a budding career as a singer. Caroline was devoted to her older brother; that devotion would change her life, and the change began to be felt in the early 1770s. William had become fascinated with astronomy.

Herschel the musician had long been interested in the mathematics of harmony. That interest led him to a textbook on the subject of music theory written by Robert Smith with the typically verbose eighteenth-century title *Harmonics, or the Natural Philosophy of Musical Sounds*. When he finished that book he immediately began reading its sequel, *Compleat System of*

5

Opticks in Four Books . . . a Popular, a Mathematical, and a Philosophical Treatise.

Caroline later remarked that her brother was given to sudden enthusiasms, and that when he got involved in something he pursued it with single-minded fervor. William was a healthy man in his early thirties, with great physical stamina. His childhood interest in natural philosophy (what we today would call "general science") and the work of astronomical pioneer Johannes Kepler was reignited. Herschel became captivated by the idea of making telescopes and studying the sky . . . in his spare time, of course.

In 1773 he continued his self-paced instruction in astronomy and mathematics. He read *The Elements of Trigonometry* and bought himself a quadrant, an instrument used by navigators to determine latitude. He bought a copy of James Ferguson's *Astronomy Explained upon Sir Isaac Newton's Principles, and Made Easy to Those Who Have Not Studied Mathematics.* It was his first book on astronomy. Later that year Herschel bought and read Emerson's *The Elements of Optics.* By November of that year he had already examined and rejected several refracting telescopes, which use convex lenses to magnify and focus light from distant objects. Herschel settled on reflecting telescopes as his instrument of choice, learned how to grind telescope mirror blanks and silver them, and set to work building his first telescope.

One wonders where he found time to spare for his now-consuming hobby. In one of his own journals from that time Herschel comments that in one week he gave music lessons to forty people. It was "a typical week," he added offhandedly.

Herschel was a man who did the best he could at whatever task he set himself to, and with his talents he did very well indeed. Before long he was making telescopes superior in magnifying power and clarity to any others being used in England or on the Continent. But no one knew—yet—about this suddenly rising star of astronomy. He was living in Bath, teaching music. Bath wasn't London, and this music teacher was totally unconnected at this point to the rest of the astronomical community.

Herschel didn't mind. He continued teaching music during the day, observing the skies at night, and sleeping the few hours in between. Caroline was pressed into service, more or less willingly, as his assistant. That this spelled the end of any singing career for her seems to have bothered William not a whit. As his sister had remarked, he had a one-track mind when it came to his enthusiasms, and he expected others simply to come along and support him. Music's loss, however, was astronomy's gain. Caroline Herschel went on to move from her brother's shadow and become an eminent astronomer in her own right.

In 1776 the British colonies in the New World were rebelling against England and King George III. Herschel was busy building three new telescopes, all superb instruments of observation. One had a mirror about 15 centimers (6.2 inches) wide and a focal length of 2.1 meters (7 feet); the second had a 23-centimeter (9-inch) mirror and 3-meter (nearly 10-foot) focal length; the third had a 30-centimeter (1-foot) mirror and a 6-meter (nearly 20-foot) focal length.

Two years later Herschel started a long series of experiments in mirror grinding and polishing, hoping to find the best materials and techniques for making telescope mirrors. In November of that year he repolished the mirror of his 2.1-meter-long telescope, using, he wrote, "the divided reducing stroke of the 170th experiment." Herschel was a man of enormous patience and endurance.

It paid off. That reground mirror in his 2.1-meter-long tube was to make possible an extraordinary discovery.

. . .

Tuesday evening, March 13, 1781. It was between 10:00 and 11:00 p.m. Herschel was involved in what he was calling a "second review of the heavens," a systematic search for double stars. He was using the 2.1-meter telescope with its newly reground 15-centimeter mirror and a 227-power eyepiece. He was looking at some stars in the constellation Gemini.

"I perceived one that appeared visibly larger than the rest," Herschel reported a month later in a letter to the Royal Astronomical Society. "Being struck with its uncommon magnitude, I compared it to H. Geminorum and the small star in the quartile between Auriga and Gemini, and finding it much larger than either of them, suspected it to be a comet."

Herschel knew that stars do not increase in diameter when viewed with higher powers of magnification, for they are too far away. Planets and comets, though, did appear larger when viewed with telescopes of higher power. So he took a look at the odd object with eyepieces of 460 and 932 power.

"[I] found the diameter of the comet increased in proportion to the power, as it ought to be," Herschel wrote, "on a supposition of its not being a fixed star, while the diameters of the stars to which I compared it were not increased in the same ratio. Moreover," he added, "the comet being magnified much beyond what its light would admit of, appeared hazy and ill-defined with these great powers. . . ."

Herschel was intrigued by his "comet," and continued to keep an eye on it. The comet got more interesting by the night.

On March 17 he "looked for the Comet or Nebulous Star and found that it is a Comet, for it has changed its place."

From observations on March 19, he reported that "the Comet's apparent motion is at present 2¼ seconds per hour. It moves according to the order of the signs [the twelve constellations which make up the astrological signs] and its orbit declines but very little from the ecliptic. . . .

"April 6. With a magnifying power of 278 times the Comet appeared perfectly sharp upon the edges, and extremely well defined, without the least appearance of any beard or tail."

A most unusual comet this was. First, its orbit was not the stretched-out ellipse of most comets, highly inclined to the ecliptic—the great circle in the night sky traced out by the plane of the earth's orbit as it intersects the celestial sphere. Instead, the comet followed a path that stayed very close to the ecliptic. Comets rarely did that. The five planets did.

Then there was the matter of its appearance. It no longer appeared hazy and ill-defined, but was rather "perfectly sharp upon the edges, and extremely well defined." Comets simply didn't look like that. And there was no tail, either.

The initial assumption that the object was a new comet was a reasonable one. Comets were very "in" at the time, and Herschel's first observations showed an object that looked like other comets, hazy and ill-defined under high magnification. That it might be a new planet was almost unthinkable. There were only five planets beside Earth. Why should there be another?

But if William Herschel wasn't thinking the unthinkable yet, someone else was: Neville Maskelyne, the Astronomer Royal, who had received reports on the new comet from Herschel and taken a look at it himself.

Maskelyne wrote to William Watson, an associate of Herschel's, on April 9 and referred to the "comet or new planet." Two weeks later he wrote Herschel:

"I am to acknowledge my obligations to you for the communication of your discovery of the present Comet, or planet, I don't know which to call it. It is as likely to be a regular planet moving in an orbit nearly circular round the sun as a Comet in a very eccentric orbit. I have not yet seen any Coma or tail to it."

The question continued to be debated by the astronomical community in England and on the Continent for the next several months. Others looked where Herschel had, and also saw the object in the sky. The word spread, and Herschel became the astronomical superstar of his day. His new friends at court lobbied to get him a permanent position as an astronomer. George III granted Herschel a stipend and knighted him. In August Herschel moved from Bath to Windsor. The professional astronomical community of the time began to accept the notion that Herschel's "comet" was something much more extraordinary: the first new planet to be discovered since the dawn of history. In any case, there was no real doubt that Herschel's discovery was a major contribution to science. In November the Royal Astronomical Society awarded the musician from Bath its prestigious Copley Medal.

Herschel never for a moment thought his discovery was an accident. He was a thoroughly precise observer of the heavens. He wrote later: "In the regular manner I examined every star of the heavens, not only of that magnitude but many far inferior, it was that night *its turn* [Herschel's emphasis] to be discovered. . . . Had business prevented me that evening I must have found it the next, and the goodness of my telescope was such that I perceived its visible planetary disk as soon as I looked at it."

The Astronomer Royal later wrote to Herschel at his new home:

"Astronomy and Mechanics are equally indebted to you for what you have done; the first for your shewing to artists to what degree of perfection telescopes may be wrought; and the latter for your discovering to Astronomers a number of hitherto hidden wonders in the heavens. . . . I hope you will do the astronomical world the faver [sic] to give a name to your planet, which is entirely your own, & which we are so much obliged to you for the discovery of."

Since Herschel had discovered the new planet, he had the honor of naming it. He decided to tag his discovery Georgium Sidus, "the Georgian Star." It was an obviously political move, designed to flatter his patron, the king. Other astronomers didn't like the name at all—especially those in Europe. They despised King George III. A number of other names were suggested: Hypercronius ("Beyond Saturn"); Astrea, for the mythological daughter of Jupiter and Themis who fled the world at the end of the Golden Age; Neptune; Cybele, who in Greek mythology was Saturn's wife; and even Herschel's Planet. Indeed, the name Herschel became quite popular for many years.

Several people suggested the name Uranus, and it was a good choice: it fit the name pattern already in use for the planets. Jupiter, the largest planet in the solar system, was named for the king of the gods. Saturn was named for Jupiter's father. Uranus, in the same Greek and Roman mythological tales, was the father of Saturn and Jupiter's grandfather.

The name Uranus eventually stuck, but it took almost sixty years. Well into the nineteenth century, some astronomers were still calling the planet Herschel in their papers.

Herschel's planet lies in the distant reaches of the known solar system. It orbits at an average distance of 2.87 billion kilometers from the sun, more than nineteen times Earth's distance, and fully twice the distance of Saturn, the next planet in. Uranus is nearly 51,000 kilometers in diameter, a giant compared to Earth and the other inner planets (Mercury, Venus, and Mars), but considerably smaller than Jupiter (142,980 kilometers

11

in diameter) and Saturn (120,540 kilometers). Still, five dozen earths could fit in Uranus's volume, with room left over for the moon. Astronomers now believe Uranus is made of a small rocky core, covered by melted ices of ammonia, methane, and water, all enveloped in an atmosphere of hydrogen, nitrogen, carbon, and oxygen, and several of their combinations. Until 1986, no one was sure how long a Uranian day is; recent guesses were either sixteen or twenty-four hours.

Herschel remained interested in Uranus after his discovery of the planet, even though his main astronomical work would continue to be the "big picture," the nature and distribution of the stars. He noted that the planet was bluish green in color, and unlike Jupiter or Saturn was not banded in appearance. Herschel also noted an oblate appearance to Uranus—it seemed slightly flattened at the poles.

In 1787, he discovered the first two Uranian satellites. His son John Herschel later named them Titania and Oberon, for the queen and king of the fairies in Shakespeare's play *A Midsummer Night's Dream*. They were the first celestial bodies not named for characters in Greek or Roman mythology (though Ovid once used the name Titania to refer to the goddess Diana).

Oberon orbits Uranus at a distance of about 586,000 kilometers (364,000 miles), with a period of revolution of 13.46 days. Titania orbits about 438,000 kilometers (272,000 miles) from Uranus, with a period of 8.706 days. They are about the same size; Oberon has an estimated diameter of 1,630 kilometers, Titania about 1,600 kilometers.

William Herschel also noticed something quite unusual: the two moons revolved around Uranus in an up-and-down manner, not back and forth like the moons of Jupiter and Saturn. If they circled Uranus around its equator as other satellites did, he reasoned, then Uranus must have a polar axis with a huge tilt. He was right. Uranus has an axial tilt greater than that of any other planet in the solar system: depending on which astronomer you talk to, the orbital tilt is either 98 or 82 degrees. (Both are technically correct, since they add up to 180 degrees.) If the former figure is used, then the Uranian north pole points *below the plane of its orbit.* This concept seems too much for many astronomers, so the figure of 82 degrees is now frequently used. That keeps the Uranian north pole above the orbital plane and its south pole below. Whichever figure one picks, Uranus seems to "roll" around the sun in its orbit. During its "year" of eighty-four Earth years, the planet's north and south poles each get continual sunlight for forty-two years at a time.

In February and March of 1787, Herschel was observing the motions of the newly discovered satellites when he spotted something else: rings, and odd ones indeed, for there seemed to be two sets of them around the planet, but at right angles to each other. Herschel himself was none too sure he was seeing something real. But in 1788 he again saw rings around Uranus. This time it was one set, smaller than Saturn's outer A ring and circling Uranus's equator. Herschel still wasn't sure. It was possible the ring was simply an optical illusion from the metal mirror of his telescope. If some flaw in the mirror was causing the ring, rotating the mirror should make it disappear from view. He rotated the mirror 90 degrees. The ring was still there, in the same position. He used eyepieces with powers of 470 and 590. The ring remained visible.

Between 1787 and 1793, Herschel saw—or thought he saw—a Uranian ring many times. He could never absolutely confirm its existence, and he himself never fully believed that what he thought he saw actually was there. In his day, no one else ever saw Herschel's Uranian ring.

Titania and Oberon were the last Uranus-related discoveries credited to William Herschel, though in 1789 he did discover two new moons of Saturn, which

13

he named Mimas and Enceladus. In 1798 he announced the discovery of four more moons of Uranus. However, other observations showed these "discoveries" of Uranian moons to be mistakes. The next discoveries connected with the seventh planet were made by English astronomer William Lassell, who in 1846 had discovered Triton, a moon of Neptune. (Neptune itself had been discovered just three weeks earlier.) In 1851 Lassell spotted two more Uranian moons, which he named Ariel and Umbriel. The names followed the general pattern started by John Herschel. Ariel is a spirit from *The Tempest*. Umbriel, though, is not a name from Shakespeare, but a spirit from Pope's mock epic *The Rape of The Lock*. Umbriel (the moon) is about 1,100 kilometers in diameter, and circles Uranus in an orbit about 267,000 kilometers (166,000) miles) from the planet with a period of 4.14 days. Ariel is still closer, in an orbit about 192,000 kilometers (119,000 miles) from Uranus with a period of 2.52 days. Ariel is larger than Umbriel but smaller than Titania and Oberon, with a diameter of some 1,330 kilometers.

Recently, evidence has surfaced that Lassell was not in fact the original discoverer of Ariel and Umbriel. It now appears that William Herschel actually spotted Umbriel in 1801, and astronomer Otto Struve saw Ariel in 1847. However, it was Lassell who firmly established the existence of the two moons by determining their orbital periods.

It was a situation that had happened before, and with Uranus itself. Between 1690 and 1771, for example, three different astronomers had "discovered" Uranus on eighteen separate occasions. But they never recognized the true nature of the object they observed, for they didn't notice that it moved against the star background. It was Herschel who not only spotted Uranus but recognized it as something different, something previously unknown.

14

Neptune, the planet beyond Uranus, was also "discovered" several times before it was finally recognized as a previously unknown planet. On May 8, 1795, fourteen years after Herschel discovered Uranus, French astronomer Joseph Lalande spotted Neptune. In fact, Lalande saw Neptune twice in three days, and even noticed that its position had changed—an almost certain indication that it was a planet. Astonishingly, Lalande thought he had simply made a mistake in noting the "star's" position.

In the years following its discovery, astronomers carefully plotted Uranus's orbit. It soon became apparent that the planet was not following the path it should. By 1840 most astronomers had reached the conclusion that a still-undiscovered planet lay beyond Uranus, and its gravitational attraction was disturbing Uranus's orbit around the sun. Two astronomers, John Couch Adams in England and Urbain Leverrier in France, separately solved the difficult mathematical problem of predicting just where in the sky this planet had to be. By mid-1846, Sir John Herschel was saying the discovery of the new planet was merely a matter of time. In Berlin, German astronomer Johann Galle took Leverrier's mathematical predictions and checked that part of the sky against his up-to-date star chart. Within hours of starting the search, he discovered Neptune. The date was September 23, 1846, sixty-five years and six months after the discovery of Uranus.

The planet beyond Neptune would not be discovered for another eighty-four years. Pluto was finally spotted by American astronomer Clyde Tombaugh in 1930 at the Lowell Observatory in Arizona.

Throughout the nineteenth and early twentieth centuries, astronomers continued to observe Uranus and its moons and to learn more about the system. They

15

refined their knowledge of Uranus's diameter, mass, and possible composition, and made better estimates of the satellites' sizes and orbital distances. However, nothing truly major happened until 1948, when American planetary astronomer Gerard Kuiper pointed his telescope at Uranus.

Kuiper was greatly respected in the astronomical community as an accurate and thorough scientist. But his specialty was solar-system astronomy, and in the 1930s and 1940s the "hot" area was stellar, galactic, and extragalactic astronomy—the study of the universe beyond the solar system. Kuiper, though, continued to follow his own chosen path, and in the late 1940s he began a massive search program for new planetary satellites, using the 2.1-meter diameter McDonald Observatory telescope in Arizona. His painstaking work bore fruit on two different occasions, and the first was with Uranus.

On the night of February 16, 1948, Kuiper took a photograph designed to measure the relative magnitudes—that is, the brightness—of Uranus's four known satellites. When he later examined the plate he noticed a tiny, faint spot of light very close to the overexposed disk of the planet. Could it be a new Uranian moon? The way to find out was to take a second set of photos, and see if the object was still there, and if it had moved in a way that would indicate it was in orbit around the planet. On March 10 Kuiper did just that. The second series of photographs did indeed show that the object existed and was moving in an orbit around Uranus. Kuiper named the newly discovered fifth Uranian moon Miranda, the heroine in Shakespeare's *The Tempest*. With the discovery of Miranda, Gerard Kuiper became the first person to find a new Uranian moon in nearly a century.

Kuiper continued his photographic survey of Uranus through 1961, but found no other Uranian moons besides Miranda. Yet Kuiper had another discovery waiting in the wings. He began a series of photos of Neptune using the McDonald reflector, and in May 1949 he discovered a second satellite of Neptune, which he named Nereid.

Kuiper's reputation as the foremost planetary astronomer in the United States was now firmly established. He had carried out his McDonald Observatory Satellite Survey with typical exhaustive thoroughness, searching for new satellites around Venus, Mars, Jupiter, Saturn, and Pluto, as well as Uranus and Neptune. He pushed the telescope and the photographic plates to the limits of the technology of his day. His search turned up nothing, except Miranda around Uranus and Nereid around Neptune.

Astronomers now know for certain that Venus— like Mercury—has no natural satellites. Only Phobos and Deimos circle Mars. Many more moons have recently been discovered around Jupiter and Saturn by both ground-based observers and the Pioneer and Voyager spacecraft. The discovery of new moons around Uranus had to await the arrival of Voyager 2 in 1986, and who knows what that hardy spacecraft will find at Neptune in 1989? Pluto's moon Charon was indirectly detected in 1978 using image intensification of a photograph. All these new discoveries of planetary moons resulted from technology far beyond what Kuiper had available in 1950, when he photographed Pluto in search of moons. But despite the mostly negative results, Gerard Kuiper's McDonald Observatory Satellite Survey remains a model of scientific excellence in ground-based planetary astronomy.

The final pre-spacecraft discovery connected with Uranus took place in 1977, and it was one of the most unexpected and dramatic astronomical findings in decades. It had to do with a kind of eclipse called an occultation.

To most people, an eclipse means a solar eclipse, when the moon swings between the earth and the sun. By a remarkable cosmic coincidence, the moon is just far enough from the earth that its apparent size is precisely the apparent size of the sun's disk. The moon blocks the sun's disk from sight for a few minutes in the middle of the day along a small part of the earth. Inside that shadow path, a temporary night falls.

The paths of the moon and of the other planets in the solar system also at times take them in front of stars other than the sun. Astronomers call this kind of eclipse an occultation. Just as the moon's shadow falls on part of Earth in a solar eclipse, so the shadow of a planet cast by a distant star falls on part of Earth during an occultation. The planets are much farther from Earth than is the moon, of course, so their apparent size is much smaller. However, the stars are thousands of times more distant still, and their disk is effectively a point. The result is that stellar occultations last much longer than solar eclipses.

In recent years, occultations have been used as natural experiments. For example, by measuring the way the light from a distant star is affected as it passes through the atmosphere of, say, Mars or Jupiter, astronomers can learn a lot about the planet's atmosphere. And by measuring how long an occultation takes—from the time the star disappears behind a planet to the time it reappears on the other side—astronomers can more precisely measure the diameter of the occulting planet.

Astronomical calculations made in the early 1970s revealed that Uranus would occult a star known as SAO 158687 on March 10, 1977. The star would seem to pass behind Uranus at the widest part of its disk. The best spot to see it would be in the southeast Indian Ocean. James Elliot, an astronomer then at Cornell University, and several colleagues had had considerable success observing a stellar occultation by Mars. Buoyed by their success, Elliot and his associates turned their attention to this new occultation. NASA's Kuiper Airborne Observatory would be ideal for the observations of the occultation, and Elliot put in his request to NASA for its use.

The Kuiper Airborne Observatory, or KAO, is a specially modified C-141 cargo jet aircraft, named for the same Gerard Kuiper who discovered the Uranian moon Miranda in 1948. The KAO is a flying observatory, with a 90-centimeter telescope and banks of instruments to control the telescope and record all the data it gathers. The KAO flies at a normal cruising altitude of 12.3 kilometers (7.3 miles). At that altitude the KAO is above 85 percent of the earth's atmosphere, and most of the water vapor which blocks infrared radiation from astronomical objects. That makes the KAO a valuable tool for infrared observations not possible with telescopes on the earth's surface. Elliot got permission to use the Airborne Observatory, and in 1976 he began intensive preparations for the occultation.

Elliot and his team wanted to precisely determine the temperature of Uranus's upper atmosphere by measuring the way the atmosphere absorbed the star's light. The Uranian atmosphere contains a lot of methane, which is a very good absorber of longer, redder wavelengths of light. That in turn meant that SAO 158687 would be brighter relative to Uranus if it was observed in infrared light rather than visible wavelengths. The Airborne Observatory would be a perfect instrument for the task.

The mission would also accomplish a second purpose. By precisely timing the moments when the star disappeared and then reappeared behind Uranus, Elliot and his colleagues would be able to calculate the planet's diameter more exactly.

About two months before the KAO mission began, a problem cropped up. The original calculations for the occultation were not entirely accurate. In fact, it was possible there would be no occultation at all. And if the occultation did occur, there was a 17 percent probability that the KAO's planned flight path would not even take it to the northern edge of the shadow cone cast by Uranus. In other words, there was nearly one chance in six that Elliot and his associates would not see any occultation at all. Nearly a year's worth of plans and money might be down the drain. But planning for the mission was already too far advanced to make any changes, and the KAO's flight plan would take it almost to the limit of the plane's range and fuel capacity. There was no way to change it to the astronomer's advantage.

On the other hand, there were five chances in six that they *would* get into the shadow cone. Elliot decided to go ahead and make the flight.

And if there was no occultation? Elliot recalled a flippant remark made by fellow Cornell astronomer Joseph Veverka, shortly before Elliot had left for Australia. If the mission produced nothing, Veverka had said, at least Elliot and his associates could use the near-miss data to put an upper limit on the distance from the planet of any theoretical rings around Uranus!

Of course, everyone knew that only Saturn had rings.

At 10:37 p.m. local time, on March 10, 1977, the KAO lifted off the runway of Perth International Airport and headed southwest. It was carrying 153,000 pounds of fuel, five crew members, fourteen passengers, and a heavy load of excitement and anxiety.

Behind the flight deck, in the cramped quarters of the KAO's observatory section, the observing team spent the first several hours of the flight getting ready for the hoped-for occultation. Three team members ran the telescope itself; another person took care of the star tracker, which helped make sure the telescope was precisely aimed at Uranus. The team included someone to run the computer and a scientist who took care of the infrared radiometer. This instrument monitored the amount of water vapor in the traces of atmosphere above the KAO and would let the team know if any clouds were above them.

The astronomy team itself included Elliot, his graduate-student assistant Ted Dunham, and computer programmer Douglas Mink. Dunham was planning to do part of his doctoral research on the Uranus occultation; he would run the data-recording equipment. Mink would handle the backup data-recording equipment, and Elliot would do the fine guiding of the photometer attached to the 90-centimeter telescope, keeping Uranus and the star in the instrument's field of view. It was the data gathered by the photometer which would make or break the mission.

About forty-five minutes before the predicted time of the occultation's start, the KAO swung into a turn onto the path it would take to track Uranus.

"Okay," said James Elliot, "we're in the turn."

"Twenty hours, zero minutes, and zero seconds," Ted Dunham said, calling out the time in Universal Time measurement. At that moment it was 8:00 p.m. at Greenwich Observatory in England; 5:00 a.m., March 11, in Perth; and about 2:00 a.m. in the time zone occupied by the KAO.

"Long way to go," remarked Milo Reisner, one of the telescope operators.

In the cramped quarters of the KAO, the three astronomers sat almost literally cheek by jowl. Elliot wore a hooded jacket and sported dark-rimmed glasses and a set of extravagant sideburns that ran from his ears nearly to the corners of his mouth. To his left sat a youthful, clean-shaven Ted Dunham. To Dunham's left was Doug Mink, in a light-colored long-sleeved shirt, metal-rimmed glasses, and hair down to his shoulders.

The observers watched the TV monitors attached to

the telescope as the moon's image crossed it. Then the image of Uranus appeared on the TV monitor. It had not yet begun occulting the star.

Five minutes after the KAO began its turn, the team turned the data recorders on. It was still forty-one minutes to occultation, but they wanted to allow plenty of time for any errors in the calculation. The instruments included a digital tape recorder, and a chart recorder that traced the data coming in from the telescope onto a wide paper tape.

Elliot and his associates checked the photometer readings for Uranus, SAO 158687, and the sky, making calibration measurements. Unnoticed by them, the pens of the chart recorder traced out a sudden dip in the light intensity of the star.

"Read those by again, more slowly," Dunham asked Elliot.

"For the sky, essentially, twenty-eight hundred in channel one, fifteen hundred in channel two, four fifty in channel three." The photometer split the light from each observed object (or, in this case, the sky) into three different wavelength bands. All three channels were recorded as electrical signals on the Cipher digital tape recorder. Two of the three channels were traced onto the chart recorder for immediate monitoring during the occultation. Elliot was giving the expected readings from the photometer for the night sky.

Said Dunham, "Okay, fine."

"Now relate that to tonight," asked Elliot.

"We've got six seventy, six thirty, and one seventy."

"Okay, so you're down by two thousand counts, that should be twenty-four eight in the top one—okay, lookit there," said Elliot.

"Pretty . . . good, pretty good," Dunham replied.

They continued checking the photometer readings.

Suddenly Ted Dunham exclaimed, "What was that? What was that?"

"What?" Elliot asked.

"This!" Dunham pointed to the chart. He had spotted the sudden dip in light intensity from SAO 158687.

"I dunno," Elliot replied. "Was there a tracker glitch?"

Nothing of the kind, came the answer from the man at the telescope console forward of the three astronomers.

"Uh-oh," from Doug Mink.

Dunham said, "No, I don't think it's anything here, it's clearly duplicated in both of these." Both traces on the chart showed the dip.

Elliot wondered if a cloud had passed in front of the star and Uranus and cut off the light. They checked with Pete Kuhn and his infrared radiometer. Nothing.

"What happened?" asked Mission Director Jim McClenahan, of NASA's Ames Research Center.

"Well, we got a dip in the signal here which was either due to a momentary glitch in the tracker, or a cloud whipping through," said Elliot in reply.

The team couldn't explain the sudden dip in light intensity. They kept watching the tape and preparing for the occultation. And then a second light dip occurred.

"Okay," said Ted Dunham, "I've got a second spike here."

"I wonder if we're getting any clouds," said Elliot, still thinking in terms of water vapor as the explanation for the "glitches."

Dunham thought not. "Pete [Kuhn, who was running the infrared radiometer] said we had eight point nine microns of water."

"There're no clouds," said Kuhn. "I mean, truthfully, there's nothing up there."

"Well," smirked Elliot, "maybe this is a D ring. The D ring of Uranus."

Everyone laughed.

"Another one," Dunham called out, as a third dip occurred.

"Yep," said Mink.

Now Elliot began to realize that these might not be glitches after all. "These are real," he said. "I guess."

There was still no sign of water vapor or high clouds above the KAO, and the telescope was solidly pointed at Uranus. Elliot started getting excited. "I think we're getting real—maybe it could be small bodies. . . . The satellite plane is [face] on or it could be just small bodies like thin rings. . . . It was too quick for a tracking glitch, I think."

"They're too quick for anything," Doug Mink added.

Ted Dunham suggested that maybe the star was drifting out of the telescope's aperture while Uranus was not, then realized the two objects were now too close together for that to happen.

"Nominal occultation in twenty minutes," said Elliot. Then, "Is that *another* one?"

"Another one!" Dunham said, confirming the fourth dip in light intensity. Elliot and Dunham, checking the traces on the chart recorder, realized that it was the starlight's intensity *alone* that was dropping and returning. The intensity of light from Uranus was unchanged. Only starlight was being removed.

"It's definitely the star being occulted somehow," said Elliot to Dunham. "I told you every occultation comes up with a new surprising thing, and this may be it."

A fifth dip appeared on the tracings. Said Elliot, "Yeah, we're always joking about this D ring. It looks like maybe we've got one."

The team was still not certain. A visible Uranian ring had never been seen from Earth, and only Saturn had rings; perhaps they'd found a belt of tiny satellites around Uranus instead.

"What'll we call them?" Elliot asked. "What are we

going to have as a name for them? Let's see, think of something classic."

Said Mink, "Uranus has its own asteroid belt, obviously. . . ."

The time of actual occultation by Uranus was getting closer, and Elliot voiced another conclusion. "With all this stuff, we can't leave the leg early, we'll run it out to the end, because they're gonna be coming on the other side." Under ordinary circumstances, the KAO would turn for home a few minutes after the end of the occultation proper. But if there was a belt of asteroids, or a ring, around Uranus, then secondary occultations should take place on the other side of the planet's disk. They couldn't leave their occultation flight path until they'd had a chance to see if that happened. "It would be nice," said Mink, "if we got them symmetrically on the other side."

The excitement built, and people started getting a little silly as the time of the planned occultation neared. Flight controller Gillespie said: "I know it will have to be checked with the altitude, but probably there are clouds of orange juice floating around out there [around Uranus]."

Everyone laughed, and McClenahan said, "Sure sign of life." "That's right," several others said. "Junk in orbit," Dunham added. "Old satellites that were launched by an ancient race of Uranians!" Elliot exclaimed. "They took to launching orange-juice cans in orbit," said someone else. The signal now started getting noiser, and a lot of spikes began appearing in the traces. The light of SAO 158687 began refracting through Uranus's atmosphere. The occultation began.

"I'm starting the burst mode on this [tape recorder] —they'll run for a hundred seconds," said Dunham. "Yeah, Elliot, that's definitely it."

"Ahhhhhh . . . !" Elliot exclaimed. The rest of the team joined in with loud yippies and hoorahs.

"Oh, look at the spikes. Boy have we got a lot of those," Dunham said.

"Another Ph.D. in the world!" McClenahan laughed. Dunham would definitely have more than enough material for his degree. They settled in to watch the monitor and wait for the reappearance of the star on the other side of Uranus. They calculated when the star would reappear, and when they might expect to see the secondary occultations of SAO 158687 from the "satellite belt."

A few minutes after the planetary occultation finally ended, the dips began appearing again. Nobody was surprised. In a matter of less than an hour the team's mood went from utter astonishment to blasé acceptance.

Dunham said, "Okay, we got one. We got a blip here." Then another one. And another.

"That was one at 21:47 [Universal Time]," Mink noted.

Said James Elliot, "They're real."

They were real, but were they rings? Elliot and the others had talked about the "D ring" of Uranus, a reference to a ring around Saturn, but they actually didn't think they had seen Uranian rings. Rather, they were sure they had found a satellite belt circling the planet. Of course, a planetary ring *is* a belt of satellites, but Elliot was thinking in terms of objects several kilometers in diameter, like tiny asteroids. The rings of Saturn were thought to be made of particles at most the size of Volkswagens. And those rings were broad, with enough "satellites" to reflect sufficient light to be seen as rings. The "satellite belt" around Uranus was quite narrow, and no one was thinking in terms of narrow rings less than 10 kilometers wide.

The KAO finally finished its long run and landed back at Perth, Australia. Jim Elliot quickly wrote a note for the astronomers in South Africa, asking them to check their occultation observations for signs of a satellite belt. He wired it to Brian Marsden of the Smithsonian Astrophysical Observatory. Marsden issues the International Astronomical Union's circulars." The circulars are the "instant news flashes" of the astronomical field, sending information on the latest findings to astronomers around the world. This was no circular, but Marsden quickly called the South African observers and passed Elliot's request to them. In the process he found that some of the South African observers had been rained out and had not seen the occultation. Meanwhile, Elliot and the others compared notes with American astronomer Robert Millis, who had been on the ground at an observatory in Perth. Millis had not seen the actual occultation of the star by Uranus, since the shadow had passed south of Perth. But he had recorded several unexplained quick dips in light intensity. They seemed to correspond with the ones seen by Elliot and the others aboard the KAO.

Though exhausted from lack of sleep, the astronomers continued to poke at the mystery of the dips. They unrolled the chart recordings—nearly 100 feet—and compared notes. They talked about possible explanations. Small satellites, or rings? Rings they discarded, for the events had lasted such a short time. No one had ever heard of *narrow* rings. How could Uranus have rings that were narrow?

But there was a problem with tiny satellites, too. The secondary occultations had not been total; the light from SAO 158687 had not completely disappeared. It was as if each dip in light intensity had been caused by a grazing occultation by a tiny satellite. The coincidences involved were a bit much. But it was the best explanation available, they thought. Elliot sent a report to that effect to Brian Marsden for immediate publication in an IAU circular.

The following day, Elliot, Dunham, and Mink left

27

Perth in the KAO and flew to Melbourne, changed planes, and continued on to America. They arrived in Ithaca, New York, home of Cornell University, on March 13. Throughout the flight home, Elliot kept thinking about the mission. Had it really been a belt of satellites? The explanation continued to bother him. The following evening he got together with Cornell colleagues Joe ("the upper limit of Uranian rings") Veverka and Jay Goguen, and went over the data with them. Rings still seemed too farfetched. But after they left, Elliot thought about it some more.

If they had seen narrow rings, then there would have been considerable symmetry in the dips in signal before and after the primary occultation, a symmetry naturally caused by circular rings. He decided to put the question to rest. Elliot and his wife unfolded the 100-foot-long paper chart in their living room, then folded parts of it over on itself to check the spacing between the dips.

The spacing was nearly perfect.

The next day, March 15, Elliot showed the results to Dunham and Mink. They made the necessary geometrical calculations and plotted it all to an accurate scale. The match was even better. They called Marsden for another IAU circular.

Marsden said no. He was too skeptical of the idea of rings—narrow ones at that—around Uranus. It was simply too unlikely. He wanted confirmation from other astronomers.

He got it. Marsden found that an astronomer at Cape Town had not been rained out the night of March 10-11. Marsden calculated when the events seen by Elliot should have been seen at Cape Town. To his amazement, the Cape Town data fitted. Marsden then checked with Bob Millis, who had recorded several short dips in signal from his site at Perth. Three of his five matched three of Elliot's five secondary occultations; the data matched perfectly.

Marsden called Elliot back. "I think you might have something with this ring business," he told him.

The IAU circular went out. Uranus, it announced, was circled by at least five narrow rings.

James Elliot, Doug Mink, and Ted Dunham had made the first new discovery of a planetary ring system in more than 350 years.

Five months later, on August 20, 1977, the Voyager 2 spacecraft was launched from the Kennedy Space Center. Nine years and two planetary flybys later, the craft would reach Uranus and its family of five known satellites and nine known rings. And James Elliot would be at the Jet Propulsion Laboratory in Pasadena, California, "Voyager Mission Control," watching the latest episode of a story in which he had played a central part.

Along, no doubt, with the spirit of William Herschel.

Chapter 2
THE PERILS OF VOYAGER 2

On August 20, 1977, a Titan-Centaur booster rocket roared off the launch pad. The rocket arrowed up into the steel-blue Florida sky trailing a tail of smoke and brilliant flame. Atop the booster was a 825-kilogram robot spacecraft, the most sophisticated such machine ever built: Voyager 2.

The solid-fuel stages burned out, were jettisoned, and fell into the Atlantic. The Titan main stage burned on, its liquid fuel and oxidizer mixing to produce a nearly invisible flame. The main stage emptied, shut down, and was blown away from the Centaur second stage by explosive bolts. The second stage fired up and carried Voyager 2 into Earth orbit.

The Centaur and its cargo coasted silently around the curve of Earth to a predetermined point in space-time, and then the second stage ignited again. In the vacuum of space the exhaust gases expanded in a fiery bloom. The machine accelerated to nearly 12,000 meters per second; the engines cut off, fuel gone; the payload separated from the booster, which fell away under the gentle urging of tiny rockets. Then the spacecraft's own solid-fuel rocket ignited and accelerated the craft an additional 2,000 meters per second, carrying Voyager 2 to escape velocity. The spacecraft had begun the greatest journey of exploration in human history, a journey that would take it past the largest bodies in the solar system other than the sun itself. If it successfully carried out its primary mission to Jupiter and Saturn, and if everything else went as planned, Voyager 2 would visit the planet William Herschel had discovered 196 years earlier.

The scientists, engineers, and technicians following the launch cheered as Voyager 2 successfully separated from the booster. A few hours later they got their first taste of "the Voyager Jinx": the spacecraft's scan-platform boom apparently refused to lock in place.

Sixteen days later, Voyager 1 followed Voyager 2 into space. The reverse order of launch was deliberate. Voyager 1, though launched later, would follow a faster trajectory and would get to Jupiter before Voyager 2. They would arrive in the correct numerical order.

Minutes after its launch, however, Voyager 1 was also in trouble. There was a real possibility it would never make it to Jupiter at all. If it didn't, then Voyager 2 would never make it to Uranus.

The Voyagers were not the first robot space probes to Jupiter and Saturn. That honor had gone to two earlier, less sophisticated spacecraft named Pioneer 10 and Pioneer 11. They were launched from Kennedy Space Center in 1972 and 1973, and flew past Jupiter in 1973 and 1974 respectively. Pioneer 11's path took it on to Saturn, which it flew past in September 1979.

Though somewhat primitive by current standards,

the two Pioneer craft returned an amazing amount of information about Jupiter. They confirmed that Jupiter emits more heat than it receives from the sun. In a very real sense, Jupiter is a sun that almost was. Were it just a few dozen times larger than it is, it would be massive enough to ignite thermonuclear reactions at its center and thus become a tiny but real star.

The Pioneers also proved for the first time that Jupiter is completely fluid, with the possible exception of a small metallic core no larger than Earth. The two spacecraft returned new information about Jupiter's powerful magnetic field and its associated magneto-sphere, that region surrounding the planet and influenced by its magnetic field which contains ionized particles and radiation belts. The probes gave scientists a more accurate determination of the masses of Jupiter's four largest satellites, the so-called Galilean moons, named Io, Europa, Ganymede, and Callisto. The Pioneers discovered an ionosphere around Io, and detected strong emissions of ultraviolet radiation—possibly from hydrogen atoms—from a region near that moon.

And, of course, the Pioneer cameras returned the most detailed and beautiful photos of Jupiter and its largest moons ever seen up to that time.

The powerful gravitational field of Jupiter flung both Pioneers off into new trajectories. Pioneer 10 headed out of the solar system. Pioneer 11's path was different; it headed to a September 1979 rendezvous with Saturn.

There it detected for the first time the magnetic field of Saturn, and found the planet's magnetic poles were aligned with its rotational poles. This latter discovery was a bit surprising. Earth and Jupiter both have magnetic fields whose poles are offset from their rotational poles by about 11 degrees.

Pioneer 11 also detected Saturn's magnetosphere and confirmed that Saturn, like Jupiter, emits more heat energy than it absorbs from the sun. It showed that Saturn is made primarily of liquid metallic hydrogen and may have a relatively small solid metallic core.

And then there were the photographs. Pioneer 11 showed no large spots or bright bands in Saturn's atmosphere. It discovered a new moon of Saturn, about 200 kilometers in diameter and orbiting the planet at about two-and-a-half Saturn radii (150,675 kilometers) from its center.

Pioneer 11 also beamed back tantalizing color photos of Saturn's rings. Those images for the first time showed hints of detailed structure within some of the five previously known rings (known as the D, C, B, A, and E rings, from the closest in to the farthest out from the planet). The spacecraft also discovered still another ring, dubbed the F ring and located between the A and E rings, and returned images that suggested the Cassini Division between the B and A rings was not an empty gap, but contained material of some kind.

After its encounter with Saturn, Pioneer 11 was flung off in a trajectory which will carry it out of the solar system. Both it and Pioneer 10 continue to function, sending back data about interplanetary space. They are also being used in a unique experiment as "gravitational antennas" that may detect the presence of a giant planet beyond Pluto, or perhaps even a star companion to the sun.

The Pioneer missions were formally approved and started up in 1969. But even before that, scientists had begun serious planning for a much more ambitious planetary mission, the so-called Grand Tour. Astronomers had long known that Jupiter's powerful gravitational field could alter the orbits of comets that passed too close to it. In fact, there's a large group of comets called the Jupiter family, because their orbits have been so modified. They never get much farther from the sun than Jupiter. In the mid-1960s, Michael Minovich, an analyst at NASA's Jet Propulsion Laboratory (JPL) in Pasadena, California, pointed out that what Jupiter's gravity did to comets it could also do to spacecraft. If a probe was correctly targeted, it could use Jupiter's gravity field to boost its velocity and thus shorten its travel time to the other outer planets.

Aeronautics graduate student Gary Flandro, then at JPL, took Minovich's observation and turned it into an ambitious proposal. Flandro discovered a rare alignment of the planets that, properly used by mission planners and celestial navigators, could be used for a Grand Tour of the outer planets of the solar system. A space probe to Jupiter would be gravitationally boosted on to Saturn, which would throw it into a trajectory to Uranus, and finally on to Neptune. The flight would take just twelve years, a small fraction of the time it would take without the gravitational slingshot technique. Opportunities for such a Grand Tour launch occurred only every 177 years. The next one would be in 1977.

Flandro's paper on the Grand Tour was published in 1966. Three years later, NASA began detailed planning for it. (The Pioneer Project continued toward its 1972-73 launch dates, and the Minovich-Flandro gravity-boost technique would in fact be used to send Pioneer 11 to Saturn.) In 1970 NASA had outlined an ambitious project involving four spacecraft. The first two would be launched in 1976 and 1977 and would fly past Jupiter, Saturn, and Pluto. The second two would be launched in 1979 and would fly past Jupiter, Uranus, and Neptune. The total project would cost about $750 million.

Almost at once the cold realities of economics and politics caught up with the Grand Tour. The glory days of NASA came to an end right after the 1969 Apollo moon landing. The enormous expenditures for the Vietnam War and a decline in apparent public interest in space programs resulted in massive budget cuts for

NASA. One of the programs canceled was the Grand Tour. The fact that the opportunity would not come again for hundreds of years meant little to politicians, who were more focused on the 1972 presidential election. The realities of politics sometimes seem as immutable as the laws of physics.

NASA shifted gear. The Grand Tour might be gone, but there would still be opportunities for Jupiter-Saturn gravitational slingshot flights. The planners scaled down their plans. There would be just two spacecraft, not four. They would fly past Jupiter and then, using a gravity boost, on to Saturn. There were advantages to be gained, in any case. They wouldn't have to worry about spacecraft degradation over long years of flight, about spacecraft power for a long trip, or about the problems of communicating with a spacecraft that would be out at Pluto, nearly 6 billion kilometers from Earth.

And the project would cost just $250 million, a third of the Grand Tour budget.

The new program was initially named Mariner/Jupiter-Saturn, and it officially began on July 1, 1972. NASA assigned the project to JPL (the Pioneer project was already being run by NASA's Ames Research Center in Mountain View, California). The project manager was Harris Schurmeier, and the project scientist was Professor Edward Stone of the California Institute of Technology, an expert on cosmic-ray and magnetospheric physics. Schurmeier later left and was replaced in turn by John Casani, Robert Parks, Ray Heacock, Esker Davis, and Richard Laeser. Stone, though, has remained the project's chief scientist for the entire duration of the mission.

Charles Kohlhase is one of many Voyager personnel who have been with the project through nearly all of its lifetime. A lean and lanky man who enjoys golf and backpacking, he always seems to have several projects in the air at once. Kohlhase has been head of the Voyager Mission Planning Office almost since the project's beginning.

In the early 1970s he was the leader of the Viking navigation development team and helped design the navigation programs that would eventually put the two Viking Landers on Mars. But before the two Vikings were launched, Kohlhase had a chance to change jobs, and he felt it was time for him to do so.

Recalled Kohlhase: "The job I had always wanted was to be mission analysis and engineering manager for a project like Voyager. And I told Pickering [Dr. William Pickering, then the Director of JPL] that. The Martin Marietta Company was trying to entice me away from JPL at the time, and Pickering told Schurmeier to keep me in mind for any new jobs that might open up on Voyager. At that time someone else had the job I have now. But later he had some medical problems and had to resign. In January 1975 this job opened up. I applied for it along with many other people, and I was thrilled to be accepted."

After the Voyager launch the Mission Analysis and Engineering Office had its name changed to the Mission Planning Office. Kohlhase has run it ever since.

Some people changed jobs; some did not. What was interesting about the project, though, was that its very name changed.

It wasn't that Mariner was a bad name. Mariner spacecraft have an honorable history. Mariner 2 made the first successful planetary flyby, of Venus in 1962. Mariner 4 was the first successful probe to Mars, flying past the red planet in 1965 and returning the first-ever closeup photos of its surface. In 1971, Mariner 9 became the first artificial satellite of another planet when it went into orbit around Mars. It returned thousands of astounding photos, including the discovery photos of the giant Martian volcanoes and the first-ever closeup photos of the two natural moons, Phobos and Deimos. Mariner 10 made the first successful use of the Minovich-Flandro gravity-boost technique. In February 1974 it flew past Venus and then used its gravitational pull to head for a successful first-ever flyby of Mercury. (Pioneer 11 also used the gravity-boost technique at Jupiter, but that took place nine months later.)

The two probes to the outer planets were to be called Mariner 11 and 12, and the project was named the Mariner/Jupiter-Saturn 1977 Project. But NASA and JPL eventually decided that the project name was too awkward for publicity purposes. "John Casani was the project manager by this time," Kohlhase remembered. "And he decided we should have a new name, since 'MJS 77' was a real mouthful. Well, a lot of names were submitted. We had names like Discovery, Argus, Odyssey, Endeavor, and Pilgrim. Voyager was a name, too, and so was Galileo. But we all liked Voyager best."

There was, though, some reluctance over the name. "There had been another, earlier Voyager program," explained Kohlhase. "This would have launched two orbiter-landers to Mars on a single Saturn 5 booster—the one that sent men to the moon. Well, that project got to be very expensive and NASA killed it. Out of its ashes rose the Viking Program, which did put two successful landers on Mars. The question was, should we be superstitious in renaming this new project after the old Voyager which had died?"

Kohlhase paused and grinned. "But we all said: 'That's ridiculous, we're all scientists, not witch doctors. Let's go ahead.'"

Project Voyager's primary mission was to make successful fast flybys of the two largest planets in the solar system. Jupiter has a mass of 1,900 trillion trillion kilograms (319 times the mass of the Earth) and a diameter of 142,980 kilometers (more than eleven times that of Earth). The planet is larger and more massive than all the other planets, moons, comets, and asteroids in the solar system put together. Saturn is nearly as large: 559 trillion trillion kilograms in mass and 120,540 kilometers in diameter. And it has its astonishing system of rings. Seen from Earth, they are a beautiful band of light girdling the planet. Even a small 7-centimeter telescope bought in a department store will show Saturn's rings. Many an astronomer was first inspired by just such a sight, through just such a modest instrument. Now scientists would have a new pair of instruments to examine these incredible celestial bodies up close.

The Voyagers were the *crème de la crème* of early-1970 space-probe technology. Each craft had a mass of 825 kilograms (just over 1,800 pounds). Each had a huge dishlike antenna some 3.7 meters (about 12 feet, the width of a small bedroom) in diameter. The dish antenna would remain continually pointed at Earth, to receive instructions and broadcast back data. The two radio receivers (one main, one backup) had a transmitting power of 22 watts, less than the wattage of an average light bulb. The giant dish antennas of NASA's Deep Space Network (DSN) were quite sensitive, though, and would be able to "hear" Voyager at distances of billions of kilometers.

. The spacecraft were "three-axis-stabilized." They had a set of electric-eye star trackers, gyroscopes, and tiny rocket thrusters that would keep the dish antenna pointed toward Earth. The thrusters and gyros could also rotate the craft around any of three axes to perform maneuvers or point scientific instruments in different directions.

The Voyagers each carried ten experimental instruments, and used the spacecraft's own radio as an eleventh. Four of the instruments, the so-called "remote-sensing" ones, were mounted on a special scan platform at the end of a boom. The scan platform could tilt and swivel in three directions by means of tiny electric motors and a set of gears and actuators. This made it possible to point the TV cameras, ultraviolet spectrometers, infrared detectors, and photopolarimeter in many different directions, and at the same target at the same time—all without having to swivel the entire spacecraft around.

The spacecraft were powered by a special kind of "battery" which was more like a nuclear reactor than a Sears Diehard. The radioisotope thermoelectric generators, or RTGs, produced energy from the decay of radioactive plutonium. The process of radioactive decay produced heat, and the RTGs—each spacecraft carried three of them at the end of a long boom—turned the 7,000 watts of heat into 400 watts of electricity to power the spacecraft. The electricity ran the radio receivers and scientific instruments—and the computers.

The space probes carried three kinds of computers: the AACS (attitude and articulation control subsystem), the FDS (flight data subsystem), and the CCS (computer command subsystem). The AACS computer essentially controlled the spacecraft's position in space. The FDS computer processed the scientific and engineering data compiled by Voyager before it was broadcast back to Earth. Finally, the CCS computer functioned as the overall coordinator of the spacecraft's actions. Instructions on when and where to point the spacecraft and its various instruments during a planetary flyby, for example, were contained in programs run by the CCS. The CCS also contained special commands called fault protection algorithms, which constantly monitored the spacecraft itself for any problems. They made the Voyagers semi-independent of Earth, and able to quickly correct some kinds of problems which might occur.

Each of the three main computers had a backup.

The computers' precoded sets of instructions, or "loads," could run the craft for days, weeks, or months at a time. The loads could be updated, modified, or replaced with new loads broadcast from Earth. The computers and their software loads made the Voyagers the most intelligent space probes ever built. The spacecraft could run by themselves for long periods of time, could check their own programs for errors, could find and correct problems before the human controllers at JPL were even aware of them, and with the proper kind of programming could even take over and command the Voyagers right through a planetary flyby without any further help from Earth.

The Voyager Project had just formally started when the two Pioneer spacecraft flew past Jupiter in 1973 and 1974. The flybys had a major impact on Voyager. The two space probes discovered ionizing radiation trapped in Jupiter's magnetic field. Jupiter had its own version of Earth's Van Allen radiation belt, but Jupiter's was immensely more powerful. A human being sitting on the Pioneer spacecraft would have gotten a dose of 400,000 rads, a thousand times the lethal dose for humans. Even inside the craft, in shielded areas, a human would have received fifty times the lethal dose. Though machine parts are more durable than human tissue, Voyager engineers knew their crafts' electronics wouldn't survive the intense radiation. The Voyagers would have to fly past Jupiter at a further distance, and some electronic parts would need extra radiation shielding. In the end, an additional 22 kilograms of tantalum shielding was added to each spacecraft, and special radiation-hardened parts were used as well. Voyager 2 was also retargeted to fly past Jupiter at a distance of 10 Jupiter radii (about 714,000 kilometers) instead of 5. That would reduce its exposure to radiation around the planet by ten times.

It would also make possible a dramatic addition to the Voyager mission. The new trajectory at Jupiter meant that Voyager 2 could not only go from Jupiter to Saturn, but also on to Uranus by taking advantage of the Minovich/Flandro gravity-boost technique. It was an attractive option. Key members of the Voyager Navigation Team, working under Kohlhase, designed a special case-optional trajectory for Voyager 2. *If* (1) Voyager 1 made it all the way to both Jupiter *and Saturn*, (2) had a successful encounter with Titan, Saturn's giant moon with an atmosphere, and (3) got good observations of Saturn's rings, *then* Voyager 2— arriving at Saturn nine months after Voyager 1—would no longer be needed as backup for Voyager 1. The spacecraft would then be reprogrammed for a new trajectory that would use a Saturn gravity boost and go on to Uranus.

The Uranus option was not an easy one to set up. "We had to sift through ten thousand different trajectory combinations before we found all the ones that might be usable for complementary Voyager missions," said Kohlhase. "We were finally able to narrow those down to something like eighty possible flight paths." The eighty were narrowed to only two when the Voyagers were launched.

Almost from the beginning, though, the two Voyager spacecraft ran into problems. Shortly after launch, ground controllers received a signal from Voyager 2 that the boom holding the scan platform had not fully extended from the craft. If true, this would mean the spacecraft would be unable to get any data from the four instruments on the scan platform. It seemed a serious problem. But when Voyager engineers checked the data carefully and ran some tests, they decided there was no problem. The boom had in fact deployed within half a degree of the correct position. The Voyager spacecraft

41

team reprogrammed the computer to ignore the spurious report from its sensor. The spacecraft's builders then quickly added a second set of coil springs to the boom-deployment mechanism on Voyager 1.

Sixteen days after Voyager 2 was launched, Voyager 1 blasted off from Kennedy. The second scare took place before the booster had even cleared Earth's atmosphere. Voyager 1 almost never made it out of Earth orbit.

The Centaur second stage of the Titan-Centaur booster has an inertial guidance system that tells it to fire its engines until it and the spacecraft get into a parking orbit. Then, when the guidance system senses that the rocket has reached the right point in space and time, it reignites the Centaur's oxygen-hydrogen engines. The spacecraft, in turn, has its own solid-fuel rocket attached, with a velocity-change capability of 2,000 meters per second. (Change in velocity is usually referred to as "delta-v." The Greek letter delta stands for "change," the "v" for "velocity." And don't forget: velocity is not just speed, but also *direction*.) When the Centaur has accelerated to within 2,000 meters per second of the final velocity needed, the guidance system shuts down the engines, the Voyager separates from the booster, and its own solid rocket gets it to escape velocity.

Kohlhase was at Kennedy Space Center when the near-disaster happened. "I was with [Project Manager John] Casani at the Cape at the Mission Control room when this thing was flying. After the Centaur got into its parking orbit I heard all this chatter over the communications net between people at the Cape and people at General Dynamics in San Diego, who built the Centaur.

"Well, it seems the Centaur had burned twelve hundred more pounds of propellant than normal to get into parking orbit. The Air Force later investigated, and found that the fuel and oxidizer in the Titan's liquid-fuel stage didn't mix properly because of a leak. So it lost performance. The Centaur guidance system essentially said, 'I've still gotta get into parking orbit,' so it burned an extra twelve hundred pounds to achieve its objective—parking orbit. But it was now lighter, and would need less propellant to get to escape velocity.

"The question was: Did it have enough? Would it have a normal burn and shutdown, or burn to depletion and not have enough to get us to Jupiter? As it turned out, the Centaur made it. But it had just two hundred and ten pounds of fuel left! That's not much left at the bottom of the tank; the Centaur's engines would've gobbled it up in just three more seconds."

Voyager 1 experienced relatively few difficulties after its initial brush with disaster. Its instrument scan platform jammed briefly a few months after launch, but the Voyager team soon got it into working order, and it never had further problems. Voyager 2, though, continued to suffer. Its next major malfunction happened in April 1978. The result of diverted human attention and two bad electrical connectons, it has plagued the mission ever since.

The CCS computers aboard the Voyagers contain a special fault-protection algorithm, a "what-if" command: "What if my primary radio receiver dies?" The answer is that the computers switch to a backup radio receiver and wait twelve hours for further instructions. Then, after this half-day wait, they switch back to the first receiver—just in case there was nothing wrong with it in the first place. Computers, of course, are totally literal machines; they do exactly what they are told. In this case, the lines of code in the CCS program essentially told Voyager 2 that if it didn't hear from Earth within a one-week period, then its primary radio receiver must be dead and it should switch to the secondary receiver.

The spacecraft engineers were distracted by the

stuck scan platform on Voyager 1. They may also have been lulled into a false sense of security by the apparently excellent health of Voyager 2. Whatever the case, the flight team forgot to call the second spacecraft. On April 5, 1978, having not heard from Earth for more than a week and concluding that its primary receiver was malfunctioning, the CCS computer switched to the secondary receiver. However, that receiver had a faulty tracking-loop capacitor. It had failed, probably months earlier when not in use and therefore without the knowledge of the people on Earth. The backup receiver was therefore unable to track the frequencies of the radio signals from Earth as the Doppler effect shifted them back and forth. Result: Voyager 2 effectively lost all contact with the mission controllers.

On Earth, the Voyager team discovered that the spacecraft had apparently turned itself off. They scrambled to figure out why, and to reestablish contact. The cause was eventually discovered—but not in time. After a further twelve hours of no word from Earth, Voyager 2 on cue switched back to the primary receiver. But now something went wrong with the primary receiver—apparently a short in the power-supply circuit. That circuit blew, and the primary radio receiver died for good. The spacecraft's computers again did the right thing; a week later, on cue, they again switched to the wounded but still-functioning backup radio receiver.

The backup receiver can still hear signals sent to it, but the exact frequency the receiver can hear wanders widely as temperatures change in the spacecraft. Simply changing the internal power loads will do it; so will maneuvering the spacecraft by firing its onboard propulsion system, or turning on the gyroscopes, or turning on a lot of science instruments at once.

When something like that happens the Voyager team waits for the radio receiver to settle down so the spacecraft can hear them again. The waiting period—

usually twenty-four to forty-eight hours—is called a "command moratorium." The team then sends commands to the spacecraft at several different frequencies, hoping to hit the right one and reestablish contact. In the years since the April 1978 incident the team developed sophisticated computer techniques of predicting what frequency was the right one. But simple human forgetfulness and unexpected hardware failures have made things harder than they should have been.

The radio-receiver incident was not the last of Voyager 2's pre-Jupiter woes. Not long into its journey, the Voyager spacecraft team realized that it was using far too much hydrazine fuel. The thrusters used for trajectory-change maneuvers were producing 20 percent less delta-v than expected. If this continued, Voyager 2's optional Uranus mission would be very risky; the spacecraft needed a hydrazine "cushion" of about 15 pounds to make a Uranus flyby navigationally possible. At one point in the flight, in fact, Voyager 2 was nearly 30 pounds "in the red." Spacecraft engineers eventually found the problem: the exhaust plume from the thruster was hitting a part of the spacecraft, forcing the craft to expend extra hydrazine to keep it in proper attitude. The solution was found by the mission planners and navigators. They rescheduled the long burn for the post-Jupiter trajectory-change maneuver, moving it from seventy days after Jupiter flyby to just two days after closest approach. They also used some other hydrazine-saving tricks, but that one shift in time saved enough hydrazine to keep the Uranus option alive.

Besides failures of radio receivers and glitches with scan-platform booms, Centaur booster rockets, and attitude-control fuel, the two Voyagers suffered a near-disaster with one of the scientific instruments. The photopolarimeter, or PPS, is a specialized kind of camera with a telephoto lens. It is extremely sensitive to light—in fact, it's the most light-sensitive instrument aboard the Voyagers. The PPS is designed to measure how light changes in intensity as it is reflected or absorbed by particles in a planetary atmosphere or rings, or by the surfaces of moons. It has four different-sized apertures or holes in a plate that rotates in front of its lens, as well as three color filters and four polarizing filters. It also has two separate sensitivities—as if it could shoot pictures with two different kinds of film. The PPS is mounted on the scan platform, along with the imaging cameras (the ISS instrument), the IRIS infrared instrument, and the ultraviolet spectrometer (UVS).

Perhaps the most exciting use of the PPS would be for recording stellar occultations of rings. It was a somewhat paradoxical use of the instrument, according to Arthur L. "Lonne" Lane, the JPL scientist responsible for the PPS as its principal investigator (PI). Lane is a small man, not more than 5 feet tall, with large, wide-set eyes, tiny hands, and a shiny pate counterpointed by a Van Dyke beard. "Here we've got an instrument with extreme sensitivity to low levels of light," he explained, "but we found a way to point it at a relatively bright light source—a star—and track that star as it seems to move behind the rings and its light is blocked by ring particles." How much light passed through semiopaque rings would indicate how thin the rings were and where any gaps might exist. The result would be a mass of information about the complex structure of planetary rings.

The near-disaster to the PPS happened because of its great sensitivity to light. Somehow, during the cruise to Jupiter, the PPSs aboard both Voyagers were left staring at a calibration plate with their sensitivity setting at a high level. The calibration plate, necessary for setting baseline responses for the TV cameras, is a bland off-white plate mounted on the spacecraft. But the sunlight reflected from the calibration plate severely damaged the sensitive decoder part of the Voyager 1 PPS.

So badly damaged was the instrument, in fact, that it was essentially destroyed.

The PPS aboard Voyager 2 suffered a similar but not so serious degradation of sensitivity. But it was bad enough. After a lot of soul-searching and not a little agony, the Voyager management decided to keep the use of the PPS during the Voyager 2 flyby of Jupiter to an absolute minimum. They hoped to save it and its dwindling sensitivity for Saturn and a possible stellar occultation of the planet's rings.

Besides the sensitivity-degradation problem, the PPS also had a serious problem with its mechanical filter and analyzer wheels. Hydrocarbon compounds outgassing from parts of the spacecraft settled on the electrical contacts of the wheels and interacted with their surfaces to form a greasy compound. As a result, the wheel would no longer turn to specific settings, but free-floated instead. That meant there was no sure way to align different aperture holes or filters with the PPS itself. Months of work on the ground eventually turned up a way to rotate the wheels and scrape off the hydrocarbon buildup.

The PPS was not originally Lane's instrument. It was designed and developed by a team of people at the University of Colorado, who proposed a simple, rugged, relatively inexpensive instrument for doing photometry and polarimetry. NASA accepted their proposal and then, in a somewhat unusual move, added some people to the investigating team. Nevertheless, the instrument was built by the Colorado team in 1973 and 1974. Lane did not become PI for the instrument until after the Jupiter encounters in 1979. Through that time he had been assistant project scientist to Ed Stone, a job later filled by Ellis Miner.

Just exactly how Lane went from assistant project scientist to photopolarimeter PI is somewhat unclear. "I think there was a personal problem involved," said one

Voyager management person. Regardless of the circumstances, Lane took over the PPS after the Jupiter flybys. "Lonne did a hell of a job [as assistant project scientist] at Jupiter," said one Voyager team member. "He pulled together the science observation sequences for the Voyager 1 Jupiter flyby, guided them through to execution, and then helped with the Voyager 2 sequences." "Lonne's a truly remarkable man," said another team member. "I mean, this guy almost single-handedly resurrected that instrument. It was dead when he took over."

Lonne Lane inspired strong responses from people. He was admired by some and disliked by others. Lane made no bones about what he wanted: he wanted a photopolarimeter that functioned as perfectly as possible and that got Class-AAA treatment from the rest of the Voyager organization; he wanted total dedication from his experiment associates and he got it; he wanted high-quality data from his instrument and did everything possible to ensure that. The fact that he finally got an enormous amount of good data from an instrument that functioned at only a portion of its potential was the biggest tribute to Lonne Lane's ability.

Project scientist Edward Stone, tall and hawk-faced with a shock of combed-back black hair thinning in front, joined the project at its inception in 1972. Project managers would come and go, PIs would arrive and disappear, but Ed Stone stayed on, providing the anchor of stability in the Voyager structure for the scientific teams.

The job of Voyager project scientist was not a full-time one (except during encounters themselves). Stone, in fact wore several hats: he was chairman of the Division of Physics, Mathematics, and Astronomy at the California Institute of Technology, JPL's parent organization, and was also leader of the team building the giant 10-meter Keck optical telescope.

"My job as project scientist has three major parts to it," Stone explained one hot June Pasadena afternoon; outside the temperature in the shade of Cal Tech's old adobe-walled buildings was in the high 90s. In Stone's enormous wood-paneled office the air conditioner kept it cool and civilized. "First, I represent the eleven PIs to the rest of the project, in different meetings with management. I also represent the project itself to NASA headquarters in Washington, D.C., and at meetings of groups like the National Academy of Sciences.

"Finally," he said, "I'm responsible during the implementation phases of a flyby to optimize the science objectives of the Voyager Project and the Voyager scientists."

There was no doubt of Stone's successful accomplishment of those tasks. He was probably the single most respected member of the Voyager team.

Candy Hansen, the experiment representative for the imaging team, began working on the Voyager project in May 1977, three months before the two Voyager spacecraft were launched. Hansen's infectious laugh comes easily in conversation. She has a dark California tan and is reputed to be a good infielder in the softball games among amateur teams at JPL. Hansen looked like someone who probably enjoyed rafting the Colorado River or camping out in the Mojave Desert—both of which she did whenever there was a day or two of spare time. "Yep, I keep my camping gear in my pickup truck. I'm always ready to go," she said.

Hansen said that she had started out as a science observation analyst. "Then I became the assistant experiment representative for the Jupiter and Saturn flybys." As Stone represented the PIs' needs to upper Voyager management, so Hansen was the imaging team's spokeswoman to the midlevel management responsible for the science of Voyager.

After the Saturn flyby in 1981, Hansen took a break from Voyager and spent several years with the

AMPTE "artificial comet" project. AMPTE was a multinational space project designed to learn more about the interaction of the solar wind and Earth's magnetic field. One of the AMPTE satellites was German-built, and Hansen spent a lot of time at West German space facilities and at the European Space Agency headquarters in Paris. "It was a great experience," she recalled. "And it was very interesting to see how others do space research, and compare it to the way we do it here in America." Among the many photos posted above her desk was one of an AMPTE-released "artificial comet," its barium-blue tail spreading out into space.

Stone and Hansen had been with the project from the beginning. Charles Kohlhase had come on board after the probes had been launched. Another "latecomer" to Voyager was Peter Doms. Small and slim, with a trim mustache and beard, Doms was no stranger to the space program. He had spent five years with the Viking Project, which had put two spacecraft into orbit around Mars and two landers on the surface to search for signs of life. He had been a UCLA graduate student when he began on Viking; he had worked with an experiment designed to detect water vapor in the Martian atmosphere.

"I switched over to the Voyager Project in 1979, as the assistant experiment representative for the radio science experiment, or RSS," Doms recalled. The RSS was somewhat unusual. It had no specific instrument aboard the two Voyagers. Rather, the spacecraft themselves and their radio transmitters were the instruments. When the spacecraft went behind a planet relative to Earth, it would beam powerful radio-wave pulses through the atmosphere. The waves would be detected by the Deep Space Network radio antenna dishes on Earth, and the manner in which the radio waves were bent and distorted would provide valuable information about the nature and composition of the planetary atmosphere. The spacecraft could also shine the radio beams through planetary rings, and the way the ring particles scattered and absorbed the radio waves would give valuable information to the scientists back home about the structure of the rings.

As the assistant experiment rep, Doms worked closely with the RSS scientists as they prepared for the Jupiter flybys in March and July 1979. He helped present the needs and problems of the RSS team members at meetings with the Voyager management. "It was one of the most rewarding jobs I ever had," said Doms. After the Jupiter and Saturn flybys, Doms moved into a new position in the Voyager hierarchy, as head of the Science Investigation Support (or SIS) team, which was part of the Voyager Flight Science Office. Dom's colleagues in SIS included the various experiment representatives, as well as people who were go-betweens between the scientists and the people who programmed Voyager's onboard computers. The SIS team and its leader were thus a vital part of the Voyager Project.

At the beginning of 1979, the two Voyagers were beginning their approach to the King Planet. Kohlhase, Lane, Stone, Hansen, Doms, and their associates were about to become participants in one of the most extraordinary periods in the history of science: the discovery of nearly three dozen new worlds.

Chapter 3
NEW WORLDS

Despite the glitches and breakdowns, the two Voyagers continued their journey to Jupiter. That journey, as well as the encounters with Saturn and Uranus, were divided by the project into several different phases. They included cruise, observatory, far encounter, near encounter (which included the planetary flyby itself), and post-encounter. For Voyager 1, the cruise phase to Jupiter ended on January 4, 1979, and it entered observatory phase. The craft was 50 million kilometers from Jupiter. The scientific instruments stepped up their observations and the TV cameras took photos of Jupiter every two hours during January, sending back hundreds of images of a planet looking like an Easter egg gone mad.

In February, Voyager 1 entered the far encounter phase. For about a hundred hours the cameras took images every ninety-six seconds, producing the "rotation movie." With the images run in rapid-fire sequence, Jupiter could be seen twirling about its axis in its ten-hour dance. When the spacecraft was much closer, and only small parts of the planet fit into the cameras' field of view, another movie was shot: the "zoom movie." The action around the Great Red Spot in the zoom movie was particularly amazing, as small light and dark spots the size of terrestrial continents were sucked in and then spit out by the counterclockwise-whirling high-pressure system.

By the end of February and beginning of March, hundreds of journalists, science writers, TV and radio reporters, and free lances began descending on JPL. Everyone worked hard, but a lot of the time was spent wandering about the auditorium looking at the latest images on the TV monitors.

Voyager 1 flew past Jupiter on March 5, 1979, and Voyager 2 made its closest approach to the planet four months later, on July 9, sending back tens of thousands of photos and reams of data from the other scientific instruments. They clocked the wind speeds in Jupiter's atmosphere; the fastest blew at 150 meters per second (about 335 miles per hour) at the equator. The famed Great Red Spot, it was found, rotates in a counterclockwise direction and is therefore a gargantuan high-pressure region in the Jovian atmosphere. The Voyagers did not resolve the mystery of the spot's color; there is still no sure answer to the nature of the compounds that cause the ruddy hue.

Voyager 1's cameras also took the first-ever photos of a thin ring of dust around the planet, picking out the incredibly faint band in scattered sunlight. It was not entirely unexpected, since Jim Elliot and his colleagues had discovered the Uranian rings two years earlier. The ring was only a few kilometers thick, and extended from about 1.72 Jupiter radii (123,000 kilometers from the center of the planet) out to 1.80 radii (129,000 kilometers), a ring width of about 6,000 kilometers. The ring particles are extremely tiny, something like smoke.

The most dramatic discoveries had to do with the

planet's system of moons. Most astounding of all were the erupting sulfur volcanos seen on the Jovian moon Io. Navigation engineer Linda Morabito was examining an optical navigation photo ("opnav" in Voyager team parlance) of Io, trying to determine the moon's position relative to background stars. Instead, she saw a curious umbrella-shaped mark hanging off one side of Io's disk. It turned out to be a plume of dust and gas being spewed out by a volcano. Eight and possibly nine active volcanos were eventually seen on the moon.

The three other giant "Galilean" moons were also quite interesting. Ganymede turns out to be the largest moon in the solar system and its surface shows evidence of tectonic motion and crustal plates, similar in some ways to Earth's surface. (However, it shows no evidence of any volcanic action.) Both Ganymede and Callisto are also very heavily cratered. Callisto is so completely cratered that it has reached the saturation point—meteor impacts creating new craters will also destroy older ones. Europa has a smooth surface that appeared made of water ice. Some scientists suggested the surface is about 5 kilometers thick, and that a moon-wide ocean of liquid water lies beneath. Science writer Richlard Hoagland later wrote an article for *Star & Sky* magazine suggesting that life might exist in the Europan seas, getting their energy from subsurface hotspots much as do the terrestrial creatures that live along the hydrothermal vents of the Pacific Ocean. Arthur C. Clarke later incorporated Hoagland's speculation into his science fiction novel and movie *2010*.

Voyager 1 and 2 also discovered several new moons orbiting Jupiter. Metis and Adrastea orbit just outside the Jovian ring. Both moons are a mere 40 kilometers—or 25 miles—in diameter. A third new moon, Thebe, is about 80 kilometers in diameter and circles Jupiter just outside the orbit of Amalthea. There are currently sixteen known moons circling Jupiter.

. . .

The two Jupiter encounters of 1979 produced a new kind of science—"instant science," attempts to come up with tentative answers to not always comprehensible questions for a mass audience that really didn't know too much about what science was or how it was done. For about a week at each encounter, the press corps would assemble every morning at 11:00 a.m. at the Jet Propulsion Laboratory's Von Karman Auditorium for the daily briefing. Several Voyager scientists would sit at the long dais and present the latest findings of Voyager 1 or 2. Then the questions would follow.

The project manager (during the Jupiter flybys it was Robert Parks, at Saturn it was Ray Heacock for Voyager 1 and Esker Davis for Voyager 2, and at Uranus it was Richard Laeser) would begin with a quick report on the spacecraft's status. Usually it was "Everything's just fine." Then Project scientist Ed Stone would say a few quotable words about the science. Next to report was usually Brad Smith, head of the Voyager imaging team. Smith, an astronomy professor at the University of New Mexico and later at the University of Arizona at Tucson, had a rugged face and a laconic manner that Marshall McLuhan would have loved. Though not a native Arizonan, he'd lived there long enough to pick up the inflections and mannerisms of a southwestern cowboy. He wore cowboy boots, too. Brad Smith was "cool" and looked great on television.

Smith would begin by calling for lights out and screen down. The latest photos of Jupiter would flash across the screen, and Smith would point out the interesting features. He always saved the best for last: incredibly colored images of the planet, image-stretched into surrealism; closeups of a particularly fascinating cloud formation; some particularly bizarre image of a moon.

Following Smith was usually Laurence Soderblom, a geologist with the U.S. Geological Survey. Smith usually focused on the planet and its atmosphere. Larry Soderblom, on the other hand, was the imaging team's "moon man." He would present the waiting media with the latest images of Jupiter's (and later Saturn's) miniature solar system. Indeed, Soderblom and the others were soon referring to the Jovian moons as "other worlds." They were each unique, each a special world. Ganymede, in fact, was larger than two official planets, Pluto and Mercury. Soderblom would usually concentrate on evidence of geological activity, such as faulting from moonquakes or cratering.

After Smith and Soderblom had finished with their slide shows, there were usually two or three other scientists with quick reports to the press. Sometimes it was Fred Scarf, principal investigator for the plasma-wave experiment or PWS. Scarf's data in its raw form would have been incomprehensible to most of the press people. He did a brilliant end run on that problem, though, by turning the data into sound. "Sounds of Jupiter," data about the strength and frequency of waves in the ionized plasma around Jupiter, usually resembled the sounds made by Rice Krispies. That was in 1979; by 1981 he had come up with some tricks that made "Sounds of Saturn" downright music of the spheres.

After the formal presentations came the question-and-answer period. Frank Bristow, of JPL's Public Information Office, moderated the affair and called on different reporters, the quality of questions depended on the specialization of the reporter. Some tended to ask "what does this all mean" questions. Others, usually the professional science reporters, had fairly insightful and sometimes technical queries. The television reporters almost always got called on first, so they could get their question asked and their film shot and be ready to make the evening news deadlines back east. Reporters for major daily newspapers also got first dibs at questions, since they had short deadlines to meet. Free-lance writers rarely got the cordless microphone. Neither did reporters for radio stations, much to their frustration; they were often on deadlines as tight as those of the TV and newspaper people.

After the briefing was over, print reporters would cluster around the dais for a few last impromptu questions. The TV people would lurk near the full-sized replica of Voyager and snag Smith, Soderblom, or Stone as he went past—"just a few quick ones, Doctor"—as the camera crew turned on the floodlights.

When the actual Jupiter flybys were over in late 1979, the work for the Voyager team's scientists had just begun. There were mountains of raw data to deal with, to make sense of, to write papers about. Within two periods of about a month each, the scientific community had learned more about Jupiter, its atmosphere, its bizarre moons, and its newly discovered ring than in the entire previous history of astronomy. It was time for some *real* work. The dog and pony shows for the media were not *real* science. However, the American public paid for the space program with its tax dollars. If it lost interest, the politicians in Washington would eagerly cut budgets and shift the dollars to other, more popular programs. But if in 1979 the general American public was not too literate scientifically, then the American science community was also not too literate politically. Within two years that would begin to change.

By November 1980, and the Voyager 1 flyby of Saturn, other events were occupying the American public: the Iranian hostage crisis; the Soviet invasion of Afghanistan and the subsequent American boycott of the 1980 Summer Olympics; the eruption of Mount St. Helens; the presidential race between Carter and Reagan. Could Saturn compete with all that?

Oh, yes.

The Jupiter-Saturn cruise phase for Voyager 1 ended, and the observatory phase began, in August 1980. By October 1, six weeks from encounter, Voyager 1 was 56 million kilometers from the planet and closing. The cameras could resolve details on Saturn and its rings as small as 1,000 kilometers in diameter, or about the distance from San Francisco to Portland, Oregon. The resolution was already three times better than achievable by the best telescopes on Earth. The rings were rippled and banded, and contained much more structure than had even been evident from the Pioneer 11 images of a year earlier. There was no empty space in the Cassini "Division" between the A and B rings; it was filled with material. Also surprising was the discovery that features in the ring rarely coincided with the resonance positions of the inner Saturnian satellites.

Resonance had long been accepted as the explanation for the divisions in the rings as seen from Earth. Saturn's inner moons—Mimas, Enceladus, Tethys, Dione, and Rhea—orbit Saturn at distances ranging from 186,000 to 527,000 kilometers from the center of the planet. Their orbital periods range from 0.94 days for Mimas to 4.5 days for Rhea. Saturn's classically known rings extend to 136,800 kilometers from Saturn's center. The rings are made of individual particles that orbit Saturn like any other satellite. So different parts of the rings have different orbital periods, just as Saturn's different moons do. The resonance theory is based on the fact that there are distinct relationships between the orbital periods of the inner Saturnian moons and different parts of the rings. For example, Mimas orbits Saturn once every 22 hours. The orbital period for a particle in the center of the Cassini Division (119,000 kilometers from Saturn's center) is a little over 11 hours —almost exactly half the period of Mimas. A particle in the inner edge of the B ring orbits Saturn once every 7.93 hours—about a third the period of Mimas. Scientists believed these fractional relationships could cause gravitational tugs at those areas of the rings, "sweeping out" particles in those resonance areas, creating gaps and divisions and relatively sharp edges at the boundaries of different rings. The Cassini Division and the observed edges of different rings were the classic proofs of the resonance theory.

Voyager 1 severely damaged the resonance theory. There was only one real "division" in the Cassini Division, the tiny 450-kilometer-wide Huygens gap at the two-to-one Mimas resonance position. The gap was filled with particles. The B ring and the A ring were not separated by 4,500 kilometers of empty space. Their "edges," though sharp and distinct, butted up against the edges of other rings in the division.

Meanwhile, Voyager 1 was plunging toward Saturn at a speed of 54,000 kilometers per hour. The resolution of the transmitted photographs improved steadily. Cloud structure in Saturn's atmosphere became visible to Voyager's cameras. There were no "great red spots" like that on Jupiter, but several smaller and lighter-colored ones did show up. One, later dubbed Anne's Spot, was first noticed and followed by the imaging team's then assistant experiment representative, Anne Bunker.

Over the weekend of October 4, Voyager 1 shot a long sequence of images of the rings. On Monday, imaging team member Richard Terrile began examining them and discovered something utterly astonishing: dark structures that radiated *across the width of the rings* like spokes from a wheel with Saturn at the hub.

The spokes were totally unexpected. They were also totally inexplicable. They should not exist. Saturn's rings are not solid structures, but a collection of trillions of relatively tiny particles orbiting the planet. Any structure made of these particles that stretched radially from the plant would soon be smeared into oblivion by the differing orbital speeds of its particles.

On October 24, 1980, Voyager 1 entered the far encounter phase of the flyby. The spacecraft controllers had reprogrammed the craft to spend about ten hours photographing the ends of the rings with images every five minutes. The resulting images made up a "movie" of the rings as their particles moved about Saturn. That morning, the imaging team's experiment representative, Andrew Collins, began looking at the movie, and he soon spotted something new: a small moon orbiting just outside the F ring. The next day, October 26, Collins found a satellite just *inside* the F ring. They were the first new satellites of Saturn to be found by Voyager.

Astronomers began speculating that these two tiny moons are responsible for the F ring's narrow form, their small gravitational fields acting to "focus" or pinch the ring matter into a small band. Science fiction writer Jerry Pournelle later referred to them as "sheep dog" satellites, and planetary scientists generally called them "shepherd" moons. Similar moons had been earlier theorized as the cause of narrow rings of Uranus. They were found first, though, at Saturn.

By the end of October the features in Saturn's atmosphere were becoming clearer. The planet's major moons were also becoming visible as distinct round shapes and not just points of light. The rings, too, were becoming more and more detailed as the imaging resolution increased by the hour. Scientists could now see at least five rings in the Cassini "Division." Encounter was just twelve days away.

One member of the imaging team had not been much in evidence during the Jupiter flybys. Dr. Carl Sagan, astronomer and writer, had been very much involved with a rather special project. It was a thirteen-episode TV special entitled *Cosmos: A Personal Journey.* With a multimillion-dollar budget and the facilities of public television station KCET in Los Angeles, Sagan had put together a remarkable journey through space and time. Charlie Kohlhase had helped with the programs, particularly in the areas of computer graphics and special effects. *Cosmos* was something Kohlhase was proud of; a *Cosmos* poster always had a prominent place in his office. In November 1980, the show was on the air and Sagan had become a national celebrity. Millions of TV viewers had the opportunity to see *Cosmos*, the real images of Saturn and Sagan himself, all on TV. Sagan again was before the cameras, but now it was at JPL and on ABC's *Nightline* with Ted Koppel.

On November 3, Saturn's giant moon Titan was looking more like a planet than a moon. In fact, Titan was at that time the only moon in the solar system known to have its own atmosphere. It was thick, orange, and nearly as opaque as the atmosphere of Venus. Computer image enhancement brought out some faint hints of banded structure in Titan's atmosphere, but nothing more. Several scientists, Sagan the most prominent of them, had suggested that there might be complex organic chemicals in the Titanian atmosphere and on its surface. The vulcanism seen on Io back at Jupiter raised the possibility that Titan's surface might have hot spots where those complex carbon compounds could have gotten even more complex. The word "life" was mentioned now and then. No one was really optimistic about it; though Voyager's cameras couldn't see the surface, other instruments aboard the spacecraft indicated the place was very cold. The conclusive data would come from the IRIS instrument and the radio science experiment on November 12.

Meanwhile, the ring movie of November 3 had been processed by the Image Processing Lab into a real movie. Ed Stone and some others took a look at it. Clearly visible were Terrile's spokes, visible as ring particles moved out of Saturn's shadows and sometimes dissipating before the particles moved back into the shadow. But they lasted a long time, much longer than they should. For that matter, the scientists couldn't figure out why the spokes even existed in the first place. Theories were soon flying around like the ring particles themselves. The spokes are still not fully explained.

By November 6, when the first formal press conference on the Voyager 1 Saturn flyby took place, the spacecraft itself was speeding toward Saturn at more than 55,000 kilometers per hour. The cameras were shooting images of the rings once a day with a resolution of 150 kilometers. Voyager 1 was examining Titan every six hours with a full complement of instruments. That evening the spacecraft reoriented itself and fired its rocket motors for about twelve minutes to make a final change in its path to Saturn.

I arrived at JPL on Friday, November 7, to cover the flyby for a local radio station. My press badge was number 595, and there were still a lot of people in line behind me. The talk in the press area (again Von Karman Auditorium) was a mixture of space and politics. The images of Saturn were already astonishing, albeit a bit blander than the swirling clouds of Jupiter. There were already mysteries to puzzle over, especially the ring spokes. As for politics, Ronald Reagan had beaten Jimmy Carter three days earlier, and everyone was wondering how that would affect the unmanned space program and the exploration of the solar system. NASA budgets had never fared well after the Apollo glory days of the late 1960s. Would Reagan as president make a difference? Some thought so. One of many rumors floating about was that Reagan was a closet space freak; he had space photos pasted on the walls of his office at "the Ranch" near Santa Barbara. Somehow this all proved that Reagan would support the space program with budget increases. How he would do this while at the same time cutting taxes and ballooning the Pentagon budget seemed to escape the more fervent true believers in the press corps.

Voyager 1 cared not about politics; its computers did what they were told and nothing more. That included a search for new satellites around Saturn and a close look at Titan in the ultraviolet region of the spectrum. Both searches were successful. A new tiny moon—the fifteenth for Saturn—was found about 800 kilometers (480 miles) outside the edge of the A ring. The UVS instrument detected the presence of atomic hydrogen in the atmosphere of Titan. It was just five days from flyby.

The first bad news was reported the next morning. A severe thunderstorm in Spain had wiped out some six hours of data transmission from the spececraft to the Deep Space Network station outside Madrid. Worse, a series of storms in the Atlantic seemed to be heading for Spain, and that might mean more data losses on up-coming passes. The rain in Spain was no joke in Pasadena. Fortunately, the next thunderstorms held off long enough that the next transmission from Voyager to the Madrid station came through.

By November 10, two days before encounter, Voyager and Saturn had captured the world. Von Karman was packed with news reporters, TV crews, science fiction writers, wives, husbands, significant others, hangers-on, and space groupies. Front-page stories were appearing in every major paper in the country. Johnny Carson and Angie Dickinson got exclusive guided tours of JPL. The working press area, a large room in Von Karman adjacent to the auditorium proper, was filled with men and women banging away at typewriters and talking on the phone. Periodically we lined up at the door marked "Photos" and received the latest packet from Jurrie Van der Woude, the picture man for the Public Information Office. Jurrie had been with JPL since the days of Mariner 2, the American space-probe flyby of Venus in 1962. He had seen it all, but the press zoo of the Saturn flybys, he later remarked, was particularly amazing.

Jurrie's boss, Frank Bristow, had his hands full, too. He and his cadre of PIO staffers kept the media fed with press releases and scheduled interviews with Voyager personnel as best they could. Periodically a group of reporters would get an escort from Von Karman, across the plaza to Building 264, which housed the Voyager Project, and into someone's office for a few minutes of talk or photos.

Bristow also had to deal with the space groupies, people who weren't accredited writers or reporters but had in one fashion or another gained access to the press area. It was an onerous task. He was particularly upset by the presence of a large continent of science fiction writers. Some members of the press welcomed them— they made for great interviews and that much more copy. Besides, some of the reporters were science fiction fans. Bristow felt otherwise. He insisted he had nothing against science fiction writers per se. But they were not working press, and he felt strongly that their presence simply made his job, and the press's job, that much harder. Also, he had not invited them; science fiction writer Jerry Pournelle had done that, through connections with high-level JPL management. There was never any love lost between Bristow and Pournelle.

November 11, 1980: the day before encounter with Saturn for Voyager 1. That evening the spacecraft flew past the moon Titan and produced exciting data for the scientists, but the pictures were uniformly dull. Titan was completely enshrouded by a high, impenetrable haze. It was a giant frozen orange; the average surface temperature, Voyager's instruments said, was just 92 degrees Celsius above absolute zero. Some of the writers and scientists had entered a "Titan pool," trying to guess what the air pressure was at the surface of the moon. No one got close; Voyager 1 returned data that suggested it was 1.6 bars (sea-level air pressure on Earth is defined as 1 bar).

Now the attention of scientists and media alike focused on Saturn itself, its incredible ring system, and its retinue of moons. In the press room people gathered around the TV monitors and watched the latest images flash onto the screens. One after another the moons appeared, seen for the first time as actual objects and not just tiny spots of light on a photographic plate. The moon Dione, some 1,118 kilometers in diameter (it would fit between Los Angeles and Portland), had an eerie white ropy pattern sprawled across it. An enormous trench, a kilometer deep, 50 to 100 kilometers wide, and more than 2,000 kilometers long, stretched across the face of Tethys. And tiny Mimas, just 396 kilometers wide, stared out of the monitors like some giant eye . . . or the "Death Star" from the movie *Star Wars*. An enormous impact crater 13 kilometers wide dominated the hemisphere imaged by Voyager 1. The impact must have been so powerful that it almost shattered Mimas.

The morning press briefing featured these and other photos from Voyager 1's cameras. Everyone was stunned The newest images of Titan showed a distinct high-altitude haze, and a detached polar hood in the north. Then Brad Smith flashed the latest image of the F ring on the screen. "In this strange world of Saturn's rings, the bizarre becomes the commonplace," said Smith. "This is what we saw this morning." The auditorium erupted in gasps. The high-resolution image showed the F ring—at least in this one place—was *braided*, composed of at least three interwoven strands. "At least they *appear* to be braided," said Smith. It was all just too much. Ed Stone had said earlier that week that everyone should expect the astounding to be commonplace. Science knew relatively little about Saturn, and even less about the details of its moons and rings. But one after another, the images had turned the encounter into a literal freak show. It was a field day of the fantastic for the news media, a nightmare for scientists who would have to explain things like spokes and braided rings and Death Star moons.

Could the braided F ring be temporary? Smith thought not. "That's stable," Smith said. "It boggles the mind that it even exists. It defies the laws of orbital mechanics, as I understand them. Obviously the rings are doing the right thing—we just don't understand the rules."

Later that afternoon, in the daily science meeting, IRIS principal investigator Rudy Hanel reported there was a strong indication of methane in Titan's atmosphere. Also detected, he added, were acetylene, hydrogen cyanide, and ethane. To the delight of the "pro-Titan-lifers," the moon's atmosphere seemed chock-full of hydrocarbon compounds. Of course, no one really expected life on Titan when the temperatures were well below −100 degrees Celsius, but there certainly was a lot of organic stuff around.

As the evening progressed, the images continued coming in from Voyager 1. The rings, at higher and higher resolution became more and more complex. There were not just four, or fourteen, or forty, or even four hundred rings; there were thousands. Rings within rings within rings. Ringlets next to ringlets. Within the Cassini "Division," for example, there now appeared to be at least fifty distinct radial features not separated by gaps.

Voyager 1 had made its first crossing of the ring plane earlier in the encounter, before the Titan flyby. It was now "beneath" Saturn and coming up from under. It made its closest approach to Saturn late that afternoon, coming within 124,000 kilometers of its cloudtops. At 7:08 p.m. Pacific Time, Voyager 1 disappeared behind Saturn, beginning its occultation by that planet. It reappeared, then passed behind the C, B, and A rings.

At 9:00 p.m. it finally came out from behind the A ring, as seen from Earth. At 9:45 p.m. it again crossed the plane of the rings, heading upward and out from Saturn. A series of images of Mimas, Dione, Enceladus, and Rhea came in the hours following close approach. The Enceladus images were from a considerable distance, and all that could be seen was that the moon seemed curiously . . . dull. There didn't seem to be any impact craters. Was this another Europa? The scientists would have to wait for Voyager 2's flyby in August of 1981. That craft would come much closer to Enceladus.

For Lonne Lane, now principal investigator for the photopolarimeter instrument, the Voyager 1 encounter with Saturn was frustrating. Nothing happened for him. The PPS aboard Voyager 1 had been so badly damaged by the 1978 overexposure incident that it was essentially useless. The Voyager 2 PPS had been used to make a map of aerosols in the Jovian atmosphere, but that had been all. It would be another nine months before he would have a chance at getting any scientific information at all from the PPS experiment. In the meantime, Lane had to sit this third giant-planet flyby out.

The time between launch and Saturn flyby had not been totally wasted, though. "We gained a better understanding of the instrument," Lane later recalled, "and we were able to accurately calibrate its response. We also developed some techniques for using it better." The work would eventually pay off, but not for Voyager 1.

On June 5, 1981, Voyager 2 entered the observatory phase of its encounter with Saturn. The great success of Voyager 1's flyby meant that Voyager 2 no longer needed to back up any failed or missed Voyager I tasks. The spacecraft engineers could adjust the spacecraft's flyby aimpoint to get the kind of gravitational boost

67

from Saturn that would fling it off toward a new target: Uranus.

Observatory Phase ran for eight weeks, through July 31. The spacecraft carried out a careful examination of Saturn's atmospheric movements and took a detailed look at the mysterious dark spokes in the rings. The spacecraft continued to probe the space environment with its fields and particles instruments. Though the team was worried about the spacecraft's only remaining radio receiver, most of the engineers felt fairly confident that Voyager 2 would make it through the Saturn system unscathed and would carry out its mission in full. But wouldn't this all be somewhat anticlimactic, after the spectacular success of Voyager 1 nine months earlier? What could possibly top braided rings, spokes, a Death Star moon, and a moon with an orange atmosphere stuffed with organic molecules? Could Voyager 2 possibly elicit anything more than a "we've-seen-this-all-before" response from the scientists, the press, and the world at large?

Oh, yes.

By August 1 the spacecraft was 25 million kilometers (about 15 million miles) from Saturn and closing in at nearly a million kilometers a day. On July 31 the far encounter phase began. Many of the more than 18,000 images of the Saturn system were pouring into the computers of JPL's Image Processing Lab. It appeared that the cameras aboard Voyager 2 were more sensitive than those on Voyager 1, perhaps 50 percent more sensitive. The images were crisper and had more detail than those from Voyager 1 at equivalent distances. Also, the lighting was better. Saturn's northern pole was now pointed slightly closer to the sun than before. The sunlight was hitting the rings at an angle of 8 degrees rather than 4 degrees as during the Voyager 1 flyby.

However, the images from Voyager 2 weren't the only spectacular ones on display. Using Voyager 1 imaging data and the known and predicted positions of Saturn, its moons, Voyager 2, the sun, and about 6,000 of the background stars during each part of the flyby, Charlie Kohlhase and JPL computer graphics wizard Jim Blinn had put together an astonishing computerized movie of the Voyager 2 flyby. Watching the movie, which ran for about five minutes, was like sitting in an imaginary spaceship flying along right behind Voyager 2. You came in closer and closer to a realistic-looking Saturn that loomed larger and larger in your field of view. Voyager 2 twisted, turned around, spun on its Earth-pointing axis as it made its observations. A moon would suddenly flash by and the space probe would swivel about and aim its cameras as it went past. Then, at the climax, Voyager 2 plunged through the place of the rings: swoosh!—the rings and their particles blurred past you. The spacecraft again moved about and continued to aim its cameras and other instruments at the passing moons. Finally, looking back at Earth and Saturn, you saw the golden-ringed planet disappear into the distance. . . .

On August 20, Voyager 2 was approaching Saturn at more than 11 kilometers per second. The cameras could now make out features in Saturn's atmosphere as small as 150 kilometers in diameter. The infrared interferometer spectrometer (IRIS) and the ultraviolet spectrometer (UVS) were sending back extensive data about Saturn's upper atmosphere and cloudtops. And the photopolarimeter (PPS) was working just fine. Lonne Lane was in business. For now the PPS was doing its workhorse job: sending back information about the aerosols and dust particles in the planet's atmosphere. During the last few hours before closest approach, however, the instrument would be trained on a star named Delta Scorpii, the fourth-brightest star in the constellation Scorpio, the Scorpion. Voyager 2's path would take it above and across Saturn's rings, and the PPS would follow Delta Scorpii as it flickered through the particles. The result, Lane and his team hoped, would be a detailed "map" of that cross section of the rings, including information on their opacity, size, and spacing.

On August 21, the spacecraft was 6 million kilometers from Saturn and closing. The first press conference formally opened up the media season for Voyager 2 at Saturn. Nearly 600 press passes had been issued for the Voyager 1 flyby nine months earlier. The number was up by 50 percent for this one. Clearly, the world's press did not think the Voyager 2 flyby would be a case of "we've seen all this before." The spectacular results of the Voyager 1 encounter had only served to whet the appetite of the media and the public for Saturn and space. Carl Sagan's *Cosmos* TV series had helped, too. Finally, there was the realization that this would probably be the last planetary encounter in many years.

Esker "Ek" Davis had replaced Ray Heacock as Voyager project manager. Dick Laeser was the mission director. Davis greeted the assembled media with encouraging words: "Everything is going very well!" A chip in one of the FDS computers had failed a few weeks earlier, but, he explained, "We found better ways to do the sequencing for the encounter, so we end up with more capabilities than were present in the original sequences."

Brad Smith showed the latest movie sequence of images taken of Saturn by Voyager 2, and stressed the importance of finding small satellites within some of the gaps in the ring system. Theoretically, the gaps were best explained by tiny moons sweeping particles up— "Moonlets between ringlets cause gaplets," as *Science News* reporter Jonathan Eberhart put it—and the "moonlets" should be large enough for Voyager to see.

Voyager 2 would come fairly close to Saturn's G

ring as it passed through the ring plane. Ed Stone, however, was sure nothing would go wrong. "I think we're
all confident," he said in response to a question, "but on
the other hand, we'll all be much happier to hear the
transmissions when the spacecraft comes out on the
other side."

On August 21, Voyager 2 had taken some photos of
Saturn's moon Iapetus. The next day they were made
available to the press. The resolution was about 40
kilometers, and the images showed the features that
made Iapetus so famous in astronomical circles: the
amazing contrast between the dark leading hemisphere
of the moon (the hemisphere facing in the direction of
its path around Saturn) and large, bright icy surfaces.
The dark areas were as black as asphalt. The border
between the dark and light areas of Iapetus resembled
an S, giving the moon a yin-yang appearance. The icy
areas were dotted with impact craters. One very large
crater looked as if it had black stuff partly inside and
outside it. No one was sure what could cause such a
dark surface, but Carl Sagan and others suggested a
tarry black organic substance formed by the bombard-
ment of Iapetus's surface by solar radiation. If true, that
meant the dark areas were surface and the bright areas
were ice covering it. Others suggested just the opposite:
the bright areas were the icy surface of Iapetus, and the
dark areas were black organic-like deposits of dust that
came from another Saturnian moon, Phoebe.
Later on the 22nd, as Voyager closed within 4 million kilometers of Saturn, several SF writers and media
people looked very closely at the Iapetus pictures. Try as
we might, though, we could not see the object that made
Iapetus famous in fictional circles: Arthur C. Clarke's
mysterious monolith from the book version of *2001: A
Space Odyssey*. We really didn't expect to see it, of

course; as one person pointed out, the resolution limit of 40 kilometers would not have made it visible. But the effort was a somewhat spooky intersection of science fiction and science fact.

On the morning of August 23, the spacecraft went through an intricate ballet of rolls and twists so some of the instruments could map out the fields and particles environment near Saturn. Voyager 2 was now within 3 million kilometers of the planet and approaching it at a rate of more than a million kilometers (25,000 miles) per hour. The imaging team released a new "spoke movie" which followed a single ring spoke as it formed and moved around the rings and disappeared into Saturn's shadow. The film was immediately dubbed "The Saturn 500."

Just as interesting was the search for moonlets in the ringlets causing gaplets. Jeff Cuzzi of NASA's Ames Research Center near San Francisco was an associate member of the imaging team and was the team's resident ring expert—the "ring leader," as Candy Hansen would later call him. Cuzzi and his colleagues predicted the existence of a 20-to-30-kilometer diameter moon in a gap at the edge of the Cassini Division. Voyager 2's cameras had taken pictures of that area for one complete ring rotation. If the moonlet was there, it would show up in the images at least once. Cuzzi and Richard Terrile (alias the "spokes man") had already looked through a third of the images taken, and had found nothing. By late evening they had looked through two-thirds of the images. Still nothing.

Earlier in the afternoon the first pictures of Saturn's moon Hyperion came back from Voyager. They were shocking. Although about the same size as the moon Mimas, Hyperion did not look at all like that innermost major moon of Saturn. For Hyperion was not a sphere. Rather, it looked a lot like a 410-kilometer-wide hockey puck. Nor was that the only surprise. The moon was small enough and close enough to giant Saturn that it would have been in a permanent "tidal lock"—like Earth's own moon, it should have had one side permanently facing Saturn. But the long axis was instead pointing off to one side. "Are you sure you know where Saturn is?" a stunned Ed Stone asked the imaging team at one point. Hyperion was, it seemed, tumbling in a random fashion, as if it had recently (cosmically speaking) been struck by another object.

Early on the morning of August 24, Voyager 2 crossed Saturn's bow shock for the first time. The bow shock is the area where the sun's "wind" of charged particles hits Saturn's powerful magnetic field. The solar wind pushes the bow-shock area back and forth, and so Voyager "crossed" the line several times before the final plunge through and into the realm of Saturn's magnetic influence at 6:52 p.m.

Voyager 2 was now just twenty-four hours, less than 2 million kilometers, from closest approach to Saturn. In front of the assembled press corps that morning, imaging team leader Brad Smith admitted total failure in the search for the moonlets in the ringlets causing gaplets. There were none to be seen, he said, that were larger than 10 kilometers in diameter. He didn't think they'd see moonlets even at the final limit of 5-kilometer resolution. It was a tough situation to be in, he added. "We now find ourselves at the point where we hoped not to be. We are desperately looking for an alternative hypothesis to explain the gaps [in the rings]."

On the brighter side, there was now a firm theory for the strange appearance of Iapetus. The scientists had an accurate estimate of the moon's mass and diameter. From those data, astronomer David Morrison calculated the moon's density to be 1.1 grams per cubic centimeter, close to pure ice. So Iapetus's bright areas were probably surface ice, and the black areas a coating of something similar in darkness to asphalt.

Other scientists were puzzling over the rings. Voyager 1 had spotted bizarre kinks and loops in the F ring, but now Voyager 2 saw nothing of the sort. Researchers had proposed several hypotheses to explain the braided F ring, but where was it? Then there were the ring spokes. How could such features exist? And what caused them? One theory for the spokes' visibility was electromagnetic levitation. Some sort of interaction between the ring particles and Saturn's electromagnetic field might cause fine dustlike particles to rise up a few centimeters above the plane of the rings. It was a nice explanation—but it didn't explain the essential *how* and *why* of the spokes.

August 25, 1981. Encounter Day for Voyager 2. The next several hours would include close approaches to the moons Tethys and Enceladus. The craft would also take close looks at newly discovered moonlets that shared the orbits of Dione and Tethys. Voyager 1 had come in from above the ring plane and had made two passes through the plane as Saturn's gravity looped it around and out toward the stars. Voyager 2 was also diving down on Saturn from above the plane of the rings, but its incoming view of the rings was better than that of Voyager 1, because it remained above the ring plane until after closest approach to Saturn. Also, it would make only one plunge through the ring plane.

Von Karman Auditorium—"Press Central" for this flyby, as it had been for the others—was packed to the rafters. A phalanx of TV cameras lined the back wall, mounted on long risers. Electrical cables snaked everywhere. Every folding chair was occupied by working press. Still photographers squeezed in where they could. A coterie of VIPs that included high NASA officials, movie stars, ex-astronauts, and science fiction writers were forced up against the sides of the auditorium. After a few false starts, Frank Bristow got the crowd quieted down. Project Manager Ek Davis announced that Voyager 2 was slightly off target . . . by all of 50 kilometers. After a two-year journey of more than a billion kilometers, the near miss was utterly insignificant. Brad Smith, cowboy-booted and smiling ever so slightly, showed the latest images of the rings. The crowd gasped in delight and wonder. Next came high-resolution images of the moon Tethys. Again the gasps. There on the screen was *another* Death Star crater, like the one seen nine months earlier on Mimas. Only this one was truly gargantuan. Mimas was a shade under 400 kilometers across, while Tethys was an estimated 1,000 kilometers. The giant crater now discovered on Tethys was itself well over 400 kilometers wide. The entire moon Mimas would fit comfortably inside it.

But the surprise hit of the press conference that morning was not pictures, but music. Out of the shadows of popular obscurity stepped Fred Scarf, the principal investigator for the plasma-wave instrument, or PWS. Plasma waves are electrical waves in a medium of electrically charged particles (the definition of "plasma"), much as sounds are waves in air. What's more, plasma waves are in the audio range of frequencies. They are what we would hear if the waves were sound instead of electromagnetic. Scarf had wondered what they would sound like if they *were* sound waves. When he discovered a new kind of computer, a so-called "home computer" called the Apple II, he figured out a way to turn the plasma waves into audible sounds. He hooked the Apple to a music synthesizer, digitized the plasma-wave pickup, and ran it through the resulting combination. The result, which he played over the Von Karman speakers, sounded like something written by Philip Glass, or from the sound track of *Star Trek*. It was eerie, and beautiful. The journalists gave Scarf and his "Sounds of Saturn" a standing ovation.

By now the VIPs were crowding into JPL. NASA Administrator James Beggs arrived to extend congratulations to the Voyager team and JPL upper management. Along with Beggs was Andy Stofan, the acting head of NASA's Office of Space Science. Later that afternoon a helicopter from the Santa Barbara White House deposited the chubby figure of Presidential Special Counselor Edwin Meese. Journalists squeezed in around Meese as he looked at the Voyager model and asked a series of questions that exposed his general lack of knowledge of things spacy. JPL Director Bruce Murray answered them with masterful tact. The journalists shouted a series of questions about the future of the space program under Ronald Reagan and Budget Director David Stockman. Meese answered them with masterful vagueness.

At 3:00 p.m., Beggs, Stofan, and Murray faced the media in a special press conference celebrating the imminent close encounter with Saturn. Each gave a short statement of congratulations and hope for the future, and then they asked for questions.

What they got was a savage raking over the coals by a surprisingly prospace group of over 500 reporters. Rumors had run rampant through Von Karman that David Stockman had boasted of his plans to destroy the U.S. planetary space program. "NASA will be out of the space exploration business by 1984," he had supposedly said. There were plans, claimed the rumors, to turn off the giant dish antennas of the Deep Space Network and leave the Pioneers and Voyagers drifting wordlessly in space; the planned space probe to Venus called VOIR would be canceled; the Galileo space probe to Jupiter would be canceled. The cooperative space mission with Europe that would send two space probes under and over the sun was in danger. The U.S. probe to Halley's

Comet in 1986 was in serious danger of cancellation. That would leave the United States as the only space-faring nation *not* sending a probe to the most famous comet in history.

The journalists who regularly covered space activities, the "space gypsies," were frankly outraged. They wanted answers, they wanted the truth, and they wanted it right then and there. It was pack journalism at its best—or worst, depending on where you were sitting in the auditorium. The three officials on the dais had expected a love feast and a few concerned questions. What they got was the Inquisition. The questions came hard and fast and were often indistinguishable from accusations. They were stunned by the ferocity of the attack, and their answers were for the most part hesitant, stumbling, and evasive.

"I cannot conceive of NASA without a strong science program," Beggs said at one point. At another point he asserted that the Halley probe was "still under consideration" in Washington. The truth, though, was that the Halley probe would be dead by the end of the year, and that the proposed NASA budget for 1983 was cut so badly that some scientists described it as "gutted." Beggs assured the press that once the space shuttle was paid for (maybe around 1986), more money would be freed up for space science. But Andy Stofan, his own acting deputy administrator for space science sitting right next to him on the dais, responded that "science is not going to be there anymore if we don't solve the problem by 1986." All in all, James Beggs's promised trimphant moment turned out to be one of the more uncomfortable days of his life. Perhaps, too, it was an omen of things to come. For by the time Voyager 2 arrived at Uranus, Beggs was gone, forced out of NASA's highest position after being charged with unethical business practices at his former job with General Dynamics.

. . .

Voyager 2 kept closing in on Saturn, oblivious to earthly politics and pack journalism. At 6:18 p.m., Lonne Lane and his team received the signals from the spacecraft that indicated the PPS had begun tracking the occultation of Delta Scorpii by Saturn's rings. Cheers exploded in the crowded office in Voyager Country. For the first time since Jupiter, Lane and his science group were in business. It was to be a glorious night and day. For more than two hours the data poured in; Lane was ecstatic. By 8:40 p.m., when the occultation ended, the photopolarimeter had traced a detailed profile of *more than 82,000 kilometers* of Saturn's rings. It took up half a mile of chart paper. The effective resolution of the rings was measured in feet, much better than the best images from Brad Smith's TV cameras. Even Smith admitted it was worth the time lost to his imaging team.

Then it was their turn. Voyager 2 twisted around and its scanning platform began swiveling about as it resumed its photographic probing of Saturn's moons. The target was Enceladus, seen only from a distance by Voyager 1 and seemingly devoid of impact craters. As the photos flashed up on the monitors in the imaging team area of floor three in Building 264, the reasons for no craters became clear. Like Io at Jupiter, Enceladus was a geologically active moon. Voyager 2 came within 87,000 kilometers of Enceladus, and the images showed icy areas seemingly wiped clean. At the edges of those areas could be seen impact craters almost literally cut in half, parts of them wiped out of existence. Other areas on the moon were indeed dotted with craters; still other parts seemed warped and twisted, the topography looking ropy and ridged. Enceladus was apparently geologically active; some internal heat source, perhaps caused by gravitational tugs from Saturn, was driving the reworking of Enceladus's icy surface. And like Jupiter's Io, Enceladus could well be *currently* active geologically. More images of Enceladus and other moons would come the next day. Meanwhile, Voyager 2 stored additional moon and ring images on its digital tape recorder.

At 9:50 p.m., Voyager 2 made its closest approach to Saturn, 101,000 kilometers above the cloudtops. At about 10:00 p.m., the imaging sequence ended and the spacecraft got ready to disappear behind the disk of Saturn. The craft would dive through the plane of the rings near the G ring at about 10:44 p.m. Pacific Time. All this would take place out of contact from Earth. From 10:26 p.m. to a minute past midnight, Voyager 2 would be behind Saturn relative to Earth and out of touch. The radio science experiment would take place as the spacecraft slipped out of sight; Voyager 2 would beam its radio waves through the edges of Saturn's atmosphere and probe its nature and structure.

For nearly two hours, journalists and scientists milled about in Von Karman, drinking coffee, joking nervously, and glancing up at the blank monitors. No one really expected anything to go wrong, but no one would know for sure until the signals from Voyager 2 were reacquired. Finally, just a few minutes before midnight, the first faint signals came filtering through Saturn's atmosphere. She'd made it! Out of the desks and nooks in the press area appeared bottles of champagne and plastic cups. Brad Smith had wandered in and was treated to an impromptu series of toasts. Cheers and whoops of joy echoed throughout the auditorium.

Voyager 2 was on its way to Uranus!

Some of the news media arrived early the next morning, bleary-eyed and slightly hungover, for the first post-encounter press conference. To their surprise and concern, they were called to an unscheduled 8:15 a.m. briefing.

Voyager 2 was in deep, deep trouble.

79

A haggard-looking Dick Laeser, the mission director and deputy project manager, told the grim story. Shortly after JPL reestablished contact with Voyager 2, it became obvious the cameras were not pointing in the right direction. Shots were off by wide margins, and eventually all that could be seen on the monitors was black space. The scan platform had frozen up. It would not move. It had happened, it appeared, fifty minutes after Voyager 2 had plunged through the ring plane. Further examination of the engineering data showed that the scan platform was jamming in just one axis, the azimuth or back-and-forth direction. The elevation axis worked fine.

There was little to be done immediately. Round-trip light time to Voyager 2 was about three hours now, and any long-distance repairs would take a while. In the meantime, the spacecraft team "safed" the instruments on the platform by having it gingerly moved in the still-usable elevation direction to a position pointing farther away from the sun. The instruments continued to operate, but the computer commands that ran the platform were disabled. The spacecraft had received and executed those instructions by the time of the briefing, and now all that could be done was evaluate, brainstorm, and hope for a successful fix before 1986.

Lost to science were images from the closest encounters with Tethys and Enceladus, stereo views of the F ring, views of the rings from the dark side, and a second star occultation with Lane's PPS. But not all was lost. At 9:00 a.m. the tape recorder began playing back the images shot earlier and stored away. They were beautiful: close-ups of the multiple-stranded F ring; images of the F ring's shepherd satellites; astounding shots of Saturn's rings seen nearly edge on, moments before Voyager 2 passed through the plane. Finally, poignantly, a small corner of Tethys appeared on the screen, all that remained of what should have been an astounding closeup of that moon.

Other images from the previous day were processed and released to the media at the regularly scheduled press conference. They included wonderful views of the Tethys trench, a vast canyon now seen to stretch three-quarters of the way around that moon, for more than 2,500 kilometers. Brad Smith pointed out an image of the "Encke Gap" in the Saturnian rings, an image showing a thin "kinky ring" running down the middle.

Later that afternoon, at the 2:00 p.m. meeting of the scientists, Fred Scarf played an eerie tape from the plasma-wave instrument made at ring-plane crossing. It sounded like a violent hailstorm slamming into a tin roof. The activity was a million times the normal energy level, Scarf said. It appeared the antennae of the PWS were recording the impact on the spacecraft of thousands of dust grains at 10 kilometers per second. It roared on and on, for several minutes before, during, and after the crossing. Everyone thought the same question: could this be the cause of the jammed scan platform?

Would Voyager 2 be able to do anything at Uranus in 1986? It could, even without an operable scan platform. The craft would have to do roll maneuvers to point the instruments on the platform, though. Charlie Kohlhase quickly calculated the remaining hydrazine fuel for Voyager's thrusters and determined there was enough to get some good scientific data from a Uranus encounter.

On August 27, Dick Laeser reported that the scan platform *was* moving—barely. "We are not yet at the point of solving the problem," Laeser warned. "We are still trying to define the problem, to understand what's happening."

Then it was Lonne Lane's turn. He proudly walked to the dais and said: "It's taken us three years to traverse the seventy-five feet from the back of this room to the front. We have a superb set of ring data." Lane showed one tiny section of the PPS occultation experiment, profiling a stretch of the ring 340 kilometers wide. It included the Keeler Gap, and it showed incredibly fine features, much finer than photos could ever produce. The PPS data also gave Lonne a new estimate of the thickness of Saturn's rings: less than 300 meters, or about 1,000 feet. The best earlier estimates had been in the range of 2 kilometers, or some 6,600 feet. Other data from the occultation showed evidence of tiny wave patterns in the rings, possibly spiral density waves similar to those that create spiral arms in galaxies. The years of frustration for Lonne Lane had ended in spectacular triumph.

On the 28th, Laeser was smiling. "There's a good chance that Saturn will be on our TV screens again by the end of the day," he said. The scan platform was continuing to respond to tiny movement commands, and could now be moved enough so that Saturn would again be in the cameras' sights.

Again, Lane came to the front of Von Karman with PPS occultation results. Now it was the wild and crazy F ring, with its braids and kinks. The PPS data had been converted into a "pseudo-image," what the F ring would look like if the PPS had been a super TV camera. The image showed the F ring made of *at least ten strands*.

At 5:30 p.m., the worst Voyager 2 picture of Saturn ever seen appeared on the TV monitors. But it was a picture! The scan platform was moving again—slowly, painfully, but moving. Perhaps there would be a full-scale Uranus encounter after all.

Chapter 4
THE "QUIET CRUISE"

In April 1985 the Jupiter and Saturn flybys were nearly four years or more in the past. The Uranus encounter was less than a year in the future, and it would be different from the others. The Voyagers had been the third and fourth probes to Jupiter and the second and third to Saturn. But Uranus was virgin territory. No space probe had ever visited this distant, cold gas giant. Voyager 2 was no longer the bridesmaid, the backup, the last in line. Now she was on point; more than that, Voyager 2 was the one and only. There would be no other spacecraft to follow it to Uranus in either the near or medium future of the U.S. space program. If something went wrong and the spacecraft was not able to return data about the planet, there would be no backup. And that simple fact made this planetary encounter by this spacecraft very different for the two hundred or so men and women on the Voyager Project. This was humanity's one and only shot at a close-up look at Uranus for a long, long time.

Voyager 2 had had a rough time of it right after its closest encounter with Saturn. The scan-platform malfunction had shaken people deeply. It also had brought out the best and most creative fix-it instincts in the team's spacecraft engineers and programmers. Richard Laeser, the deputy project manager under Esker Davis for the Saturn flyby and now Davis's successor for the Uranus encounter, brought me up to date on the four-year-long Saturn-Uranus "cruise" phase.

Laeser is a bear of a man, with a barrel chest and thick arms. He looked to me as if he could bench-press an 825-kilogram interplanetary spacecraft with ease. He enjoyed bicycling and cross-country skiing in his leisure time, and he and his wife and two teenage daughters would get onto wheels and skis whenever they could.

Dick Laeser commanded an enormous amount of respect from the rest of the Voyager team. He had an intimate knowledge of the team organization, of who was doing what, and how; he knew whom to talk with to get answers to questions; he let his middle-management people do their jobs, and drew from them the best they were capable of; and he knew how to deal constructively with the people at NASA headquarters in Washington, D.C. All these skills came in handy during Voyager's "quiet cruise" from Saturn to Uranus.

At least, it was *supposed* to be a quiet cruise. That had been the plan before the Saturn encounter. " 'Quiet cruise' turned out to be a joke phrase around here," Laeser said during my first meeting with him. Laeser's corner office was on the fourth floor of Building 264, located next to the cafeteria at JPL. Most of the Voyager personnel were on floors three through five. "Once or twice a week, I guess, someone in the hall would cry out, 'Where's the quiet cruise?' "

Several things had conspired to defeat it. First, the Voyager team had committed themselves to a major restructuring of the spacecraft's computing capabilities, to provide greater information return from Uranus. Then there was the scan-platform problem. Could it be used, or would they have to do something else? That problem turned out to be a monster.

On top of all that, it turned out that the activity level on the spacecraft was significantly greater than anyone had expected. In part that was because the team needed to test solutions to the actuator problem. But they were also testing new capabilities for the spacecraft, making sure it could be used in ways it had never been used before. "We did all these extra things," said Laeser, "but we had to do them with the lean resources intended for a 'quiet cruise.'

"After Saturn, we got a heavy push from NASA headquarters to reduce costs and personnel. Ek Davis and I put together a plan for a lean team to carry Voyager 2 through to Uranus encounter. So we dropped from two hundred to about one hundred and eight people on the team, with the idea of a long quiet cruise. Then at the end of 1984 we would start hustling to get ready for the encounter. But the scan-platform problem took a lot of work to get squared away.

"The unfortunate side effect has been that there are some people in the organization who are a little tired. It's been like running a marathon: you get to the last few miles and you're wondering if you can make it the rest of the way."

The Voyager engineers had managed to get the faulty scan platform moving again within a few days of its failure at Saturn encounter. The spacecraft was even able to return some photos and other scientific data. They also soon determined that the problem was with the platform's azimuth actuator, a set of gears that moved the platform left and right. But getting the platform to move was just the beginning. They needed to find out why the azimuth actuator had jammed in the first place, if it would stick again, how to prevent that from happening, and, if all else failed, what alternative techniques they could use for the scan platform's instruments. The result, Laeser explained, was "several years of intense testing and engineering analysis.

"Specifically what we did was attack the problem on four fronts. The first front was on the two Voyager spacecraft themselves, with tests on the actual actuators. The second front was by using a duplicate actuator on the ground. The engineers tested it to destruction, and it failed at the same point in its lifetime as Voyager 2's actuator. The engineers then took it apart, examined it, put it back together, and tested some more."

The azimuth gear train was at the heart of the problem, so the engineers then built a number of duplicates of the gear's shafts and bearings in the platform azimuth actuator. These were, essentially, simple metal boxes with gearworks and lubricant inside. As these failed the engineers did various tests on them, including examinations of the bearing surfaces with electron microscopes and analysis of the metal shavings and lubricants.

But what if, despite all the work, the scan platform could not be used during the Uranus encounter? To answer that what-if question, Laeser set up a "tiger team" to determine what it would take to roll the whole spacecraft around to replace azimuth movement of the scan platform.

It was a long, wearying job. "We started in late 1981 to solve the scan-platform problem," Laeser recalled, "and we literally just finished at the end of 1984." The actuator's greatest sensitivity, it turned out, was to high-rate motion. When it was pushed too hard, the gear lubricant began to migrate or flow away from the areas between the fastest-turning gearshafts and their bearings. The parts began scraping together, metal on metal, and the by-products of metal shavings built up as a bump on the bearing shaft. Soon the clearance between the bearings diminished until they wouldn't move at all and the scan platform jammed.

The solution finally reached by the team was to never move the platform at its high rate of speed, only sparingly at its medium rate, and whenever possible at the low rate. Said Laeser, "One consequence of this was that we've placed limitations on the amount of actuator motion allowed during the Saturn-Uranus cruise period, up to encounter, and during the encounter time period itself. And we watch it very closely."

The team didn't stop there, however; they also developed a technique for freeing up the actuator if it should jam again. This involved cycling the temperature of the actuator. The gears would expand and contract, finally crushing the bumpy buildup of spalled metal shavings on the gear bearings.

It also turned out that running the actuator at low rate tended to polish the gear-train surfaces—an unexpected but welcome side effect.

Even more amazingly, Laeser reported with a grin of satisfaction, the Voyager engineers developed a technique to actually detect an impending failure. "The scan platform is moved by a nine-thousand-to-one reduction-gear train," he explained. "So that big, massive scan platform is actually run by a little stepper motor the size of my thumb that spins around like a son of a bitch, and slowly—*slowly*—moves the platform." The imminent-failure test essentially measured the increasing level of resistance of the gear train to movement. If the actuator was starting to stick, it would take more effort for the tiny stepper motor to move the platform. Trial-and-error testing eventually determined what the danger levels were. The technique was first tested on Voyager 1, and it worked superbly.

While all this was going on, finally, the team's scientists, engineers, and computer programmers were building a Uranus encounter plan that was a hybrid of

87

the tiger team's contingency plan to roll the whole spacecraft, plus the scan platform's revised capability to move in azimuth at low rates only.

Said Laeser: "The azimuth actuator on Voyager 2 now looks as good as new; we have a strategy that should keep us out of trouble; we have contingency plans in case we get in trouble; and we have a test to determine if it is failing.

"So the bottom line is: if we use the azimuth actuator conservatively we should have enough lifetime left in it to get us through both the Uranus and the Neptune flybys."

The Voyager Project management had decided before Saturn encounter to do a major reworking of Voyager 2's computer software. At Uranus, Voyager would be twice as far from Earth as it had been during the Saturn flyby, some 3 billion kilometers. Voyager's radio signals would thus be only a quarter as strong as at Saturn. All other things being equal, the spacecraft would be able to return only 25 percent of the amount of data it had sent back at Saturn. But the Voyager engineers and computer programmers had a few tricks up their sleeves that would enable Voyager to send back nearly as much data from Uranus as it had from Saturn. The tricks were dual processing, image data compression, and Reed-Solomon coding.

Dual processing and image data compression made use of the two flight data subsystem (FDS) computers aboard Voyager 2. Ordinarily just one FDS computer was used to handle the onboard processing of scientific and engineering data acquired by the spacecraft. The other FDS was the backup, just in case the first failed. Dual processing meant using both FDS computers: one would process all scientific and engineering data *except* imaging, and the backup would take care of the data gathered by Voyager's cameras.

Image data compression, or IDC, was a special software routine the backup FDS used to process the imaging information. Normal Voyager television images contain 800 lines with 800 pixels (short for "picture elements") per line. Each pixel consists of eight bits of data that coded for a specific level of brightness. Each picture thus contained 640,000 pixels, and over 5.1 million bits of information. Much of that information was black space or features with very low contrast. IDC reduced the level of redundant information by up to 60 percent in a very simple fashion.

The first pixel in the first line would encode the actual brightness level seen by the camera. Each following pixel would encode *only the difference in brightness* between its position and that of the previous pixel. This meant that fewer bits were put into the data stream being broadcast to Earth, "compressing" the important information into the data stream.

One side effect would be that the images might have ragged edges, caused by "busy" scenes or by a loss of continuity in the data stream. But even that could be overcome with a coding scheme that added extra bits to the data in a way that allowed reconstruction of information lost in the static or chopped off at the picture edges. The standard coding process added one extra bit for every bit of raw science data, effectively doubling the amount of data to be broadcast back to Earth. For the Uranus flyby, the Voyager team instituted an experimental scheme called Reed-Solomon encoding. This added one extra bit for every three to five bits of raw science data. Reed-Solomon encoding also dropped the error rate from five in 100,000 to one in a million. A "black box" installed on Voyager 2 almost literally just before launch encoded the data. Back at JPL, another "black box" decoded the data sent from Voyager.

Still another technique would be used at Uranus to improve the quality of the images. It was called target motion compensation, or TMC. Imaging team experiment rep Candy Hansen likened it to taking pictures of a racecar speeding past. "If you just shoot a picture holding the camera still, all you'll get is a blurred car," she said. "But if you pan the camera, swing it along the direction of the car's motion as it moves past, there's a lot less blur. In fact, if you do it just right, you get a perfectly clear image." TMC was just panning the camera, by taking the spacecraft off its radio lock with Earth and physically swiveling it about by moving its internal gyroscopes. The team had tried the technique at Saturn with Voyager 2 for some images of the moon Rhea, and it had worked quite well. Now it would be used more extensively at Uranus. "TMC will be especially important for the pictures of Miranda," said Candy. "We're going to come within twenty-nine thousand kilometers of Miranda at closest approach. We will have to use TMC if we want to get good details of the surface." The Miranda images, along with just about all the others, would be stored on Voyager's on-board digital tape recorder and played back to Earth on Saturday, January 25.

Even the tricks of dual processing, IDC, and Reed-Solomon encoding would not be enough to return adequate scientific data from Uranus without the additional use of antenna arraying. Arraying involved the electronic linking together of two or more dish antennas. Dishes arrayed together in this manner would perform as if they were a single dish with a signal-gathering area almost equal to that of all the separate dishes added together. For example, in Madrid, Spain, a 34-meter dish was to be arrayed with the main 64-meter dish. A radio dish with a diameter of 34 meters has a signal-gathering area of about 900 square meters. A 64-meter diameter dish has an area of 3,215 square meters. Arrayed together, though, the two dishes would perform as if they were one dish with an area of just over 4,000 square meters.

The Madrid station was one of the three major components of the Deep Space Network, and the least important for the Uranus flyby. The Goldstone DSN facility in California included a 64-meter-wide dish antenna and two 34-meter dishes. They would be arrayed. The Canberra, Australia, DSN facility also had one 64-meter and two 34-meter antennas to be arrayed. In addition, another 64-meter radioastronomy telescope in Parkes, Australia, would be arrayed with the Canberra dishes. This last set would result in the equivalent of a single giant radio dish with an area of 8,230 square meters. That would be the equivalent of a single giant radio antenna dish over 100 meters wide. Most of the important observations would be done by Voyager when the Australian stations were facing it.

By arraying antennas in the Deep Space Network the Voyager team would be able to increase considerably its ability to "hear" the data Voyager 2 would send back to Earth. At Saturn the maximum data rate from Voyager was 44,000 bits per second. At Uranus, twice as far from Earth as Saturn, the maximum data rate would ordinarily be only about 10,000 bits per second, a quarter that of Saturn. Arraying would increase the rate to 21,600 bits per second, enough to ensure an adequate return of scientific information from this unique historical event. And image data compression and Reed-Solomon encoding would increase the information rate and decrease the project's vulnerability to garbled bits.

"The story of this summer will be testing," said William McLaughlin, head of the Voyager Flight Engineering Office (FEO). Bill McLaughlin is tall, thin, and bearded; he reminded me of the Russian writer Alexander Solzhenitsyn. The sun coming through his office window illuminated a bar-graph transparency taped on the window, turning it into a stained-glass memorial to mathematics. "August will be the month when we train individuals. We'll have videotapes available with lectures on the FDS, the CCS, various scientific instruments on the spacecraft, on how to read the computer sequence products. In September and October we will shift from inside-the-team training to joint team activities. We'll test things like what we'd do if the actuator on the scan platform jams again. Then we'll move into the encounter period with the beginning of the Observatory Phase in November. Finally, February 25, 1986, will be the end of the post-encounter period.

"We're like a football team when the big game is almost here," McLaughlin said. "We're certainly getting excited. It's like Ravel's *Bolero*—it builds up that way." He laughed at the image.

McLaughlin, like Dick Laeser and Charlie Kohlhase, had an extensive knowledge of many different facets of the project. He himself was a man of many interests and skills.

"I read a lot of science fiction as a kid in the forties and early fifties," he recalled. "I don't read as much now as I used to. I grew up on Ray Bradbury and Isaac Asimov, Heinlein, Jack Williamson. I think many people in the space business read SF as children. I met Bradbury during the Viking Project; he's a great guy." McLaughlin paused a moment, then continued. "In 1944—for some reason I remember this, I was nine years old—for some reason I started getting interested in astronomy. It's been a passion of mine ever since. I know the constellations rather well with the naked eye. I have a four-and-a-quarter-inch telescope at home, and I get a great deal of pleasure from the stars. Amateur astronomy has always been a great interest of mine. And I've been able to participate in astronomy in the only way you can now in the modern world, by being a space-mission engineer. So I've really done what I wanted to do."

McLaughlin worked on a Ph.D. in mathematics from the University of California in Berkeley. Then came an opportunity to work on the Apollo Project for the Bellcom Corporation, which was an adviser to NASA. He recalled it as "the most exciting thing I ever did." When the Man on the Moon project wound down in the early 1970s, he discovered opportunities for work in space science at JPL. He has been there for more than fifteen years. First he worked on the Viking Project, writing computer software. Then he worked on Seasat (an Earth-orbiting satellite that probed the world's oceans) doing mission analysis. Then IRAS, the infrared astronomical satellite, came along in 1976. McLaughlin joined that project and eventually became the mission design manager. Among other astounding triumphs, the IRAS satellite discovered several new comets and provided the first evidence for objects orbiting other stars in the galaxy.

"Getting the IRAS survey of the infrared in the bag was a great accomplishment," McLaughlin said. "But Voyager has had so much success as well. In fact, Voyager is probably the greatest space mission we've ever had."

He smiled and shook his head. "To be a part of all this . . . it's been incredible luck to be in these positions. It won't happen again, you know. Once we've explored the solar system there will be plenty of neat things to do. But there's a first time, and we're doing it for the first time."

Besides being a mathematician, computer programmer, and space project manager, McLaughlin is also a writer. "Oh, I'm just an amateur writer, like the guy who likes to go out in his backyard and look through his telescope. But it's fun." His "fun" included writing a monthly column for the British magazine *Spaceflight*, as well as articles for local newspapers.

He has also had published a couple of professional papers in astronomy, including treatises on extraterrestrial intelligence and on various connections between astronomy and philosophy. And finally coming full circle to the inspiration of his childhood, there was science fiction. "Yep," McLaughlin said proudly, "I actually wrote a science fiction story in the late sixties. It was published in the old SF magazine called *If*. Fred Pohl used to edit that. I was in grad school at that time. I think it was more luck than anything else that it sold." Luck probably had very little to do with it. More than likely it was skill.

In late June 1985, the temperature in Pasadena was over the century mark on the Fahrenheit scale. In air-conditioned "Voyager Country," the third through fifth floors of Building 264 at JPL, the tension and excitement were starting to build. Uranus encounter was now just seven months away. Several staffing changes had been made to put the team in a better position for the upcoming periods of test and training from August through October, and the beginning of observatory phase in November.

One of the key members of the project was very ill. Charles Stembridge had been head of the Flight Science Office, which worked directly with the scientists on the Voyager team and looked out for their needs. Stembridge had cancer of the pancreas and was undergoing treatment for it. The prognosis was not promising. Stembridge was still working part-time, however, and was determined to beat the cancer if he could, or at least hang on through Uranus encounter the following January.

However, Stembridge was no longer able to continue as FSO manager, and Pieter de Vries had taken over that position. De Vries had worked for Charlie Kohlhase in the past and had also been deeply involved in the planning for a proposed mission to Mars called the Mars Sample Return Mission. De Vries was no stranger to the ways of NASA, JPL, or Voyager, and he quickly fit into the team. Peter Doms reported to de Vries now instead of Stembridge.

Meanwhile, Laeser was beginning to worry about the condition of NASA's Deep Space Network. Not only were DSN's huge dishes being arrayed for the Uranus flyby; NASA was also introducing a sweeping upgrade of its software and hardware called the Mark IV-A. "I've been at the lab most of the time the DSN has been in existence," noted Laeser, "and I can say that except for the initial building of the network, this has been the most sweeping change the DSN has seen. They had a lot of schedule problems, and then when they got it on line last November, it didn't perform up to the standards that we've seen it do before." By the end of June 1985, it still hadn't. Laeser's concern was a legitimate one: if the DSN couldn't function properly come January 24, 1986, the Voyager 2 flyby of Uranus would be a disaster. The people on Earth wouldn't be able to talk to Voyager, and the spacecraft wouldn't be able to send scientific data back to Earth.

There were also some lower-level problems. "We basically have a concern about the entire data system, from end to end," said Laeser. "So much of it is new. In the Control Center in Building 230 we have a brand-new computer system. MIPL, the Multimission Image Processing Laboratory, is a new system for image processing. Combine that with the fact that we've changed the data system on the spacecraft, with the dual-processor configuration of the two FDS computers—well, the whole thing from end to end is a major redesign for this encounter.

"Now we're seeing funny little things in the data, and the trick is to find where the problems are in this huge new system, and then isolate and solve them. None of the problems yet are biggies, show-stoppers. But we need to clean it up so we can trust the data."

Laeser had still more to worry about. He was now

spending a lot of time working on the NASA budget process. In fact, Laeser was working on two planetary encounters: the Voyager 2 encounter with Uranus in January 1986, and the spacecraft's flyby of the planet Neptune in August 1989. "Someone's got to worry about the Neptune mission," he said wryly. "We have to make sure we have enough money lined up for the Neptune encounter.

"We're talking about a roughly hundred-million-dollar budget, maximum, including reserves and a built-in inflation factor." In other words, the Voyager project would not be allowed to spend more than that to get to Neptune. Laeser and his budget people were able to make things look better by transferring nearly $7 million of their costs to the Multimission Office at JPL. That dropped the Neptune budget to $93 million, he explained, "but once we compensate for what we'll learn from the Uranus mission we'll be up bumping against the hundred-million-dollar limit again."

One saving grace, though, was the built-in inflation factor. It helped the Uranus mission's budget, and Laeser expected it would help the Neptune mission as well. The Uranus mission would cost $93.424 million, Laeser said. "We had a six percent inflation factor built in to our budget, but it turns out the Reagan administration has done a good job of holding inflation down to less than that. And it's truly amazing how quickly one or two percent, compounded over a number of years, can add up to substantial savings. We were able to hold that extra in our hip pocket for emergencies. Now it looks like we will underrun our Uranus budget by about three million. And we'll carry that over into the Neptune mission."

It was a major change from late 1981 and early 1982, when rumors had been that the Reagan administration, goaded by the Office of Management and Budget, would turn off the Deep Space Network and abandon the Voyagers and Pioneers to the void. It hadn't happened, but there had been a lot of very worried scientists and space-program managers.

Some of the scientists had not been content with merely sitting in their offices and worrying. They did something almost unprecedented in space-science history: they got their hands dirty in Capitol Hill political skirmishes. Leading the charge was University of Hawaii astronomer David Morrison. Morrison had sent an open letter to his colleagues in early 1981, warning them that if they didn't abandon their traditional stance of "noninterference in politics," they would wake up one morning and find the U.S. space program kaput.

Morrison's apocalyptic prediction nearly came true. The preliminary 1983 federal budget saw NASA's planetary science and exploration program nearly gutted. The specter of a dead program galvanized the space-science community. Several eminent scientists testified before Congressional hearings in 1982, warning of the disaster that would follow if the Reagan budget was adopted as it stood. They included astronomers Morrison; the University of Arizona's Dr. Eugene Levy, chairman of the Committee on Planetary and Lunar Exploration; Dr. Werner Suomi of the University of Wisconsin; and Dr. George Field, director of the Harvard Smithsonian Center for Astrophysics. Morrison's testimony set the tone. "I find it remarkable that I am here today facing what is the collapse of the program of planetary exploration. As you know, there have been no new launches since 1978, there have been no new [space program] starts since 1978, and the Galileo mission is the only mission we now expect to have a planetary encounter during the [1980s] other than the Voyager continuations. . . .

"In addition," he continued, "planetary exploration has received a steadily shrinking fraction of the NASA budget. With the budget now proposed for fiscal 1983, the process of slow fiscal strangulation is being replaced with a precipitous decline, a decline that I think can only be described as a going out of business budget for planetary exploration.

"I will pull no punches: the proposed budget is a disaster for planetary science and exploration. . . . [The] proposed budget for fiscal 1983 is so bad that it will destroy the base that is necessary to be maintained if we are to establish [a] program of missions in the future."

Morrison was not crying wolf. The 1983 NASA budget would have turned off the Pioneer Venus Orbiter probe; turned off Pioneers 10 and 11, already on their way to interstellar space; ended further analysis of the data from the Viking missions to Mars; reduced the ability to analyze data from Voyager 1 and 2; and led to the firing of 500 of NASA's best scientists, engineers, and technicians.

The disaster did not happen; eventually some of the proposed cuts in the planetary exploration program were reinstated. Much damage had already been done. There would be no U.S. space probe to Halley's Comet in 1986, for example. The harm to morale in the space program was much worse. It would be several years before people in the planetary-exploration business started feeling even halfway safe.

Changes in management and problems with the DSN were not the only new events in June. Voyager 2 was still half a year from flyby, but it was already sending back interesting scientific data. One example was the first color image of Uranus from the spacecraft. MIPL produced some nice prints that were posted on bulletin boards throughout Voyager Country. Voyager 2 was still more than 300 million kilometers (180 million miles) from Uranus, and no features were visible on the tiny blue marble. But it was indeed a *blue* marble.

Uranus was definitely azure, not the blue-green or turquoise cited in most astronomy textbooks. Even this small finding was enough to call for rewrites. The Voyager team's adrenaline level rose another notch. People were now getting caught up in the excitement. Uranus was *real*. It was really out there. And Voyager 2 was closing in.

Later that month came the first spacecraft pictures showing Uranian moons. The image was for optical-navigation purposes. The narrow-angle camera aboard Voyager 2 took a very long-exposure photo of Uranus and the surrounding star field. The long exposure time made Uranus look like a burned-in white blob, but it did make visible the stars, so the navigation team could precisely determine Uranus's position in the sky. At the same time, the image revealed four of the five Uranian moons: Ariel, Umbriel, Titania, and Oberon. Only tiny innermost Miranda escaped visibility.

The image made vividly real one of the truly bizarre aspects of the Uranian system, said Bill McLaughlin. "The satellite systems of Jupiter and Saturn are kind of classical systems; they're laid out like on a plate, and your spacecraft does a tour of the system, passing one moon at a time as it flies through. But with the Uranus satellite system you go *whack!* right through it. Because it's tilted to the plane of Uranus's orbit by nearly ninety degrees, and it looks sort of like a cosmic bull's-eye." That, McLaughlin explained, made the problem of celestial navigation a particularly difficult one.

"Classically when you chase a satellite and you're trying to figure out where it is, mainly your error is where it is along the 'wire' of its orbit. The big problem with, say, Miranda, which we will make a very close approach to, is we pretty much see where it is *along* its orbit—but where is the *plane* of its orbit? We believe we'll get the relative uncertainty of that position down to under a hundred kilometers. Of course," he added wryly, "anytime you do anything different, you have a chance to reap opportunities and get some really great new stuff.

"You also have a chance to get zorched."

Dick Laeser's work days had been fairly normal as late as April. "I just live over the foothills from the lab," he had said then. "I usually don't come in on weekends or evenings, but if things are quiet at home, sometimes I will. Or," and he had laughed, "if my wife and my two teenage daughters are yelling at each other, sometimes *then* I sneak over and work a little!" By the end of June things had changed. "My days now mean coming in at seven-thirty a.m. or so and staying until six p.m. Basically, I'm now working a ten-hour day. Maybe it has something to do with the sun, too. Longer days during the summer and all that."

Laeser and Mission Director George Textor were also spending a lot of time on the fifth floor of Voyager Country. After much thought and planning, JPL had decided to do a major rearrangement of that floor. It had been years since new carpet had been put in, let alone new desks or other office furniture. The building's third floor was home to the science people, and the main management people had their offices on the fourth floor. The fifth floor, home for Voyager's Flight Engineering Office and Operations Office, looked like a tattered old office building. Parts of it were positively dumpy. The lab planned on replacing everything: new carpets, new modular office furniture, the whole ten yards.

"You've got several hundred people, and they're into their work but they need some creature comforts, too. This is going to be a lot like a magician pulling a tablecloth from the table and leaving the neatly set table in place," said Laeser. "Except we'll also replace it with a new tablecloth."

One of the people on the fifth floor was Robert

"Bobby" Brooks, a sequence integration engineer (SIE) for the Voyager Project. SIEs were computer programmers, and the computers they programmed were the ones on Voyager 2. Brooks was one of the best. He was also one of the genuine characters on the Voyager team. His normal working attire included a flannel shirt, old blue jeans, and giant motorcycle boots. He sported a huge mustache and hair down to his waist that he usually kept in a ponytail. "One of the nice things about working at JPL," he said one afternoon in June, "is that nobody really gives a sweet goddam what you look like or what you wear. The only thing that's important here is that (a) you do your job, and (b) you do it as best you can."

Brooks had worked on several of the computer sequences, or loads, for Voyager's command computer. The most important was the B752 load, which would command the spacecraft through the final hours of the Uranus flyby on January 24, 1986. Each computer load had a number identifying which spacecraft it was for, and which part of the mission it would be running. In this case, "B" was the "B spacecraft," or Voyager 2, and the 75-series loads were for the near encounter phase of that flyby. B752 was the second near encounter load, and it was Brooks's baby. He was writing it.

Bobby Brooks was a joker, a humorist, the sparkplug of the SIE area on the fifth floor of Voyager Country (identified by a sign on the ceiling as Disneyland). But he was a hard worker, as well, and almost always busy on some sequence or another. "Right now," he said one day in late June, "we're trying to get the first portion of the near encounter, from about minus two days to about minus fourteen hours, all squared away. The scientists gave us a massive number of changes to make in the second half of the sequence. So what *should* have been done three or four weeks ago has been delayed for another month."

Brooks was looking forward to the encounter in

January with a mixture of dread and excitement. "For me, when one of my sequences is running, it's absolute hell. I just sit there waiting for something to happen. 'Jesus, did I forget anything, did I do this, did I remember to do that?' Plus I worry something will go wrong and people will start razzing me and getting on my case, and then I'll have to start working twenty-four-hour days helping to figure out what the hell went wrong."

Though he loved the Voyager Project, Brooks didn't plan to stay on after the Uranus encounter. "Oh, I'll still be here at the lab, but I want to get a little bit tighter on the software end of things. I'll probably try to get involved in multimission software—all kinds of it. I'll do that for as long as I can, but I have my heart set on CRAF, the planned mission to a comet in the 1990s. That's what I want. If I can get on CRAF in a management position, a team chief, I'll be satisfied. It'll be a neat project."

While Brooks was digging into computer loads for Voyager on the fifth floor, Charlie Kohlhase a floor below was worrying about "what-ifs." It was part of his job. "We worry about contingency planning, with how the project should deal with unforeseen problems. Even earthquakes. Our office tends to worry about things with probability of happening that's on the order of one-half of a percent or higher." And what if an earthquake knocked JPL's computers out of action, or disabled the Goldstone DSN antenna? "Hmmm . . ." He started digging around on his desk and came up with a thick document. "*Mission Design Guidelines and Constraints* is a document that my office issues to the project," said Kohlhase. "It lists all kinds of things that could go wrong, and what we'd do about them. We should have *some* kind of plan. . . . We did the earthquake contingency plan in 1984. . . ." Kohlhase looked up. "But you know? I don't think it's been updated since then."

Other contingencies were better covered. "Suppose we lost one of the onboard computers?" he continued by way of example. "Well, then we have to build computer sequences that fit in half the space. Can we afford to build these backup sequences while we're still building the standard ones?

"Or suppose the scan platform stuck again. We figured out what caused that. But it is so important to use that, rather than disallow its use, we found ways to use it if we slew it slowly. This document specifies the constraints on using the scan platform. Or take the narrow-angle TV camera. On Voyager 2 it is degrading a little more rapidly than on Voyager 1, but only if you use it. As time goes by and the supply of electrons from the cathode tube diminishes, we can increase the voltage on the plate and increase the number of electrons. But we can only do that for so long. So we've decided to not put quite as much use on the camera. We allocated fifteen hundred hours to it through Uranus encounter, which should be plenty for what we want to do."

And then there was Neptune, Voyager 2's next destination after Uranus. "One of my people made a presentation on Neptune yesterday at the Science Steering Group meeting," said Kolhhase. "We've already set a preliminary trajectory for the Neptune encounter in 1989. Voyager 2 will come over the north pole of Neptune at oh four hundred hours on August 25, 1989. It goes over the north pole and dives down to within ten thousand kilometers of Triton, Neptune's giant moon.

"Now, you know there have recently been some indications that Neptune has rings, and they may extend as far out as three Neptune radii, or close to twenty-five thousand kilometers. Well, our aiming point comes in at three point one nine Neptune radii, just right over the top of these possible rings! Should we move the aim point out a bit, or do we have enough information to chance sending the spacecraft through? So far it seems okay. But how long can we wait before we finalize it?"

Kohlhase smiled and shrugged his shoulders. "Part of my job," he said.

Neptune's rings, California earthquakes, and crashing spacecraft computers weren't the only things on Kohlhase's mind in late June. He and a colleague had devised a computer game called Wilderness Survival that was just hitting retail stores. It was more than a "text game" of survival. It included detailed computer graphics and illustrations which gave the user the sense of actually being in the wilderness and having to find a way out. The first version ran on Apple computers only, but an IBM version would be out by the middle of 1986. Kohlhase's game was being distributed by Electronic Arts, and doing very well.

"They've bought eight thousand units in the first few weeks," said Kohlhase, "and many stores sold out the first day! I sent a copy to Jerry Pournelle at *Byte* magazine. He likes it and will write it up as the game of the month in the October issue. I sent one of Arthur C. Clarke, and he likes it, and said he plays it a lot. Now it looks like B. Dalton's, the big bookstore chain, will try it out.

"If we could sell half as many as Flight Simulator— well . . ." Kohlhase laughed. "I guess I might still work at JPL, purely out of love for the space program. My partner and I get a dollar fifty per unit, and we split that. But even if we sell just twenty thousand units, that's still good money." He paused a moment and then grinned. "But I wanna sell *two hundred thousand* units!"

Chapter 5
THE PERILS OF MARK IV-A

With the arrival of August and the hottest temperatures Pasadena had seen all summer, a major problem was heating tempers and raising the stress level for Project Voyager. It was beginning to look as though the biggest threat to a successful Uranus encounter might not come from spacecraft glitches but from ground-based difficulties. The Deep Space Network was having some serious problems.

For more than twenty-five years the DSN had been the unsung hero of the American planetary space program. The network was essential, for without it the robot probes into the solar system would have broadcast their scientific discoveries to a deaf world. The DSN was the ears of the planetary science program. The antenna dishes were so sensitive they could pick up spacecraft radio signals measured in millionths of a watt. During the first few years of the American space program the network had had its share of problems. But by the time of the Mariner probes to Mars in 1969 and 1970, the space community had come to expect nearly flawless performance from the DSN.

The problems, ironically enough, were rooted in a program designed to make the network even better than it already was. Laeser's June worries had not gone away. The Mark IV-A upgrade of the DSN was a top-to-bottom updating of the network's hardware and software. It was necessary, at the very least, to make operational the arraying of the DSN antennas at Madrid, Goldstone, and Canberra/Parkes. Arraying would be the most visible change in the DSN upgrade, but not the most important or extensive. The major change contained in the Mark IV-A upgrade was to computer programming. The software for the DSN computers was being totally rewritten, and most of the computers were being replaced. The purpose was to make the network fully capable of tracking and handling data from more spacecraft simultaneously, while doing it automatically. That was where the glitches began creeping in.

"DSN just isn't reliable like it used to be," said Doug Griffith, sitting at his desk in the fifth floor of building 264. Hanging in the window was a striking stained-glass panel of Saturn, made by Griffith and his wife.

Griffith, a handsome man with dark eyes and a soft Southern drawl, had been with Project Voyager since 1974 and head of the Voyager Flight Operations Office, or FOO, since 1980. "The upgrade was a good plan, but somewhere along the way it just didn't come out like it was supposed to!" He laughed, but didn't seem too amused. "It's given us trouble since it came on line in November '84."

Not everyone on the Voyager team agreed with Griffith's assessment. "Doug is our doomsday personality," one team member noted dryly. But a series of tests held during early 1985 went poorly. In the meantime, Voyager science experimenters needed to gather data

106

from their instruments. They also had to calibrate the instruments for the upcoming encounter. Those sessions did not always go as planned, either, as the new DSN software burped and gurgled along.

Lonne Lane was becoming particularly upset with the situation. During a DSN test in June, Voyager 2 carried out a calibration test for his photopolarimeter instrument. "The spacecraft did just fine," Lane said at one point, with frustration in his voice. "But DSN lost all the data."

If Lane was upset, the radio science people led by Len Tyler of Stanford University were becoming positively frantic. The radio science experiment was the only one without a specific instrument aboard Voyager 2— the "instrument" was the spacecraft's radio transmitter and the DSN dishes. As Voyager flew behind Uranus relative to Earth, its radio signals would pass through the planet's atmosphere. The ways the signal warped and changed would tell Tyler and his cohorts about the Uranian atmosphere's structure and composition. It would help determine, for example, if the atmosphere had an ionosphere layer. But if the DSN was having problems gathering in the radio signals, or if glitches garbled those signals during their transmission from the DSN dishes to the JPL computers, then Tyler and the others would have no way of deducing accurate information about the Uranian atmosphere. It would be a case of "data in, garbage out."

Lane's and Tyler's problems were typical of those of any DSN user during 1985. It didn't matter if it was engineering tests or science calibration or getting science data. DSN's tracking and data-handling abilities were seriously overloaded, and would have been even if the Mark IV-A upgrade had been fully operational. By August the station arraying at Canberra/Parkes and Goldstone had been demonstrated. Arraying tests were, for the most part, going well. But the Madrid station was still down, nonoperational, the Mark IV-A system still being implemented. DSN's own testing program was taking up huge chunks of DSN time, leaving less and less time for spaceflight projects, including Lane's photopolarimeter tests, optical navigation photos by the Voyager navigation team, and just about anything else connected with Voyager science calibrations. Things were beginning to look a bit dicey. By the middle of August, Dick Laeser was worried.

August 1 had been the latest date when the DSN ground systems were supposed to be ready. They were not. "We went through a test and training readiness review in late July and it was clear at that point that they would not make the deadline," Laeser said one morning, as we talked in his office. DSN was being hesitant to project when it would be done, he added. "So I took a shot and estimated about September 1. I figured they were a month behind, and I just told them to be ready by the first of September. We scheduled another very detailed review of all the components of the ground data system, including reports from the operations people of how well the system was delivering data to them. I scheduled two days for that, September 5 and 6, because I anticipated"—he smiled faintly—"that it would be a long and painful process."

At least one person on the team thought the July DSN test failure was the best thing to happen to the project. "I came in the next morning [after the July DSN test]," Charlie Kohlhase recalled, "and Bob Neilson, one of my staff, came to me and said, 'A terrible thing happened last night. The Mark IV-A system was set for a demonstration, and DSN wasn't ready to support the test. The spacecraft did its little things perfectly and the ground failed totally.' And my response was, 'Great!'

"You see, the project has been worried for a long time about the numbers of errors we've been seeing in the Mark IV-A system. But the DSN management never seems to have gotten a picture that's worried them enough. So to me the best thing that could have happened was to have them fail in support of our first big test. And it had *exactly* the right effect. Top JPL management got *really upset*, and now the trees are shaking! That failure," said Kohlhase, "may well be the reason we do well at encounter."

DSN's deadline slipped to September 15. "We're all a little on the nervous side now," Laeser said, "because it's not only nip and tuck with the schedule for the encounter, it's also not real clear that the *system design itself* is all going to play together properly, as we would hope it would. It is a very complex implementation, more than we realized when we enthusiastically endorsed the undertaking." The Deep Space Network might have bitten off more than it could chew in the time allotted for dinner. "Do we live with the problems for Uranus encounter, or do we risk changing the system one more time? And remember," Laeser warned, "every time we change it, we run the possibility of introducing *other* problems."

But the DSN was by no means inoperative. A few days earlier, two Soviet spacecraft had flown past Venus and dropped two balloons into the planet's immensely dense and poisonous atmosphere. The DSN's antenna dishes had helped track the movement of the probes as the Venusian winds had carried them along. Said Flight Operations Office manager Doug Griffith, "Those DSN people are working awful hard, six and seven days a week. But DSN will be the key to a successful Uranus encounter. The potential is still here to perform well. They supported the Russian Venus balloon experiment, and did very well. But you know what they did? They put an additional expert on every system during the whole duration of that activity, which was only a few days, just to handle any problems as they might crop up. They put all their engineers out there to watch everything and they were able to pull it off.

"But we're going to have so much to do during the

Uranus encounter, and for so long, that I don't know if they're gonna be able to do that again. I mean, we're talking from early November to March, with the most critical period from 10 January to about 4 February.

"The thing looks achievable," said Griffith, "but it's not going to be easy by any stretch of the imagination. And I think we will not have as successful a data return as we had at Jupiter and Saturn."

By the end of August, Dick Laeser's goals for DSN readiness had changed again. "We hope we get it all squared away by October," he said. "But we may well have loose ends dragging up closer to the encounter than we would like." Added Griffith: "We're trying to get the system to operate as best we can until we get past Uranus."

Not everyone on the team was feeling deeply pessimistic about DSN. Kohlhase was sure the "tree shaking" would eventually put DSN's house in order. So was Bill McLaughlin, head of the Voyager Flight Engineering Office (FEO). "The DSN, I personally think, will come through," he said one afternoon in mid-August. "All in all, I feel good about the encounter in January. It's sort of like a waiter on a busy night in a restaurant, going through the dining area with a loaded tray of dishes on his hand. I feel good about it in that sense. Of course, if you lose your concentration, or relax . . . ! We still have some key stuff ahead of us. The tests could flush out some problems. But I think, overall, we're in good shape."

The spacecraft did not seem to be a source of problems. In fact, Voyager 2—more than eight years old and with over 4 billion kilometers behind it—was performing better than in years. Spacecraft team chief Howard Marderness was quietly pleased. A small, slim man with dark hair and a whispery rasping voice, Marderness was called by some on the project "the human spacecraft." He probably knew more about Voyager 1 and 2 than any other human being alive. "We haven't had any changes in

110

the status of the spacecraft," he said. "In fact, we haven't had any faults with it since 1981. The actuator on the scan platform looks good." Marderness smiled ever so slightly and his eyes sparkled. "So it's looking good."

For his part, Bill McLaughlin was beginning to sound positively poetic. "Y'know, this is really an exciting time. After this long cruise, we're finally beginning to smell the methane wisps coming from the planet!"

Around the corner from McLaughlin's office, Charlie Kohlhase was putting together a 170-page book called *The Voyager Uranus Travel Guide*. An in-house publication, the *Travel Guide* would essentially be an "everything-you-have-ever-wanted-to-know" book about the upcoming encounter. Every member of the project would get a copy, as would the JPL Public Information Office staff and other people at the lab connected with the flyby. "The *Travel Guide* will have chapters on what we know about Uranus, would like to know, what we will do, scientific objectives, what's new like data compression and arraying, and some 'gee whiz' facts. That last," said Kohlhase, "will be stuff like the total cost of the Voyager mission equaling twenty cents per person per year, or the cost of a candy bar. Or like the Defense Department spends the total cost of the Voyager mission in *two days*; that kind of stuff."

Kohlhase was also working on a computer-generated "Uranus Encounter Movie" with computer graphics wizard Jim Blinn. It would be similar to the one of Voyager flying past Saturn. This latest Blinn-Kohlhase collaboration, drawn entirely by computer, would show Voyager 2 sweeping through the Uranian system of moons and rings, turning this way and that as it took pictures and gathered other scientific data. The project had started in June, but was now falling behind. "It's true: I'm late on the full five-minute film," he sighed.

"I'll start on the storyboard next week. That won't be done until end of September, and we won't have the film until the middle of December. It takes about two hundred hours of computer time to produce the film," he explained. "It'll all go onto one-inch videotape. We'll deliver the one-inch color videotape movie to the Public Information Office in the middle of December. All we've gotten done so far is a line-drawing picture system for the eventual full-color computer animated movie," he said. "We used that to make a ninety-eight-frame flip picture for the corner of the *Travel Guide*."

Other MPO projects were being completed on time. Kohlhase's people delivered the final Uranus "ephemeris," information on where Uranus was located, where the satellites were located and—vital for navigation purposes—an updated best value for the astronomical unit or AU, the standard yardstick measurement of the distance from the sun to Earth. In fact, the only Uranus-related work left for Kohlhase's Mission Planning Office was to finish the rest of the contingency guidelines—including an updated one on California earthquakes. Everything else on their agenda was concerned either with Uranus-Neptune cruise planning or the Neptune encounter itself in 1989.

And Kohlhase's Wilderness Survival game was doing very well. "Yeah!" he said brightly. "We've sold *eight thousand* so far, and it's selling at the rate of eighteen hundred a month. The reviews all seem to be good ones. Now we're told there'll be a review in *Playboy*, a review in *Futurist* magazine and in some games magazines. I guess we can't complain, can we?"

By the end of September, Len Tyler's feelings about the DSN crisis had not changed much. "At this point I'm just feeling numb," he said one sunny afternoon, in his office at Stanford University, south of San Francisco. "Earlier this year I was feeling outraged, but now . . ."

He shrugged. He was now hoping for the best at encounter, but fully expecting the worst from DSN. "They've had problems just keeping the antennas pointed in the right direction," he exclaimed. For some of the radio science experiments Tyler and his team would need at least fifteen uninterrupted minutes of data or the experiments would be worthless. At times it seemed DSN couldn't even keep an antenna pointed at Voyager 2 for fifteen continuous minutes.

Four hundred miles south, at JPL, Dick Laeser was feeling slightly more optimistic than Tyler. The DSN situation was beginning to look a little better. The network had been steadily working through Mark IV-A's gliches, or "liens" as they called them. Said Laeser: "The network has told us that they have come up with a lien-free set of capabilities for the Uranus encounter time period. It's to be delivered, tested, checked out, and operational by October 5."

High-level NASA management was also becoming involved in the DSN situation. A major review of the problem was set for October 17 at the Goddard Space Flight Center in Maryland, not far from NASA head-quarters. The top brass, including James Beggs, wanted to know what could be done to assure a successful Uranus flyby. Laeser laughed and shook his head. "If things were to get worse for any perverse reason we'd probably have Congress in on this—which is the *last* thing we want!"

Meanwhile, FEO chief Bill McLaughlin remained the optimist. "We'll get everything fixed by encounter. We'll hammer it into shape if we have to; we'll take an *ax* to it! It'll work! This is all a period of meetings, evaluations, soul-searchings, actions, training, the whole bit," he said. "I've got a real feeling that it's all coming together. We'll have the big near encounter test at the end of October, and observatory phase will begin in November and things will flatten out a bit.

"But you need a period where your actions can

113

reach a state of equilibrium and gain a kind of maturity, where you're not always doing *ad hoc* fixes to things. So when we go into the really heavy stuff in January," and his voice rose in pitch, "we can consciously *rise up like a lion and smite the planet!*" MacLaughlin grinned. "That sounds biblical, doesn't it?"

The spacecraft itself was continuing to perform like a champ. One example was the "antismear campaign," to reduce Voyager 2's normal slight wobble by shortening the pulse times of its attitude-control thrusters. That in turn would reduce any smear in the pictures. The scheme, implemented by Howard Marderness's space-craft team, was working like a charm. Candy Hansen looked quite pleased as she pulled a recent image from a pile on her desk. "This was taken with the narrow-angle camera through the orange filter," she said, and handed the black-and-white photo to me. "It is slightly smeared at the edge," she continued, "but this was a *fifteen-second exposure!* Before the smear campaign we could have expected seven to fifteen pixels of smear with an exposure that long. This might have three pixels of smear at the most." In other words, the campaign was in this case reducing image smear by a factor of five. I peered closely at the image. I couldn't see any smear at all.

On September 23 the principal investigators and their experiment representatives gathered at JPL for the last quarterly meeting of the Science Steering Group, or SSG. During these daylong meetings any unresolved conflicts between experiment teams were resolved. The imaging team, for example, might want to take pictures of a moon at some particular time, while Lonne Lane might want to use the PPS to examine Uranus at the same moment. If the two groups had not been able to work out the conflict at lower management levels, the

SSG and Ed Stone would make the final decision. The September meeting, though, was mostly devoted to Neptune.

Voyager 2's trajectory for the Uranus flyby had been carefully computed to send it via gravity boost on a path to Neptune. As Charlie Kohlhase had noted in June, the spacecraft would fly past the gas giant on August 25, 1989. The actual Neptunian "target point," that place in space and time the navigators would aim Voyager at, was still open for negotiation. Most of the scientists favored the so-called "polar crown" option: a target point that would send Voyager 2 on a path streaking over Neptune's north pole, just a few thousand kilometers above the cloudtops. A few hours later it would fly within 10,000 kilometers of Neptune's giant moon Triton. That moon was an important part of the flyby: evidence from Earth-based observations suggested Triton might have seas of liquid nitrogen.

But other recent observations called the polar-crown option into doubt. It had now been confirmed that Neptune—like Jupiter, Saturn, and Uranus—had rings, or at least arcs, or partial rings. One such ring/arc lay right across Voyager 2's proposed path. Later on in the meeting, Bob Cesarone of the Voyager navigation team presented some of the different targeting options the scientists could choose for the Neptune encounter. All of them had some drawbacks: the fields and particles scientists would get wiped out if one alternate target point was used; the plasma wave people would suffer from another one; the close Triton encounter would be lost from still another.

The scientists made various comments, but a lot of the discussion focused on events of very low probability. What if Voyager 2 hit a ring particle? Grazed the top of the Neptunian atmosphere? Hit Triton? The speculations multiplied as people continued talking.

Finally, Ed Stone stepped in. With the concurrence

of the PIs, he suggested they stay with the polar crown as a target point for the Neptune encounter. If by April 1987 astronomers discovered more ring arcs in areas that would threaten the spacecraft, they'd still be able to move the target point farther away from Neptune.

Meanwhile, the news media were already starting to show interest in the Uranus flyby in September, four months before the actual event. "I get three or four calls a week," said Ed Stone during a break in the SSG meeting. Dick Laeser, too, was spending more time with news media. He didn't think he would have to devote a significant fraction of his time to the Fourth Estate for another two months or so. Bill McLaughlin was also getting press queries. "Yeah, I get calls from people, for example from the *Space Calendar* published up in Santa Clara. And I was recorded for a BBC radio program."

McLaughlin expected public interest in the flyby to begin rising soon. But he also saw some public-relations problems for the flyby. One was that the space shuttle was scheduled for a launch on January 22, two days before the Uranus flyby. And it would be carrying, among other passengers, America's first "teacher in space," Christa McAuliffe. "Dick Laeser has been trying to work this out with NASA headquarters, to see if maybe they can delay the launch by a week or something. Because if the shuttle gets into serious trouble, they could grab some of our communication lines, or some of the thirty-four-meter DSN station antennas and ground communication lines, and that could cause us some really severe problems with receiving data from Voyager.

"And then there's the Super Bowl on the 26th!" McLaughlin added in mock despair. "My God, the competition!" He laughed, totally unaware of the prophetic nature of his comments.

.   .   .

116

Early in October, Charles Stembridge died. The former head of the Flight Science Office had been battling pancreatic cancer with great courage for well over a year. He had hoped to live long enough to see the results of the Uranus flyby in January. He didn't make it.

In the halls of Voyager Country in Building 264 there were expressions of sorrow; people had liked Stembridge a lot, and he had made important contributions to the Voyager Project in years past. But as one person put it, the prevailing feeling was one of "relief." He had fought a terrible battle with an implacable foe, and in the last few months it had been difficult to see him in such obvious pain. Some team members didn't like being reminded of their own mortality. Most everyone, though, remembered the cheerful man who had put so much time and energy into the earlier Voyager flybys. And they were sad he wouldn't be around for the event he had worked so hard for.

As Voyager 2's four-year-long cruise phase to Uranus neared its end, the project geared up for a week-long rehearsal of the encounter with the seventh planet. Running on and off through the week of October 20, 1985, the near encounter test or NET would be an exercise for all the different segments of the project: spacecraft team, sequence engineers (the programmers), scientists, management, celestial navigators, and of course the Deep Space Network. Voyager 2 was currently running the final Saturn-Uranus cruise program, B624. A major part of the NET would involve changing parts of the program and fooling Voyager 2 into thinking it was flying past Uranus. It would carry out nearly all the activities of encounter: twisting, turning, shooting pictures (often of star fields, since there was actually no planet nearby), and carrying out other scientific observations. This would be done by means of an LSU, or late stored update, to the B624 program in Voyager's CCS

117

computer. An earlier test of the LSU procedure had gone fairly well. So had a test of the LEU, or late ephemeris update, a revision of the sequence based on navigational data which would give Voyager the latest known positions of spacecraft, planet, and moons.

One morning early in the week, Bill McLaughlin and his deputy, Donna Wolff, discussed one of the more sensitive parts of the NET, the test of the scan platform. "Our medium-rate slews of the scan platform worked well when we tested them on Voyager 1," said Wolff. "We'll also do them on Voyager 2 during the NET. We tested them first on Voyager 1 because we wanted to make sure that with the reduced pulse width patch in, for the antismear campaign, we don't overload the AACS computer with medium-rate slews and the patch running at the same time."

"As you can tell, Donna's the brains of this outfit," McLaughlin said. She smiled and shook her head in exasperation. "No, really," he insisted. "Listen, I was talking with my daughter Eileen last night—she's taking introductory statistics in college."

"Again?" Wolff laughed.

"Yeah, she likes it. We were going through it, and I showed her the work you had done on the Voyager slew analysis. To test various factors on the actuator," McLaughlin added in an aside, "Donna came up with some tests. So I gave my daughter a copy of our paper; and she was just—in *awe*! Because it was a *real-life* example of using statistics. I showed her how you used statistics to reach conclusions that we take actions on. Which is probably the only time in the history of introductory statistics that that's ever been done!"

Some members of the Voyager Project began working on the NET on October 20. By Wednesday the 23rd it was in full swing, and the SIS team began picking up its part in the test. That morning began with the 8:30 a.m. science operations report—or SCORE—meeting. Dan Finnerty, Peter Doms's deputy and head of science operations for the SIS (Science Investigation Support) team, chaired the meeting. Doms wouldn't be in until the afternoon, since he was pulling a late shift during the beginning of NET. SCORE meetings were normally held on Wednesdays; this one, of course, focused on the near encounter test. Finnerty noted that the NET had in fact begun, and there had been no problems yet that he knew about. Not that there hadn't been other problems. Two days earlier the spacecraft had played back a series of images stored on its tape recorder. The DSN station receiving the playback lost some of the pictures.

The experiment reps then reported on the status of their instruments aboard Voyager 2. The photopolarimeter (PPS) was doing fine, as were the planetary radio astronomy (PRA) experiment and its cousin, the plasmawave experiment (PWS). Jim Warwick's PRA had *still* not detected radio emissions from Uranus. Most planetary scientists were totally baffled. Nearly everyone was expecting Uranus to be like Jupiter and Saturn, a powerful emitter of radio waves. The screaming sounds of theories going down in flames could almost be heard in the meeting room.

The imaging playback, Candy Hansen confirmed, did indeed take a serious beating. Altogether, ten of eighty-six frames were seriously damaged. The images were needed for target maneuvers at encounter, and they were important. "With careful and expensive data processing we can meet the objectives of the target maneuver," she said.

It also now appeared that the DSN had lost some calibration data for the IRIS, or infrared interferometer spectrometer instrument. That meant the IRIS scientists would have to go through encounter with no calibration data except pre-Saturn, and any post-Uranus calibrations

119

they'd later be able to get. The IRIS people were not happy.

The good news was pointing accuracy. The ultra-violet spectrometer or UVS on Voyager 2 had been looking at a subdwarf binary star, explained experiment representative Susan Linick. "We haven't missed a target in the last four or five computer loads. We are very happy about that." The PPS had also been blessed with superb pointing, especially during the late part of cruise phase. Lonne Lane and his people were quite pleased.

"Maybe someone should tell the spacecraft people," somebody said. Finnerty made a note to do just that.

The meeting finally ended with Flight Science Office chief Pieter de Vries giving a few words of fatherly advice about the upcoming NET: "Have fun, have a good time during this test. It will be over all too soon!"

Shortly after lunch, key members of the project gathered for an NET navigation meeting. One of the navigation team members noted that "the navigation numbers for the Uranus aimpoint and the Miranda aim-point are not gospel. They could be off by at least a factor of two." Bill McLaughlin's wry response was that in his opinion "the Miranda mosaic is *very* success-oriented."

At about the same time, Peter Doms arrived for work—but not, at first, for the NET. He and other SIS people had to attend a meeting about the B702 load, the second of the observatory phase loads. Doms was already feeling and sounding frustrated. "We're trying to do non-NET things in parallel with the NET and that makes today the hardest day of NET for us," he said, rushing off with an uncharacteristic frown on his face.

During the afternoon the pace of the near encounter test seemed to slow down. Business as usual continued in other areas of Building 264, which housed not only Voyager but also the Galileo, Mars Observer, and Ulysses projects. The NET was still in the late stored update phase. And that had been tested just a few weeks earlier. Things had gone fairly smoothly then, and no one expected any problems from LSU this time—even though the teams involved now had thirty hours instead of seventy-two in which to run through it. In fact, the third and fifth floors were quiet, almost deserted. The optical navigation (opnav) pictures for the test wouldn't arrive from Voyager 2 until nearly 7:00 p.m. About twenty minutes after that Voyager 2 would start taking thirty-eight narrow-angle frames of Uranus. Bobby Brooks wouldn't come in until 7:30 p.m. The second navigation meeting for the NET wasn't scheduled until 8:30 p.m.

At 8:15 p.m. came the first hint of problems. The Canberra, Australia, DSN station suffered a glitch. Dan Finnerty, Peter Doms, and I had been watching the opnav images in Finnerty's office when suddenly part of an image was just gone. The top half of the screen was completely blank. Finnerty made a quick call to the "Ace," the mission controller on the fifth floor. The Ace confirmed there was a problem of some kind; Canberra was screwing things up. After watching the half-blank TV monitor for another several minutes, the three of us decided nothing was going to change anytime soon. We left the building and found a vending machine elsewhere on the JPL grounds. That was dinner.

Back on the third floor of Building 264, quiet reigned in the imaging team area. "The NET feels good right now," said Candy Hansen. "We know what needs to be done." She was feeling quite optimistic. She went on to talk about the imaging team meeting held the week before. One of the things the team members discussed was a "color problem." It had nothing to do with race. Some scientists and journalists had recently complained about the color images of Jupiter and Saturn that were released to the public during the flybys of 1980 and 1981. They charged that the colors of the planets were not "real," and that the public had been deluded into thinking that Jupiter and Saturn really do look like colorful Easter eggs. Of course, Hanson admitted, there wasn't much that could be done about it. The images released to the press had been identified as being "false-color images" generated by computer techniques. Hansen and the others felt that the news media—particularly commercial television and weekly general newsmagazines—should be more accurate in their identification of said images. But she didn't think that would happen.

At about 10:30 p.m. I wandered up to the fifth floor and the SIE (sequence integration engineers) area— "Disneyland," as the sign above the door proclaimed. Bob Brooks had been in since 7:30 p.m. but had nothing to do until the maneuver and engineering files for the spacecraft were finished by the spacecraft team elsewhere on the floor. "We should get those, oh, in about an hour," said Brooks. "About eleven-fifteen p.m. You gonna stick around for it all?" I demurred, and decided to retire to my motel room in Pasadena. Things seemed to be going well, aside from the apparent problem in Canberra. "Too bad," Brooks replied. "You'll probably miss all the *hot action*." He laughed. He was hoping there would be no "hot action," that the ancient Chinese curse "May you live in interesting times" would not befall the NET. The best thing that could happen during the test would be for nothing unusual to happen.

By the next morning the Voyager Project was living in interesting times. The computer sequence for the NET late stored update, which should have been finished and ready to beam up to the spacecraft, was not. Events had fallen far behind schedule. First, the maneuver and engineering (M&E) file for Voyager 2 was very late arriving at Bobby Brooks's desk from the spacecraft team. Because of that delay, Voyager management elected to cancel the third navigation meeting scheduled for after midnight. Brooks and the other sequence engineers instead took what navigation data were already available, plus the data from the M&E file, did the computer work, and ran it through the two mainframe computer programs that generated the sequences for the Voyager 2 CCS computer.

However, the M & E file had serious errors in it, and the sequence being generated was fatally flawed. Brooks was forced to start from scratch. "Hell, we're at least one-and-a-half to two hours behind now," Brooks grumbled. He'd been up all night, and by now had expected to be on his way home.

By 8:00 a.m. the LSU update had finally made it successfully through the sequence-generating program. The resulting coded sequence was then plugged into a computer-simulated Voyager dubbed COMSIM. If the sequence made it through that, it would be ready to send to Voyager 2.

Brooks and other Voyager personnel decided to go ahead and review the LSU sequence even though it was still being computer-checked for accuracy. The humans, too, wanted to check for errors that would need to be corrected before the program was sent to Voyager 2.

Computer printouts lay scattered across the large table in the fifth-floor conference room. As the meeting progressed, people started getting punchy from lack of sleep. Mike Urban, head of the Advanced Software Development Group, babbled 1960s jargon as they went through the printouts by eye: "Totally cosmic, man," he said, reading through the tiny printed lines of code. "Oooh, grooovy." Randii Wesson of the SIS team was making awful jokes and puns. Brooks was being typically loud and scatological and talking in a Swedish accent.

Two people got into a loud argument about changes in the platform slews and the correct number of computer words allowed. Angry and tired, they started yelling at each other. Wessen, who was chairing the meeting, tried to act as peacemaker. "Hey, ahh, are we getting tired?" he asked. The combatants finally calmed down and people got back to work. Finally Wessen said: "The movable block looks good. Miranda slews look good. Let's go with it."

The NET was not out of the woods yet, though. Even though it was a test, the LSU and the modifications to the B624 load were not "dummy programs." They were real sequences that would make the spacecraft do real things. They had to be sent to the spacecraft during a specific "broadcast window"; if not, the NET would really be in trouble. And trouble was getting close, said Dan Finnerty, the science operations chief of the SIS team. "That uplink window begins in just ten minutes and it stays open for two hours officially," Finnerty explained. "We have to send a load to the spacecraft three times, to make sure it has indeed heard and received it. We're getting short on time."

It took about five minutes of transmission time to start each broadcast of the LSU load on its way to Voyager 2 (the probe, of course, was so far away it took the radio waves nearly two hours to reach it). For this particular situation, it would not be an entire computer load. The late stored update made changes to memory locations in the B624 load already in the CSS. A total of thirty minutes was all that was needed for all three broadcasts including initial cues and other things before and after.

Finally, at 8:45 a.m., the LSU finished running through the simulated Voyager—and there were no errors. Brooks was ecstatic. People gathered around a UNIVAC terminal as the confirming messages from the mainframe flashed onto the computer, laughing and slapping one another on the back. Then Brooks rushed off to get the appropriate papers photocopied and signed. The uplink meeting, originally scheduled for 7:30 a.m., was called for 9:30. The "uplink window" to send the sequence to Voyager had already opened, but there was still time.

Brooks chaired the uplink meeting, and arrived on time with a stack of papers for people to sign. Representatives from all the major offices of the Voyager Project were present, including the Flight Engineering Office, the Flight Science Office, Operations, the spacecraft team, the sequence engineers, and SIS (Science Investigation Support). Brooks formally summarized the situation: the LSU was ready to send, it had run successfully through simulation. He held up the stack of papers. "Any criticisms?" he asked. "Yeah," replied Mike Urban. "Get a haircut." Everyone laughed and the tension finally broke. Then they all started signing the paperwork.

The first broadcast of the B624 late stored update finally began at 10:20 a.m. The preliminaries took about five minutes, and the load began its light-speed journey to Voyager 2 at 10:25. The "official" window closed at 10:30, but Dan Finnerty confided that there was also a one-hour buffer, and they could actually go until 11:30 a.m. The first sending of the LSU ended successfully. The second was successfully completed at about 10:48. Then the third broadcast began—and aborted. "Oh for Christ's sake," Finnerty groaned, watching a monitor in Peter Doms's office. The Ace, the mission controller, had briefly forgotten that he had to wait until 11:00 a.m. to do the third uplink broadcast because of a conflict with another activity aboard the spacecraft. We waited some more. They tried again—and at about 11:15 the third uplink restarted. It went successfully. It was nearly noon. The first part of the NET was over.

The next morning, Doms called the NET "mildly successful." He said, "We had a problem last night [the night of October 24] with the Miranda image motion compensation, and with a couple other areas. Basically, though, I'm reasonably satisfied with the results."

125

Candy Hansen also felt good about it. "The pictures we got last night were good," she said. "The commands did indeed load and execute." The monitor on the ceiling in the imaging team area was ominously blank, however. "Oh, that's okay," Hansen said brightly. "It's supposed to be."

Bill McLaughlin was a bit less enthusiastic. "Well, it's true we got the sequence up to the spacecraft," he said later Friday morning. "We had thirty hours to do the job and we got it up with five whole minutes to spare! Hey, it was a breeze, no problem." He and his deputy, Donna Wolff, laughed loudly at the sarcasm.

"Actually, the NET pointed out some important things to us," McLaughlin continued. "We learned of two key areas for which we need more people. One is the target motion compensation calculations for the spacecraft's imaging of Miranda. We need two people working on it, not one as we had during the NET. The TMC calculations are very complicated. We also need to have a small computer program that can check the TMC calculations for accuracy."

"I'm putting something together for that," Donna interjected.

"Second," McLaughlin continued, "we need to have two people doing the maneuver and engineering file that the spacecraft team delivers to Bob Brooks and his people. We only had one person, and it took much too long. As you know, there was a great delay there."

The sequence itself, though, worked pretty well, he said, considering that the Uranus flyby would be the most complicated encounter Voyager 2 would make in its nearly nine years of life. The tail end of test and training would run through November. McLaughlin revealed that the Voyager management had decided to rerun the first part of the NET on November 9, even though it would be after the official beginning of the encounter and the start of observatory phase.

126

The cruise phase had been anything but quiet, from beginning to end. What about observatory phase, which would run from November 4, 1985, to January 10, 1986? "If I could predict a quiet time during observatory phase, it would be the time through December 15," McLaughlin said. "Voyager will be behind the sun, relative to us on Earth, and we can't talk with it. Then on December 23 we have TCM B-13, trajectory correction maneuver number thirteen, and things will start picking up again."

Chapter 6
CLOSING IN

The Observatory Phase for the Uranus encounter began on Monday, November 4, 1985, at 7:30 a.m. Pacific Standard Time. The next day the encounter readiness review took place. It went fairly well. The review board's only real concerns centered on the Deep Space Network, which had missed several milestone dates its operators had said they could meet in getting the Mark IV-A system cleaned up. Nevertheless, both the board and Project Manager Dick Laeser were feeling much better about the encounter, and the DSN's ability to support it.

"I think the picture's a lot more optimistic," Laeser said one morning in late November. "The DSN can't fully support the near encounter at this point, but they *can* support observatory phase. And it looks like most of the liens against the system will be cleared up by the end of this month." The most serious problems were some irregularities in the data from the spacecraft. There was

128

a good chance, though, that the irregularities were really the result of still-untested and untuned electronic equipment and computer programs at some of the stations. The other major problem, as Laeser and others saw it, was the delay in training operators at the ground stations. "However," said Laeser, "we have nineteen more training sessions scheduled for the Australians. And because the Australian DSN stations are the critical ones for the Uranus flyby, they are now focusing all available time and energy on getting ready for that encounter." Everyone was expected to be trained by January.

In the meantime, the "Yellow Alert" proclaimed by NASA headquarters for the Uranus encounter had not yet been lifted by Thanksgiving. Laeser pointed out that there was always a lag time because of the timing of the periodic meetings where such matters got discussed. The cautious nature of NASA's management also played a part. The conditions causing the Yellow Alert might be cleared up several weeks before the alert would finally be lifted. "Of course, we would have liked to have told the review board we were ready," he added, "but there are still one or two more tests to be made."

One was a rerun of part of the near encounter test, which took place November 9. That test went well—or, as Bob Brooks put it, "It ran like shit through a goose. It was great!" The trip-up during the NET in October, said Brooks, had been caused by serious software errors in the maneuver and engineering file produced by the Voyager spacecraft team. The M&E errors and the file's delayed arrival in Brooks's area forced Brooks and others to fall several hours behind in their work. Another problem, as Brooks and others recognized after the fact, was trying to do both a late stored update and the NET at the same time. "It didn't double the work," Brooks growled. "It squared it."

The rerun, he continued, "retested us to make sure

129

we could indeed do the LSU. The guidance and control people on the spacecraft team did a lot better, too, because they automated some of their work. So the whole thing just zipped through real smooth on the 9th."

Bill McLaughlin was also satisfied with the results of the retest on November 9. "One of the things the spacecraft team was working on was practicing the calculations for image motion compensation," he explained. "Well, they did pretty good; they went from twelve hours to do the calculations to six hours, and then to five hours. For the test on the 9th, they did it in two-and-a-half hours. It was great!"

As for the first weeks of observatory phase, Mc-Laughlin felt confident. "We're sitting in a good position," he exclaimed. "It's all working well. The B701 load, Voyager's first computer program for observatory, executed with no problems. We're getting some ultraviolet scans of the entire Uranus system with the UVS instrument. We just did a Uranus movie and it looks good. We're on schedule in developing the computer loads for Voyager. And I'm as busy as before—but I'm not panic-stricken."

Donna Wolff, McLaughlin's assistant, was equally busy, but not on Uranus. "I'll be working on Neptune all next month," she said. "helping with the schedule for Voyager's cruise to Neptune. We're already thinking about that part of the mission, even though it's several months away. If we don't work on it now, during observatory phase, we'll never get to it."

The Uranus movie McLaughlin had mentioned was put together from a series of images made on November 6. "It lasted about thirty-six hours," explained Candy Hansen. "Voyager 2 was about one hundred million kilometers from Uranus at the time, or around sixty million miles." There wasn't much to see; Uranus still showed no discernible markings in its atmosphere and the rings were not visible in the movie images. "You

130

can see the moons moving around, though," said Hansen. The next movie would be shot on Thanksgiving Day, and the spacecraft would be about 30 million kilometers closer to the planet.

The Uranian rings, however, had finally been seen by Voyager—at least part of one. Parts of the epsilon ring, the widest one, appeared in an optical navigtion image early in November. Hansen took me into the darkened room with the interactive video hookup. After a few false starts she got the image onto the screen, worked some computer enhancement wizardry—and there it was. A faint arc of gray above the burned-in white disk of Uranus, the ring was barely visible on the screen. I could see it better by not looking at it, but rather glancing just to one side of the screen. Hansen punched a few more buttons and another enhanced image popped onto the screen. Now I could see a part of the epsilon ring below the planet as well—and was that it off to the right side? Hansen assured me it was. "We haven't made a normal photo of this image," she said. "It would be a waste of time. The ring image is so incredibly faint you can barely see it on the CRT. A photograph is too coarse, too grainy, to pick up the ring. We'll wait awhile longer."

Hansen's work load increased steadily as encounter grew nearer. For some, observatory phase would be a time to catch the breath and regroup. For the science teams, including the imaging team, the work load would get greater and greater. "I just find myself in the office longer and longer and longer," Hansen said wistfully. The weekend trips to the Mojave Desert or the Colorado River would soon become a thing of the past.

Peter Doms was seeing his work load increase as well. "I've managed it okay so far," he said. "I'm still managing to stay out of the office most weekends. My housemate's daughter is into early teenage now, and that's a whole new experience for me." He laughed. "So I really do try to keep weekends as free of the project as

131

possible. Most of the people who are working more usually try to extend their weekday hours." And Doms's opinion of the first weeks of observatory phase? "It's not as exciting as some of the other observatory phases have been."

Ed Stone did not quite agree. "Oh, I think there have been some surprises already," he said one afternoon. I had managed to catch the project scientist for a few fleeting minutes between meetings. As he hurried down the corridor toward me, Stone looked like one of those long-legged birds that chase the surf at Malibu. "For example, Jim Warwick and his people with the planetary radio astronomy experiment have *still* not heard any radio emissions from Uranus. This is very, very strange, because we do see some ultraviolet emissions from Uranus's south-pole region. So far they have been attributed to auroras. But if that's the case, there should be a strong magnetic field around the planet, and radio emissions from Uranus's magnetic field. Well, now the signature of those UV emissions is beginning to look like atomic hydrogen. So perhaps we are not looking at an aurora. Is it airglow?

"Here's another one for you. There is now some evidence for a very high amount of helium in Uranus's atmosphere. I mean, in the range of as much as forty percent. It comes from an evaluation by Glenn Orton of ground-based studies of Uranus. Now, that's really strange. The percentage of helium in the atmospheres of Jupiter and Saturn is around eleven percent, the same as that in the sun. Why so much helium at Uranus? If the figures are right, we will have to rethink a lot of our theories about the origin of the solar system." Stone smiled gleefully. "We know so little about Uranus," he continued, "that I'll be very surprised if this encounter *doesn't* produce a lot of surprises."

Meanwhile, more and more of Stone's time was now being devoted to Voyager. He was spending parts of several days a week at JPL, and working more closely and continuously with the PIs and coinvestigators for the experiments. He was also spending more time with the news media doing interviews.

With the NET and the retest out of the way by mid-November, Bob Brooks had moved on to other Voyager 2 computer programs. He was now working on loads B703, the spacecraft's final CCS program for observatory phase; an updated version of B752, the program that would command Voyager 2 during the forty-eight hours that included the actual flyby; and C752, a backup load for B752 in case either one of Voyager's CCS computers crashed. Then there was the pre-BML or backup mission load. It would "hide" in the CCS and conduct a minimum Neptune encounter in 1989 if Voyager's faulty radio receiver finally failed after Uranus and before Neptune.

Brooks was busy, but he still took spare time to continue checking out post-flyby jobs. The Multimission Software Project position had been dropped along with 1987 funding for that project, and CRAF, the comet-rendezvous project, was in trouble in Congress. Brooks was now talking with people about a possible job with the Mars Observer Project. He was also looking into possible positions in NASA's Space Station Program.

In a tiny office crowded with computers, filing cabinets, piles of papers, and shelves of books, Lonne Lane summarized the status of the PPS. "The instrument is ready for encounter," he declared. "During the near encounter test it did what we asked of it, and did it well. There were no hiccups. Well, that's not quite true. There were a couple of hiccups, but they were in the sequence, not the instrument.

"For one measurement," he explained, "we did miss one star target. But the slew to Beta Persei, Algol, one

133

of the occultation stars at Uranus—that was dead on, within twenty-five pixels of point."

Since the NET, things had gone smoothly, too. The first PPS measurements during observatory phase had just been completed, said Lane, and it looked as if they had gone well. "The instrument itself is in fine shape," he added. "The science measurements we're getting are extremely accurate, and the engineering data look very good, too." Lane was quite pleased.

The PPS's three major priorities at encounter, Lane continued, would be data about the rings, the Uranian atmosphere, and the satellites. "The rings and the atmosphere are equally important," he said, "with the moons in third place. You have to realize, these may be the only continuous and close-up data we get on Uranus itself for a long, long time."

The next major observations by the PPS would not occur until late December. That gave Lane the tiniest bit of breathing space: space to begin catching up on his background reading for the encounter, and space to work on some of his other projects as well. Lane had his fingers in several pies, including the Galileo probe to Jupiter and the long-running International Ultraviolet Explorer (IUE) satellite. Lane was also involved in studies of Pluto and its strange moon Charon and an ultraviolet astronomy experiment that was to fly on the space shuttle in 1987. Not even he was sure how or where he found the time to do everything. But he managed.

As Voyager 2 closed in on Uranus, the job of the navigators became more and more important. The orbits of the planets in the solar system closer to the sun (and Earth) were better-known than that of Uranus. Astronomers had reasonably accurate information about the size, mass, and distance from Earth of bodies like Jupiter and Saturn well before the Voyagers had been launched. Uranus, though, was so distant from the Earth that even those basic data were uncertain. That in turn meant that Voyager 2's path to Uranus would need to be adjusted several more times before encounter, to make sure it hit its imaginary target point in space. Without accurate data on the planet's size, mass, and distance from Earth, those changes in trajectory would inevitably be imperfect; its path past Uranus would not be the best possible and that in turn would affect Voyager's path to a Neptune encounter in 1989. Closer to home, uncertainties in the data about Uranus could easily mean missed observations of moons or rings.

One of the Voyager navigators was Bob Cesarone. His office, like those of the other navigators, was on the second floor of Building 264. Halfway through the observatory phase, Cesarone commented on the importance of accurate navigational data. "We'll have maybe three more updates of our data before the flyby," he said. "The last one will be just one-and-a-half days out, and it will go into that final late stored update or LSU that we'll do. That's a large part of what the NET in October was all about. For the navigation people, what's important during the LSU is to determine at least two things: how the Earth-occultation ingress time has changed, and how the ring-plane crossing time has changed." Earth occultation would occur when the spacecraft swung behind Uranus (the ingress moment) relative to the observers on Earth.

Changes in the planet's mass, size, or distance could easily change both of those times. A revised measurement of Uranus's radius, for example, would change the time the spacecraft disappeared behind the planet's edge. A bigger planet would mean an ingress time occurring earlier than originally expected. If the planet and its rings were farther from Earth than originally thought, it might mean Voyager 2 would cross the ring plane later than expected.

The navigators used several sources of information to revise their data. Among the most important were Voyager's optical navigation photos of Uranus, its satellites, and background stars. As the spacecraft closed in on the planet and the photos became larger and more detailed, the opnav photos became more valuable.

The two final chances to change Voyager's path to Uranus were the trajectory-correction maneuvers for Voyager 2 (the "B" spacecraft; Voyager 1 was the "A" spacecraft), TCM B-13 and B-14. "We're working on the data for Burn 13 right now," explained Cesarone. "Burn 14, the fourteenth in the entire Voyager 2 mission, will take place at encounter minus five days, or January 19."

Also on Cesarone's mind was the mission to Neptune. New data on the eighth planet now showed it to be somewhat larger than formerly thought. That was going to affect the so-called polar-crown path that Voyager 2 was supposed to take over Neptune's north pole in August 1989.

"We really haven't put that much effort into Neptune, and the data we were using were pretty old," he said. "Recently we've had a few informal meetings about the effect of the new data.

"Essentially what's happened is that Voyager's flyby of Neptune is now twenty-two hundred kilometers closer to the pole than before. We have gone from a point about thirty-five hundred kilometers above the polar cloud tops to about thirteen hundred kilometers of clearance." The spacecraft was in no danger from the closer passage, said Cesarone, and no one on the project would do anything to jeopardize its safety. "We're not gonna crash into Neptune," he said dryly. What might be in jeopardy was the quality of the science data to be gathered at Neptune, and also at Neptune's giant moon Triton.

Nearly as large as Earth's own moon, larger than the planet Pluto, Triton would be a major second target at the Neptune encounter. Some astronomers thought

Triton had areas of liquid nitrogen on its supercold surface. The areas could be as small as tiny lakes, or as large as oceans—at least, relative to Triton they'd be ocean-sized. Astronomers wanted very much to get a good close look at Triton. The polar-crown encounter at Neptune would fling Voyager 2 down past Triton at the relatively close distance of 10,000 kilometers.

The change in Neptune's estimated size, and a resulting change in the spacecraft's distance of passage, could in turn change its close-approach distance to Triton. "We could see the Triton flyby distance go to eleven, twelve, or maybe even sixteen thousand kilometers," Cesarone explained. "At this point, management is still sticking with the polar crown."

Management didn't have to. Voyager 2's aimpoint —the imaginary bull's-eye in space that the spacecraft had to hit—could always be changed. The current aimpoint, almost on the plane of Neptune's equator, was about 3 Neptunian radii distant from the planet and very near an area where recently discovered ring arcs might exist. The possibility of a too-close encounter with ring particles, coupled with the uncomfortably close passage over the north pole, could persuade Voyager management to move the aimpoint farther away from Neptune. It would guarantee the spacecraft's safety, but would adversely affect the quality of fields and particles observations made close to Neptune. It would still, however, maintain a close encounter with Triton.

There was still plenty of time to make a decision. As had been agreed at the SSG meeting in September, the cutoff date was early to mid 1987. Said Cesarone: "Sometime around April 1, 1987, we will decide on one or another strategy."

By the middle of November the Mission Planning Office had made final revisions to the contingency plans

137

for earthquakes. Robert Frampton of MPO typed them up in a four-page memo to Kohlhase. As Frampton noted in his report, the JPL buildings in the Arroyo would not have to come tumbling down to knock out the data circuits between JPL and the DSN network. Even a moderate earthquake in the Los Angeles area could accomplish that by damaging delicate electronic or computer equipment. If it happened in the last few weeks before the actual flyby, it could prevent the important CCS computer loads from being sent to Voyager 2. If *no* command could be sent to the spacecraft for a week or two, the CCS would revert to its command-loss logic and begin switching circuits associated with the already damaged radio receiver. It could well be a repeat of the disastrous days of April 1978, and no one wanted *that* fiasco to happen again. It drove the project to extremes of contingency planning.

The earthquake contingency plan had several features. For example, loads could be sent to Voyager ("up-linked," in technical talk) over both Goldstone and Canberra stations. Also, the end of each CCS computer program ordered general science and engineering data returned to Earth at a transmission rate of 4,800 bits per second. Even if a newer computer load never arrived, Voyager would at least send back data from the fields and particles, plasma, plasma-wave, and planetary radio astronomy instruments at a high signal-to-noise ratio. The project would get some science return from Uranus.

That was a "passive" feature. One "active" feature was an arrangement with the Pacific Telephone Company to provide emergency communications between JPL and the DSN stations in the event of an earthquake. This could include, for example, a van with microwave transmission equipment standing by at JPL. The van could handle telephone and high-speed data transmission between the lab and the DSN stations around the world.

Another feature involved a "hard freeze." Voyager's command loads were usually transmitted by high-speed data lines from JPL to the DSN station that would broadcast it to the spacecraft. A computer called the command processor assembly at the station would then either beam it to Voyager 2 at once or store it until Voyager was in position to receive it. However, the computer could store it for only one day. The Deep Space Network communicated with many space probes besides Voyager, and different communications software was often needed to talk with different probes. That meant Voyager 2 commands could not be kept for long in the DSN stations' command processor.

A "hard freeze" essentially meant "freezing out" every other spacecraft from the DSN network. Only Voyager 2 would be served by the DSN during the critical period of flyby. It had been done at Saturn and would be done at Uranus, too. This would allow Voyager commands to stay in the command processor for more than one day. The current plans had the hard freeze in effect for two consecutive "passes" of a DSN station, so commands could be kept in the command processor for up to thirty-six hours at a time. If necessary, of course, the hard freeze could be extended even more.

Finally, there were ways to manually command the spacecraft by actually typing commands into the command processor assembly at a transmission station. If an earthquake knocked out all connections between JPL and the DSN, it was thus possible to type the CCS load into the command processor and then beam it out to Voyager. No one hoped *that* would be required. There were simply too many possibilities for making a typing error. And in this case, a typing error could be catastrophic.

The contingency plan also looked at earthquake-protective measures for the Neptune encounter of 1989. One possibility, for example, would be to store a CCS load on magnetic tape and then store copies of the tape at the different DSN stations. This CCS load would be a preliminary version, without the final changes always requested by the scientists and engineers. However, it would serve as a backup in case an earthquake prevented the development of a final version, or kept a final version from being sent from JPL. If tape recorders were hooked up to the command processors (something not available for the Uranus flyby), the emergency backup command file could be loaded from the tape into the computer and then sent to Voyager.

On December 6, Bob Brooks talked about how the encounter was progressing from the viewpoint of the sequencing crew. "Things are pretty hectic," said Brooks. "We're really cranking out a lot of computer sequences for the spacecraft. We have all these backup or contingency loads to finish up. These are the ones we might use if something on the spacecraft crapped out." It was everyone's devout hope that the contingency loads would sit quietly on the shelf and gather dust all through the encounter. However, the management and science teams all felt that it was necessary to have the backup loads there, just in case. There would only be one shot at Uranus; it had to work the first time.

Besides the contingency computer loads, Brooks was fine-tuning the main computer programs for Voyager 2. "There are a bunch of detailed, tiny little things to correct in the sequences," he explained. "It's a case of cleaning things up. All the sequences have SCRs—sequence change requests—turned in by the science and engineering people. So far we've got SCRs on all the upcoming loads except the post-encounter ones."

Brooks summarized the status of the spacecraft's CCS computer programs. Observatory phase (OB) would run through January 9, 1986. Its three computer loads were numbered B701, B702, and B703. B702 was now on board and working. B703, the last OB load, was going through its final review process. It would take over on December 30 and run through January 9, 1986. The far encounter phase, running from January 10 to the morning of January 23, would see Voyager 2 closing in on Uranus, its velocity increasing as the planet's powerful gravitational field exerted its influence. The two computer loads for far encounter were B721 and B723; B722 had been incorporated into the other two. These loads were being updated by Brooks and the other sequence integration engineers. Near encounter phase was just that: the part of the mission that included Voyager 2's closest approach to Uranus, including the actual planetary flyby itself. Near encounter ran from January 23 through 25. The two loads for near encounter, B751 and B752, were in the "costing" stage: various members of the Voyager Project had turned in SCRs and now the sequences were being checked to see how big they were and how many computer words they used. If the sequences were too big to fit into the command and control subsystem (CCS) computer, they'd have to be edited down.

The near encounter loads had a lot of changes requested, said SIS team member Randii Wessen. "There were something like thirty change requests on B751, and forty of them on B752," he said in exasperation. Wessen and others on the SIS team and in the Flight Science Office would have to look at all the science SCRs, evaluate them one by one and determine how valid they were, rate their importance, and then decide which would be recommended for implementation and which would get thrown out. It was a very time-consuming job, especially for Wessen. "Things have gone smoothly so far," he said, "but now they are getting *very hectic.*"

On Friday the 13th of December, FOO manager Doug Griffith reported that the project was ready for the next major event in the encounter: the December 23 trajectory-change burn, TCM B-13. "It won't be much of a change," he said, "just one and three-quarters of a meter per second delta-v. It takes place on the 23rd, which is a holiday, which means I'll be here anyway." On the phone Griffith sounded extremely tired. I imagined how he must look: curly hair mussed, dark bags under his eyes.

All in all, Griffith was feeling better about the encounter. "We're coming together," he said. "Things are getting done and it's all settling in. There have been some difficulties, but really not too many, and they haven't hurt us." Yet Griffith remained cautious. "It's less than forty days to flyby, and now we are beginning to enter the crunch time. There's an awful lot to do, and a lot of it during the holiday period, like the trajectory burn."

Griffith was feeling somewhat better about the status of DSN and the Mark IV-A system. But he was not completely comfortable. "Well . . . it's tight, it's tight. And I don't feel comfortable going into encounter. I *think* we can pull it off," said Griffith. "But I cannot in all honesty say that I'm *sure* we can pull it off. But a lot of things have been improved in the last four to five weeks, and that's good."

One area that was still a problem, Griffith said, was antenna pointing. "They thought they had it fixed, but then it started acting up again." What was worse, the problem was in the antennas at the Australian DSN station. Most of the critical science data from the encounter would come through the DSN station in Australia, so a pointing problem there was a serious problem indeed. "It's a funny oscillation in the sixty-four-meter antenna, and it causes glitches in the telemetry."

In addition to the pointing problem, Griffith singled out the need to do some good maintenance work on the DSN's electronic equipment, and to finish training for personnel. "However, the project and DSN are working hard to get everything done," he added. "And the spacecraft is performing just fine. No problems at all."

In the middle of the month, Charlie Kohlhase suffered a partially collapsed right lung. "It was pretty strange," Project Manager Dick Laeser recalled. "Charlie was sitting in his office when Layne Whyman, our secretary, went in to see him about something. And he looked just *awful*. He said to her, 'I think you'd better take me out to my car. I have to drive to the hospital because my lung is collapsing.' Well, Layne came and told me and George [Textor] and we rushed into his office. It seems this happened to Charlie about two years ago, and he remembered what it felt like back then. That's what it felt like again, he told us. So he thought he should go to the hospital.

"Well, I sure as hell wasn't going to let him drive himself. So George and I kind of helped him down to his car, and we drove him to the hospital. We took him to the emergency room, and Charlie told the doctors he had a collapsed lung. The doctors, of course, at first didn't believe him; but sure enough, Charlie had correctly diagnosed himself." The upshot was that Kohlhase would be out of action until the first of the year. But as Laeser put it, "If there was one time we could stand to lose Charlie from the team, this is it. Unlike the rest of the project, he's essentially finished his work on the Uranus flyby."

By late December, observatory phase was in full swing. On December 15 the spacecraft went behind the sun as seen from Earth, and most of the scientists had to wait several days before they could get more data from the spacecraft. For the radio science people, the solar

143

conjunction was another experiment. They had Voyager 2 beam radio pulses toward Earth past the sun in a test of Einstein's general theory of relativity. The sun's gravitational pull actually bends energy, including light and radio waves. By measuring the amount of bending to the Voyager radio beam, Len Tyler and his associates could refine the accuracy of Einstein's theory.

Less esoterically, Lonne Lane was getting good data from the PPS. "We've done our latest star calibrations," he said in a phone call on December 16, "and those went well. The photopolarimeter itself is looking very good indeed. We also did our first measurement during observatory. It was a look at the Uranian atmosphere, and the data were consistent with earlier measurements." The next block of instrument time for the PPS would be Thursday evening the 19th. However, "the first really significant block of observations won't come until January 4 through 9," he said. "Then we should start seeing some interesting stuff."

Lane was still trying to catch up on his reading and study for the flyby. "I've got so much other stuff going on," he said, "that I've fallen behind on my own preparations for the encounter. So I'm doing a lot of reading." He and the PPS team were also involved in the final revisions to the B752 load for the encounter. Lonne called it "tweaking the sequence." They were putting in requests for tiny adjustments to the spacecraft's computer commands for the flyby. Their hope was to fine-tune the timing of PPS observations and generally optimize the conditions for their experiments. "So we tweak this and we tweak that," he said with a laugh.

On a more somber note, Lonne was experiencing some personal difficulties that added to his stress level. His parents had been very ill for several weeks and he was very worried about them. His wife's father was close to death, and she had been with her family on the East Coast for two weeks. That left Lane at home with their three children. It was getting hectic. What it would

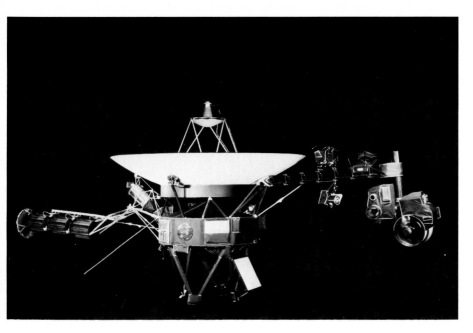

A full-scale model of the Voyager spacecrafts. Voyager 1 and 2 are virtually identical.

The Voyager Control Room, where engineers monitor the operations and temperatures of each of Voyager's instruments and major spacecraft systems.

Principal scientists and managers for the Voyager 2 mission to Uranus. FRONT ROW, L. TO R.: Pieter de Vries, Flight Science Office manager; Lonne Lane, photopolarimeter; Rudy Hanel, infrared radiometer spectrometer; Edward Stone, cosmic ray experiment and chief scientist; Len Tyler, radio science; Jim Warwick, planetary radio astronomy. BACK ROW, L. TO R.: Von Eschelman, radio science; Ellis Miner, assistant project scientist; Larry Soderblom, imaging science; Brad Smith, imaging science; Fred Scarf, plasma wave instrument; Tom Krimigis, low-energy charged particle instrument; Herbert Bridge, plasma science instrument; Lyle Broadfoot, ultraviolet spectrometer; George Textor, mission director; Norman Ness, magnetometer; Richard Laeser, project manager.

SIS team chief Peter Doms and his deputy Dan Finnerty confer on details of the near encounter test for the Uranus flyby.

Bill McLaughlin, manager of the Voyager Flight Engineering Office: a literate and witty Solzhenitsyn look-alike.

Bobby Brooks: biker, aging hippie, and computer programming ace. His program ran Voyager 2 during the actual Uranus flyby.

Candy Hansen: imaging team experiment representative. She helped plan many of the photographic sequences for the Uranus flyby.

Charles Kohlhase, head of the Voyager Mission Planning Office, explains uncertainties in the "polar crown" trajectory for Voyager 2's Neptune flyby in 1989.

A live image of Saturn as it appeared on the TV monitors at Jet Propulsion Laboratory during the Voyager 2 encounter with Saturn.

Len Tyler, leader of the radio science team, monitors the progress of the radio science experiment during the Uranus flyby.

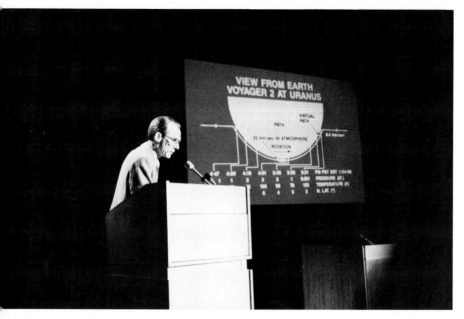

Project scientist Edward Stone explains the radio science experiment.

In the press room, reporters and writers grimly watch a replay of the *Challenger* explosion. At that moment, Voyager 2 was transmitting spectacular images of Uranus. The author is third from the left, seated.

A Voyager 1 view of Jupiter's Great Red Spot and the surrounding turbulent cloud systems.

This Voyager 1 image shows a violent volcanic eruption taking place on the Jovian moon Io.

A Voyager 2 image of Saturn assembled from several pictures.

A Voyager 2 image of Saturn's C-ring and part of the B-ring (at bottom and left), showing more than sixty bright and dark ringlets of varying surface compositions.

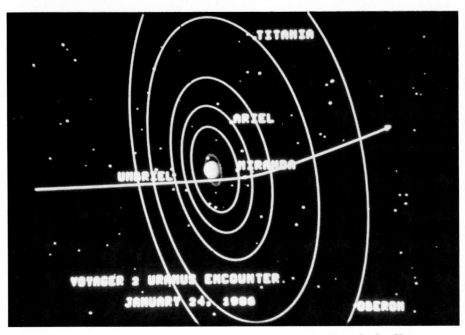

A computer graphic image showing Voyager 2's path through the Uranus system.

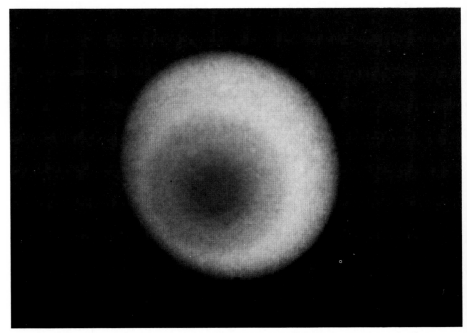

This Voyager 2 image of Uranus is the first photograph showing the haze cap and banding in the planet's atmosphere.

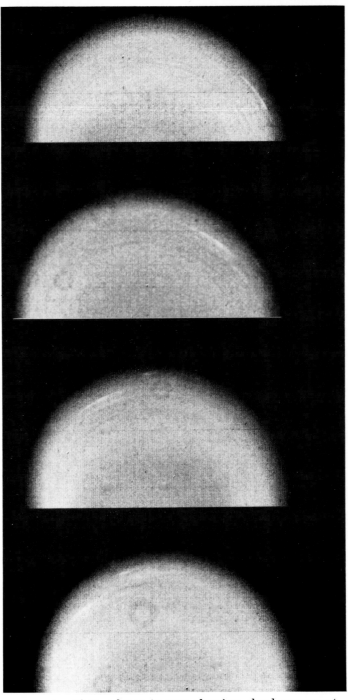

A series of time-lapse images showing cloud movement in the atmosphere of Uranus.

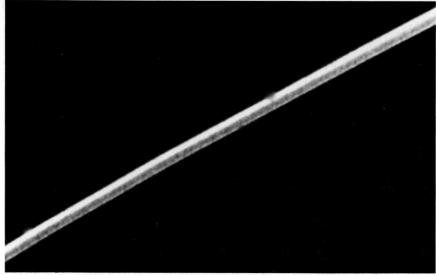

A high-resolution image of Uranus's epsilon ring showing considerable structure.

The single most extraordinary image of the Uranus flyby. A solitary ninety-six-second exposure looking back at the Uranian rings revealed a thin expanse of fine dust stretching between the known rings.

A composite "family portrait" of the five major moons of Uranus. The individual images were taken at distances of from 5 to 6.1 million kilometers.

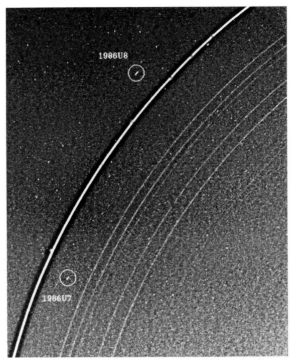

This is the discovery image of the two "shepherd satellites" for Uranus's epsilon ring. All nine of the known Uranian rings are visible.

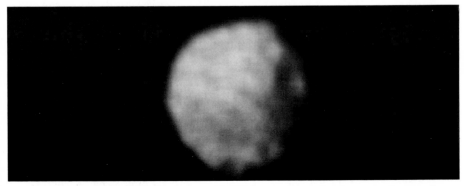

This image of the Uranian moon 1985U1 was the only close-up of any of the newly found Uranian moons.

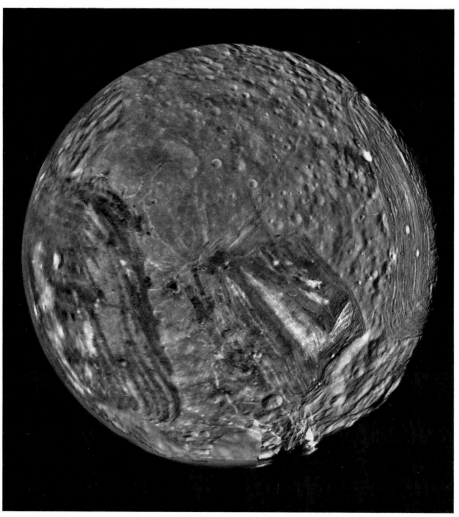

A dramatic computer-assembled mosaic image of Uranus's innermost major moon, Miranda.

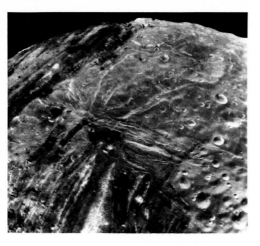

A high-resolution image of the "Grand Canyon of Miranda," which stretches over the horizon. The layered structure in the canyon's walls is visible.

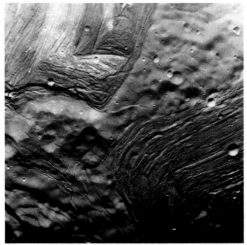

This Miranda image shows the "chevron," a Ganymede-like race-track, some hummocky lunarlike terrain, and impact craters.

An extraordinary closeup image of the dramatic fault scarp, or cliff, on Miranda.

This four-image mosaic is the highest-resolution photograph of Uranus's moon Ariel.

The most detailed image of Uranus's moon Umbriel.

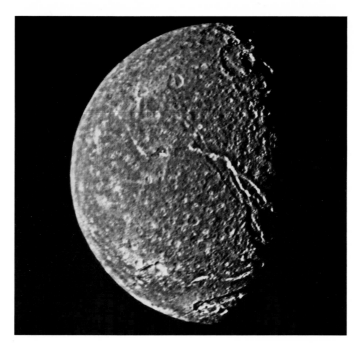

This composite of two photographs is the highest-resolution image of Uranus's moon Titania.

The best photograph of Uranus's outermost moon, Oberon.

Voyager 2's "Goodbye Uranus" image, shot on January 25, 1986, as the spacecraft "looked back" over its shoulder and took a picture of the planet's sunlit limb.

This painting by Don Davis depicts Voyager 2's encounter with Neptune and its giant moon Triton on August 24, 1989, three years and eight months after the Uranus encounter.

come down to, Lane admitted, was that he would end up working through the Christmas holidays. "I'll take a day off here and there," he said, but for Lonne Lane, Christmastime was going to be mostly work and worry, and very little play.

"Well, the mission is now past the halfway point of observatory phase," Dick Laeser reported in a telephone call on December 16. "And I must say, OB has turned out to be not nearly as productive as we'd like it to be." He paused and started chuckling. "I mean, Uranus hasn't proven to be very interesting, you know. Only the cameras recognize that the planet even exists! The UVS instrument hasn't seen anything of the planet in the ultraviolet, and that's particularly frustrating. We blocked out a lot of OB time for the UVS people to do these big scans of the entire system—and there's nothing! It's a little frustrating, and it means we're eating up a lot of time and budget spinning our wheels, as it were.

"It wasn't a mistake to block out all that time for UVS," Laeser added hastily. "The lack of any data from UVS at this stage is important, too."

The ultraviolet instrument wasn't the only one aboard Voyager that hadn't yet detected the planet. "No," Laeser said wearily, "Jim Warwick's PRA instrument *still* hasn't detected any planetary radio waves. They haven't heard a thing. So maybe there isn't any magnetic field there after all."

Voyager 2 was less than six weeks from flyby and closer to Uranus than Mercury is to the sun, so the lack of any radio emissions this late in the encounter was one of the biggest mysteries of the Uranus encounter so far. Jupiter and Saturn had huge magnetic fields that generated powerful radio bursts. Uranus, though smaller, was also a gas giant, and most astronomers had simply assumed it would be pumping out radio emissions. Both

145

Voyagers had heard Saturn months before flyby; radio astronomers on Earth had been listening to Jupiter's radio emissions for decades. Only James Warwick, the physicist from Boulder, Colorado, in charge of the PRA, was not surprised by the lack of any radio emissions. Years earlier, he had predicted in a paper in the science journal *Icarus* that Uranus would have a weak magnetic field, if any at all. Now Warwick's instrument aboard Voyager 2 seemed to be proving him correct.

In Washington, D.C., the big opening press conference for the Uranus encounter went off with nary a hitch. "We released the latest fuzzy-blue-tennis-ball picture then," said Laeser. " 'Cause that's all it still looks like, a fuzzy blue tennis ball." The press conference also featured the computer-generated Uranus flyby movie. Kohlhase, Jim Blinn, and Blinn's associate Sylvie Rueff had, in Kohlhase's words, "killed themselves" to get the movie finished in time for the press conference. It was certainly more exciting to look at than the fuzzy blue tennis ball. Would the real thing ever succeed in outshining the computer animation? The answer was less than six weeks away.

Also more exciting than the blue tennis ball was a new image of Uranus's rings. The day after Thanksgiving the imaging team took a series of heavily overexposed images, blended them together in the MIPL computers, and came up with a picture showing Uranus's epsilon ring completely encircling the planet.

"It's very neatly defined," said Laeser, "and the good news about that is that it means we will indeed be able to see the rings going into the system, and not just looking back over our shoulder as we leave it behind."

The trajectory burn on the afternoon of December 23, TCM B-13, went off without a hitch. "However, some last-minute navigation results resulted in a change in the spacecraft's aimpoint from the original design," reported Bill McLaughlin a few days later. Most of the change came from a revised estimate of the mass of Uranus. The planet massed three-tenths of a percent more than astronomers had originally estimated—"and that's a large increase!" McLaughlin exclaimed. That meant moving Voyager 2 about 340 kilometers farther away from the planet in order to get the same kind of trajectory to Neptune via the gravitational slingshot effect.

Voyager 2 was thirty-two days from its encounter with the seventh planet in the solar system. It had journeyed eight years and 4.9 billion kilometers. So far it had used about 85 liters of its hydrazine propellant, averaging 57 million kilometers per liter—pretty good mileage. Voyager engineers hoped to "hit" the imaginary target in space near Uranus with an accuracy of 100 kilometers. If they pulled it off, it would be equivalent to sinking a 2,520-kilometer-long golf putt.

Chapter 7
FAR ENCOUNTER

"Things look great. And I feel *really* good about it. With the exception of only one problem, the spacecraft is working just fine." Dick Laeser was beaming. It was January 10 and the far encounter phase of the Uranus flyby had begun. The problem, said Laeser, was with the IRIS instrument, the infrared interferometer spectrometer and radiometer. Inside the IRIS was a neon bulb that emitted a light at a very precise wavelength. The light both provided a timing standard for the experiment and served to trigger the vital back-and-forth movement of a mirror in the instrument. The neon's intensity had apparently started oscillating on January 2, causing disruptions in the data return. It quickly disappeared, said Laeser, but "then we saw it again on the 6th. We canceled an IRIS health check on the 8th because of it." The concern was that if they ran the IRIS any more than necessary, it might cause further degradation of

148

the neon calibration system. "But Rudy Hanel says he's getting good data from IRIS anyway. He still feels he can calibrate out the interference with only a small loss of information." Hanel was the IRIS principal investigator.

Laeser also felt "pretty good, but just a little nervous" about the status of the Deep Space Network and its Mark IV-A system. "Officially all the liens are removed," said Laeser. But some of the DSN station personnel were still not "settled in the saddle." That was causing occasional problems. And there were still some bugs cropping up in the Mark IV-A, Laeser noted, "and when they do sometimes we don't catch them for a while, because of our lack of operator proficiency.

"So that's the situation we'll go into encounter with. But all in all it's a workable situation."

Then there was the matter of the Soviets. A year earlier, Brad Smith had approached Laeser with the news that there *might* be one or two Soviet astronomers "sitting in" with the imaging team during the flyby. At least, Smith had sent some invitations. Laeser had heard nothing about it since. "And I *still* have heard nothing about any Soviets participating on the imaging team," he said. "I guess I need to talk with Brad about this. I haven't heard anything from him about it." He shrugged and laughed. "Actually, I don't know what's going on with it. My fear is that I'll get a call from visitor control, saying there're three people here wearing funny fur hats and talking in a weird accent, and saying they belong to Voyager!"

Laeser also had some comments on the prudishness of the press. A few days earlier the project had released a computer-enhanced photo of Uranus, showing a dark circular marking over the south pole of the planet. Most probably it was some kind of Uranian smog. But the south pole and its dark spot were pointing slightly to one side of the planet's center. Some people were calling it

149

"the eyeball." Others just snickered. Still others took two of the images and pasted them next to one another. . . .

Said Laeser, "No one seems willing to run the photo of Uranus showing the markings on it. Do you think they're embarrassed by what it looks like?" He joked about a certain prestigious space-related magazine having it and never running it. "Maybe they think they're not 'that kind' of magazine!"

More seriously, Laeser described the press interest in the flyby as "a compressed spring waiting to break loose. I'm frankly amazed at the intensity of the interest. I would have thought that it would be less than the Saturn flybys, because it's been so long, four years. But it's incredible. The interest is really out there!"

Two doors down from Laeser, Bill McLaughlin held forth on the atmosphere in the project itself. "There's an electricity in the air now," McLaughlin exclaimed. "We're definitely in encounter! You can tell from people's attitude; they're up on the balls of their feet, like boxers." McLaughlin leaned back in his chair, his halo of hair illuminated by sunlight shining through his office window. The temperature in Pasadena was in the mid-80s. McLaughlin had warm words for his engineers and computer programmers. "Right now we can say that the spacecraft engineering has held up very well. The anti-smear campaign is working well. IDC [image data compression] is fine; the imaging sequences are working fine.

"From the point of view of the Voyager Flight Engineering Office, the spacecraft team has done about ninety percent of its work for encounter. Now," he added mischievously, "the navigation people have only done about ten to twenty percent of *theirs*; they are still to be proven in the fire!"

McLaughlin concluded, "A week from this weekend —the weekend of January 18 and 19—that's when the heavy stuff begins: TCM B-14, LEU, LSU. It'll sort of be the sprint at the end."

Charlie Kohlhase wasn't supposed to be doing any sprinting. In fact, Kohlhase shouldn't even have been walking around so soon after his right lung collapsed in December. Kohlhase, however, did as he pleased. "The doctor told me that the only people who suffer such spontaneous collapsed lungs are young athletic types or people flying at high altitudes." He grinned wickedly. "So I figure it's just us athletic jock types who get these things!

"Two weeks after the lung collapsed I played eighteen holes of golf. And I shot a seventy-three. So I guess I'm completely recovered. In fact, I feel marvelous, in great health. It's wonderful, and I'm ready for the next two weeks."

As he had at previous encounters, Kohlhase was involved with the various special guests who would be at the lab for the Uranus flyby. At least 600 VIPs would be at JPL on January 25 and 26, staying in six different meeting rooms. Kohlhase said, "One of the jobs of the Mission Planning Office will be to provide people to float in those rooms and give the guests updated reports and behind-the-scenes info on the encounter. I and two others from MPO will each take two rooms and take care of them. My own plan is to find out which rooms will have what groups, and then I'll have to decide between Angie Dickinson and the science fiction people."

Even as he prepared for Uranus VIPs, Kohlhase was working on the next phase of Voyager 2's epic journey. "The final review package for the Uranus-Neptune cruise guidelines is now done and should be released today. We hope that in the next two weeks the Neptune encounter guidelines and constraints will be out. Probably, though, that won't be ready until April.

"Then on Monday afternoon we'll have an MPO meeting to get the latest values for Neptune's and Triton's radius and mass, and Neptune's polar tilt. All those data are essential to a final decision on our Neptune encounter trajectory."

Finally, the Wilderness Survival computer game was doing quite well. Yellowstone Park rangers had taken copies of it to a conference of park rangers, said Kohlhase. It was possible the game would eventually be used as a training device for park rangers. On the downside, problems with the IBM version had delayed its release until April at least. But sales were going well, he said. "The distributor bought fifteen thousand and about ten thousand have been sold so far!"

The DSN's nagging problems were still causing occasional problems for scientists. However, for the most part the DSN glitches were more nagging in nature than truly serious. Some of the data outages turned out to be outages in appearance only: a picture that didn't show up on the real-time TV monitors, for example, would later be recovered from data stored on tape at the ground station. Dan Finnerty usually had as much good news to talk about as bad news. On the 13th, for example, he cheerfully reported the successful start-up three days earlier of the first far encounter computer load, and a successful calibration test of the planetary radio astronomy (PRA) experiment aboard the spacecraft.

In other good news, Linda Horn, the experiment representative for the infrared interferometer spectrometer (IRIS), said that the problem with the instrument's neon signal bulb seemed to have gone away. With apparently no help from anyone, the apparent oscillations had disappeared as mysteriously as they had appeared. In any case, the complications caused by the oscillations were not too serious. Said Horn, "It just means that we need more data to get our signal-to-noise ratio back to normal."

. . .

Up in "Disneyland," home base for Bob Brooks and the other sequence engineers, the pace was getting frantic. Brooks was as garrulous as ever, but he was also getting more tense as the flyby approached. "There is a lot of stress here now, a lot of tension, a lot of pressure. I personally am very pissed with the piecemeal way the requests for changes to the computer sequences are coming in. It's a bullshit way to do business! I mean, it takes hours to run the modified sequences through the different computer simulations and checks, and right now we're having to do this *each time we get a change request!*"

Brooks calmed down and grinned a silly grin. "Someone recently asked me why we weren't all excited and up for the encounter. I told him that when you are five foot six inches tall, and standing in a bucket filled with ten feet of shit, it's hard to see out. That's sort of where we are right now. There's so much our particular group of people has to do in the next few days that we're totally focused on that—on the LSU and that stuff.

"But right after the near encounter loads begin running, the stress level will drop and we can begin to appreciate what's going on. I'm real happy they installed monitors in our area," Brooks added, "so we can see the images as they come in. Otherwise we would have had a really serious morale problem up here."

Brooks himself was finishing work on the final edition of B752, the program that would run Voyager during the critical hours of Uranus encounter on January 24. "It's running in the computer simulator right now," he said. "It goes to review meetings tonight, then we make any necessary final adjustments to it to get it ready to go." Yet he felt he wasn't working too many extra hours. "Oh, I guess I'm working eight to sixteen hours extra per week. And I've been coming in a little bit on weekends occasionally, but really it's not too bad. It certainly isn't as bad as I expected it to be."

153

. . .

Later that day several Voyager managers met to discuss the final trajectory-correction maneuver for Voyager 2's encounter with Uranus. TCM B-14 was scheduled for the early hours of Sunday, January 19. The meeting brought together members of the Voyager navigation team led by Don Gray and people from the Flight Engineering Office (Bill McLaughlin), the Flight Operations Office (Doug Griffith), the Flight Science Office (Pieter de Vries), the Mission Planning Office (Kohlhase), and top management (Laeser and Mission Director George Textor). Gray's people briefed the gathering on the latest navigation numbers for Voyager.

The information sounded bad—but it was actually good. Voyager 2's trajectory was drifting away from the one they had calculated it would follow. The probe was not going to hit the imaginary target in space they had aimed for with the last TCM, or trajectory-correction maneuver. The craft instead was heading about 250 kilometers up and to the left—inward toward Uranus—of that aimpoint in space. None of the navigators were sure why this was occurring. Perhaps the drift was simply a result of having more accurate data from optical navigation images. On the other hand, it was possible that some of the recent trajectory-change maneuvers had been "burning short." Voyager could be falling short of its target a little like a bullet aimed at a target beyond its range. Of course, Voyager would get to Uranus with no difficulty; it would merely be off its target point by 250 kilometers or so.

Other navigation team members joined in the presentation, and a sheet of paper was passed around to meeting participants with the parameters of TCM B-14. The burn would be a tiny one, just 0.4 meter per second change in the spacecraft's velocity. It would move the spacecraft back toward the ideal point in space that the

154

project wanted to hit, giving Voyager 2 a near-ideal gravity-assist aimpoint for the Neptune flyby of 1989. It would also benefit the planetary occultation experiment planned by Len Tyler and the radio science experimenters.

On the other hand, said Gray, they might not have to do the burn at all. And that was an extraordinary statement. Never in the previous eight years of the Voyager Project had there ever been a situation when the project could *cancel* a trajectory-correction burn. Usually the opposite was the case. And now, this far from Earth, in regions of the solar system never explored before by spacecraft, could their navigation be turning out to be so accurate that they could *skip* a TCM? Despite the drift? It couldn't be true.

But it was. Voyager's aimpoint was drifting toward the planet, which would benefit both the scientists and the navigation for Neptune; and it was not drifting too fast, so there was no possible way the spacecraft could, say, hit Uranus. Finally, no burn meant no change in the temperature levels in the spacecraft, and therefore no two-day-long command moratorium during the final days before encounter. Therefore, Gray continued, he and his people had developed some criteria for deciding whether or not to even execute TCM B-14. Their bottom line was that if it looked as if the final, actual aimpoint was within 200 kilometers of the ideal gravity-boost aimpoint, then the burn should *not* be done. They wouldn't need it. If the aimpoint looked as if it was shifting farther away, then they would all get together again Friday evening, grit their teeth, and make a final go/no-go decision.

Kohlhase's Mission Planning Office had also looked into the situation. Kohlhase told the group that MPO's bottom line was (1) to allow a maximum error of 350 kilometers if there were significant Uranus-related gains without the burn; (2) to allow a maximum error of 225

155

kilometers if the gains were minimal; and (3) if they wanted a single number to focus on, make it 275 kilometers.

The group finally decided that if the shift was between 200 and 350 kilometers, then they would meet at about 10:00 p.m. Friday night to decide whether or not to do the burn.

Tuesday, January 14, began with a SCORE meeting. The flyby was ten days away, and encounter fever was already in the air. The adrenaline level was starting to rise in a parabolic curve—slowly at first, seemingly flat, but then turning vertical with exponential swiftness.

Peter Doms announced that "The MacNeil/Lehrer Newshour" would be filming part of the SCORE meeting on Thursday for a report on the flyby to be broadcast on the 24th. If people didn't want to reveal preliminary information in front of the cameras, said Doms, they need not. He would have a second go-around with the instrument teams after the camera crew left.

Next, Dan Finnerty reported that there had been some sporadic data outages from one of the Australian DSN stations the previous evening. They had happened during the narrow-angle movie of Uranus. The damage was not serious, though. FSO manager Pieter de Vries added: "Please note that there are two data streams coming in from the DSN stations. So there may be data outages in one stream—for example, the data from arrayed antennas—and no data outage from the other stream. So you may not be missing data after all."

Dave Bliss, the assistant experiment representative for the imaging team, talked about the last far encounter movie, still going that morning. "In the frames taken through the ultraviolet filters we are seeing some visible features in the upper atmosphere, at high latitudes." A murmur of excitement ran through the room. At last, features on Uranus!

Linda Horn said the IRIS now seemed to be working all right. The instrument would begin its formal observations of Uranus the next day, although it had already been getting some data by "riding along" with the narrow-angle movie action. The IRIS was on the scan platform with the TV cameras, and the IRIS experimenters had simply turned the instrument on and let it take readings of whatever the cameras were pointed at.

Next, Lonne Lane reported that the photopolarimeter looked fine. He and his associates had taken some measurements of Beta Persei (or Algol), one of the two ring-occultation stars, and the brightness curve had been right on the theoretical curve.

Fred Scarf's plasma-wave instrument, the PWS, had been detecting a radio emission at a frequency of 1 kilohertz. However, the scientists weren't yet sure the emission was from Uranus. The activity was related to an oscillation in the solar-wind plasma, a kind of emission that could be detected anywhere in the solar system out to 19 astronomical units, or more than 8 billion kilometers from the sun. So detecting the emissions was not in itself unusual. The plasma-wave people were trying to see if there was any change in those emissions as Voyager 2 closed in on the planet. However, they had not yet seen any such changes.

Jim Warwick, the principal investigator for the planetary radio astronomy instrument, had arrived from Boulder, Colorado, the previous afternoon. His group's computer had been set up in a tiny cubbyhole on the third floor of Building 264 and was running well. Added Warwick, "But I have nothing else to report, and I'm as puzzled by that as everyone else!"

"So we still have a radio-silent planet," quipped Ed Stone. Everyone chuckled, but the mystery of Uranus's missing radio emissions was apparently continuing. Voyager was only about 10 million kilometers from Uranus, and with the possible exception of Scarf's 1-kilohertz emission it had still not picked up any radio signals from the planet.

The discussion then turned to press releases and pictures. Stone announced that no more information or pictures about new moons would be released until later that week. "Then we'll do a package release on all we have," he said.

"However, we do have a minor leak," said Ellis Miner, Stone's deputy. "A reporter called and asked 'about these new moons you've seen.' " The new, sixth and seventh moons had not even been officially reported to the rest of the Voyager team, but someone was whispering the information to "outsiders." Project management insisted on confirmation of any potential discovery before the information was released. Miner was not pleased, and the tone of his voice said so.

Later that day, Candy Hansen confirmed Bliss's report on markings on Uranus. Banded structure in the planet's atmosphere was showing up nicely in computer-processed images. She also talked about the steadily increasing workload for herself and the others on the imaging team. "I'm kicking myself for not doing some things last week; the problem is, there are some things that couldn't get done until now. I'm working from about eight-thirty in the morning until about seven each night, and weekends as well. This Saturday, for example, the team will meet to decide on last-minute exposure for our images."

Rumors of a newly discovered Uranian ring had begun spreading around the lab, but Hansen said the evidence for it "is really shaky. It depends on who's telling the story." As far as new moons were concerned,

158

said Hansen, "We've already announced the discovery of one new moon, and as you know there are two more we are absolutely sure of. We'll publicly announce them pretty soon, as Ed Stone noted in the SCORE meeting this morning. But before we can do that I need to call Brian Marsden at Smithsonian Astrophysical Observatory and give him the data on their diameters and distance from Uranus." She sighed heavily. "*But*—I need to get the data before I do that! The radii of the moons are very uncertain."

The scientists were pleased with another, more certain piece of information. Voyager's instruments indicated that the albedos, or light-reflection characteristics, of the five major moons agreed nicely with the ground-based estimates of Robert Hamilton Brown. Formerly an astronomer at the University of Hawaii and now at JPL, Bob Brown was one of the world's foremost authorities on Uranus's moons. The albedos, said Hansen, were "Callisto-like"—they reflected light in much the same way Jupiter's moon Callisto did. Would the moons *look* like Callisto, with its surface covered with craters? The answer would come in ten days.

"Everything is now moving at warp speed," said JPL public information specialist Henry Fuhrmann. It was still nearly two weeks from the flyby, but the pace was already verging on frantic for the Public Information Office. The phones in the office were ringing off the hook as requests for information poured in. Fuhrmann, Mary Beth Murrill, Frank O'Donnell, and the others were not members of the Voyager team, but rather JPL employees in their own separate department. They acted as "buffers" for the Voyager people. Requests for interviews had to go through the Public Information Office, rather than directly to the scientists, engineers, or managers involved. It was the only way to keep the team members

159

from being swamped. The system was not entirely successful, but most of the people who got direct calls from reporters immediately referred their questioners to the PIO.

As the Voyager story began appearing in newspapers and on television, JPL's PIO started getting some unusual phone calls. Murrill took a call from someone who wanted information about chromium. She passed him on to the Bureau of Mines. Fuhrmann talked to a woman who said she had "important information for the top people at NASA." He gave her the appropriate addresses in Washington, D.C. The woman then revealed that her "information" was about an alien spaceship somehow connected to a radio station in Los Angeles. Fuhrmann sighed. "I knew she was a little off when she said she was calling from a phone booth."

The PIO specialists had been assigned specific jobs during the week of the flyby. O'Donnell was coordinating television coverages. Murrill would work with print media and radio reporters. Alan Wood was handling radio updates. Fuhrmann would have the early shift in the press room, from about 2:00 a.m. to 2:00 or 3:00 p.m., working with TV people from the United States Information Agency and the early-morning American television news shows. From about 7:00 a.m. onward he would switch to writing captions for the Uranus pictures to be released that morning. Fuhrmann didn't mind coming in early. "It gives me a shot at a primo parking spot," he said, revealing himself as a typical Southern Californian.

January 15—flyby minus nine days—started with some bad news from the Deep Space Network. As luck would have it, it had started raining the day before at all the Australian DSN stations. Data from an IRIS full-disk observation of Uranus were affected—the rain caused the loss of twenty minutes of the transmission. It was beginning to sound like a replay of the "Rain in Spain" problems that had plagued the Voyagers during the Saturn encounters. Fortunately, the twenty-minute loss would not cause serious harm to the overall infrared studies of Uranus. But the rainout could be a sign of things to come. January and February were the rainiest months of the year in Australia, and the Voyager teams would fearfully watch the weather forecasts from Down Under for the next ten days. As it turned out, clear skies reigned in Australia throughout most of the encounter.

While DSN fretted over rain outages, the denizens of "Disneyland" continued work on the next several computer loads. "Everything's still right on schedule," said Randii Wessen. "The sequences in the pipeline right now include B723, the final far encounter sequence, which will be loaded into Voyager 2 on Friday the 17th, and B772, the second post-encounter load."

That day also saw the first version of a "family portrait" of Uranus's five major moons. At the morning's SCORE meeting, Hal Masursky held up a preliminary hard-copy version of the portrait. "This shows the five satellites," he said in his smooth, slightly whispery voice, "and as you can see there *are* variations in brightness, which fits right with our Earth observations.

"Oh," he added, "Rich Terrile has been checking for new rings, but at this point we cannot say we have found one. Anyway, Steve Synnott"—a member of both the imaging team and the Voyager navigation group—"has gone over our data on the five newly discovered moons and he says he can only vouch for the legitimacy of two of them." (Masursky was still speaking of five new moons, even though a total of seven had been tentatively identified. The imaging team's moon people were still not ready to speak of the others even to the rest of the project.) Masursky paused, and delivered the punchline: "So we have two legitimate and three illegitimate new satellites." The crowd in the room roared with laughter.

On the TV monitors scattered throughout Voyager Country the planet was looming larger and larger. Only weeks earlier it had been a small dot. Now its disk was close to filling the screen. Masursky also reported that the imaging team found "what seems to be a dark spot [in the Uranian atmosphere] in the images shot with the ultraviolet filter. Someone asked me what color that would be, if the image is in UV light. Well, it could be red. That means we may have found a Great Red Spot on Uranus!"

"Meaning it's 'great' we found something," someone said.

"If it is in fact there," Masursky continued, "it may help give us a rotation rate for Uranus."

Voyager's cameras were not the only instruments seeing Uranus. Principal investigator Rudy Hanel, of the Goddard Space Flight Center, told the SCORE meeting that the IRIS instrument was seeing "nothing dramatic so far. The instrument does see the planet, though."

"So it really is there!" said Ed Stone jokingly.

"Well, that's better than many other instruments," Hanel retorted, in a gentle dig at Jim Warwick and the planetary radio astronomy instrument.

Warwick for his part said that he and his associates would get a look at PRA data from the 13th some time in the next several hours. But there was still no sign from his instrument of any magnetic field around Uranus.

Henry Fuhrmann caught his breath for a few moments. He was setting up the shoot for "The MacNeil/ Lehrer Newshour," which wanted to film a Voyager meeting in progress. He was also working on the Galileo pamphlet, which had to be finished by the next evening

—a project that would turn out to be in vain. "You may want to get a picture of this," he said. "None of the phones are ringing and it's in the middle of the work day!" At that moment the phone lines lit up again.

"So much for that," said O'Donnell, picking up his extension.

The public release of new pictures from Voyager moved slowly. Everything still had to go through NASA headquarters in Washington, D.C., before it was released. That would change during the week of the flyby. Images would be coming in so fast that JPL would simply release pictures directly to the gathered media.

A more serious problem for the Public Information Office would be the names for the new moons. The first one, discovered in late December, was officially known as 1985U1. It was the first ("1") Uranian ("U") moon discovered in 1985. The other six were discovered in January, so they were numbered 1986U1 through 1986U6. Project Manager Dick Laeser, among others, feared confusion arising in the minds of the news media between 1985U1 and 1986U1. None of the new moons would get standard names until well after the encounter. But that had not stopped people from informally naming them. "I understand that 1985U1 is being referred to as Puck by some people on the third floor," noted Laeser. "And Frodo is also pretty popular, too."

Later that day, spacecraft team chief Howard Marderness discussed the status of Voyager 2. "Things are looking better than they had in the last couple of days," he said. One problem was with Lonne Lane's photopolarimeter. The PPS had suffered a recurrence of its "floating filter wheel," probably again caused by a buildup of an organic film on the surfaces of its electrical contacts. To solve the problem, said Marderness, they performed the "wheel-wipe" sequence developed

163

years earlier. It worked quite well, and now they were thinking about doing it one more time before the flyby. "But we'll have to decide pretty quickly," he added, "or we won't have any more time to include the commands in the computer load."

Marderness also noted that the most critical test for the spacecraft was still to come—the torque margin test, or TMT, set for early Monday morning. This would be the final health check on the scan platform. "The previous TMT on December 27 went well," Marderness said. "I expect it would go well on Monday. No one's worried very much about the scan platform in some time." The repair job by Marderness's spacecraft team had been so good it was working perfectly. Everyone was sure it would work right through Uranus encounter without a hitch.

And everyone would unconsciously hold his breath until the final TMT was finished and the results beamed back 2.6 billion kilometers to Earth.

The other major milestone for the spacecraft, besides the TMT, would be TCM B-14, still set for Saturday morning. The spacecraft team would begin working late Friday evening on implementing it, even though there was now a possibility the burn would not be needed. Whether or not the burn took place, Marderness was feeling extremely confident about Voyager 2. "If it keeps going the way it has been so far, the spacecraft will sail right through encounter."

The radio science experiment (RSS), however, still faced two serious problems. First, the two hydrogen masers (the radio equivalent of a laser) at one of the DSN Australia antennas had broken down. The masers were used to provide accurate frequency and timing information for the radio science experiments. If they were not fixed the RSS data would be seriously degraded. The second problem was crosstalk, similar to hearing another, extraneous conversation in the background on a telephone. In this case, data transmissions from antennas 42 and 43 at the Australian Deep Space Network station were overlapping and causing serious interference. The DSN might have to point antenna 42 straight up into the sky, and off its linkage with Voyager, in order to eliminate the crosstalk with antenna 43. That, too, would mean serious degradation of the data from the radio science experiment, since it would take one of the three Australian antennas out of commission during that part of the encounter.

Up to this point in the flyby, though, everything else about radio science had been going very well. The scientists had been able to perform their tests of Einstein's theory of relativity while Voyager 2 passed behind the sun as seen from Earth (the theory of relativity still stood), and had also studied the gigantic envelope of plasma surrounding the sun. Given all the problems the project had had with the Mark IV-A upgrade of the Deep Space Network, the radio science experiment was in surprisingly good shape at this point. Six months earlier, Len Tyler and his colleagues had been wondering if they could even point the DSN antennas in the right direction.

Thursday morning's SCORE meeting had three special guests: a team of TV people from public television's "MacNeil/Lehrer Newshour." They taped about fifteen minutes for inclusion in the show's special report for Encounter Day, and then quietly left. An unusually large number of people crowded into the room for the meeting, many of them just happening to sit in range of the camera. "MacNeil/Lehrer's" presence signaled the real beginning of the media season for the Uranus encounter. In the next ten days the one camera crew would multiply into two dozen.

The meeting produced four significant announce-

165

ments. One was a report from Peter Doms that vending machines for food and drink had been placed on the second floor; a raucous cheer greeted his announcement. The others were more scientific in nature. Imaging team leader Bradford Smith, newly arrived from the University of Arizona, announced that the six Uranian satellites discovered since the beginning of the year had now been reported to Brian Marsden. Their discovery was now official. Three of the moons had first been detected only three days earlier. "That makes seven new moons for Uranus, and a total of twelve in all," he said. "They [the new moons] all have diameters of thirty to fifty kilometers, and they all lie between the outer, epsilon, ring and Miranda. We expect to see many more."

Smith also had information on what seemed to be a feature in Uranus's atmosphere. It seemed to be at about 70 degrees south latitude, and they were tracking its movement. "It appears to indicate a rotation period for the planet of about thirteen point nine hours. However, this is just a very rough estimate, and it should not go beyond this room," he warned. It was a good thing Smith hedged on the rotation estimate; it later turned out to be off by several hours.

The final significant piece of new information was negative in nature, and came from Jim Warwick. "We have looked at data from PRA for the 13th, and still see nothing from the planet," he said. "Data from day fourteen were analyzed yesterday at Goddard Space Flight Center because we had a computer problem here, and our first reports are that there is nothing in that set, either. We will start looking through yesterday's data later today, but at this point we are still drawing blanks."

After the SCORE meeting, the members of the imaging team gathered for a confab of their own. About eighteen people were in attendance, and the number would grow in the days to come as more team members arrived at JPL. Brad Smith chaired the meeting while Larry Soderblom, the deputy team leader, actually led the group through the points for discussion. Almost everyone at one point or another had something to say, but most of the comments and observations came from Soderblom, Torrence Johnson, Robert Hamilton Brown, and Hal Masursky, who could always be counted on for a quick one-liner.

Soderblom began by urging caution regarding the "marking" in the atmosphere. "Let's not get excited," he said. "This feature is actually fainter than all the blips on the screen."

Smith, too, was more downbeat than he had been at the SCORE meeting. "It may be spurious," he said, "an artifact of processing." Spurious or not, the feature already had an unofficial name: "the phone handle."

Tobias Owen remarked that the pole of the planet seemed slightly brighter in red light than in blue; that might indicate a reddish-brown haze over the polar region. "It's the Los Angeles of Uranus," Masursky quipped. In fact, acetylene gas had long been known to exist in the atmosphere. The chemical breakdown and reaction of acetylene (a molecule with two carbon and two hydrogen atoms) with other compounds would lead to the creation of organic compounds called polymers— which have a reddish-brown color. Garry Hunt, a British member of the imaging team, suggested that the haze might be a layer in Uranus's stratosphere.

The team then turned to Uranus's first five moons, the ones discovered before Voyager 2. "The satellites are pretty much as we expected," said moon expert Bob Brown. "Umbriel is larger and darker than Earth-based observations suggested. Ariel is a little smaller and brighter."

Torrence Johnson, another member of the imaging team's satellite working group, then showed the "family portrait" photo of the moons, pointing out in particular

167

a bright spot on Ariel. A hush descended on the room as the family portrait passed from hand to hand and Brown and Johnson made their comments. The composite image was a historic one. For two hundred years the five major moons of Uranus had been nothing but faint points of light in a telescope image. Now, for the first time, they appeared as true celestial bodies—tiny *spheres* of light and dark with surfaces and hints of real markings on four of the five. It was the Jupiter and Saturn encounters all over again. Uranus's dark polar region and the moonlet known as 1985U1 had been the first *new* discoveries at Uranus by Voyager 2; but the revelation of the five classical moons as true solid bodies was a watershed in the mission. Like the man depicted in the famous medieval woodcut, Voyager 2 had passed through the ancient "crystal sphere" that held the planets and stars and into a new realm of reality.

The team then went on to discuss the rings. Carolyn Porco noted that all the rings were showing up in the images now—including the innermost and extremely faint 6, 5, and 4 rings in the best images. "However, you can look at the data if you want to," she added, "but I see nothing to indicate any new rings."

Bob Brown interrupted to stress the extremely tenuous nature of any new ring discoveries. Johnson agreed, and urged caution in talking about new rings. "But I do think we'll find a lot of junk in the system."

"And by the way," Porco added, "I've looked and looked and I can't find *any* resonances between the new satellites and the rings."

Brad Smith then brought up a rather volatile point: "The team is leaking again," he announced. "A writer for *Aviation Week and Space Technology* called Rich Terrile about noon yesterday to ask about the quote seven new satellites. It wasn't until midafternoon that Synnott was firm about the orbital elements of the six new ones!

"Now, that leak was traced to PIO, and it was because of *Av Week*'s deadline. But we have to work harder to *keep some information within the team!* And that includes PIO, 'cause they'll grab and go with anything they can get their hands on."

"You need to go out and get a plumber, Brad," said Hal Masursky. Others chimed in with comments and suggestions, and the discussion went on for several more minutes. Torrence Johnson wrapped it up with an analysis of the root of the problem:

"The thing is, the spacecraft is much farther from Earth now than it was at Jupiter and Saturn. So it will take more time and more analysis of the data before we can confirm discoveries. And we are all just going to have to live with that."

For the Public Information Office, the pace had gone beyond frantic—and there were still eight days to the actual flyby. Frank Bristow, manager of public information for the office, remarked that this encounter—in fact, all of 1986—was shaping up as the busiest he had ever seen. "We will have ninety-five desks and seats in the press area at Von Karman, and they are all completely assigned," he said. "We have twenty-four TV crews accredited, and they run from two to ten people in size. Then there are another twenty-four people accredited just for the press briefings. We've set up seven big trailers for television crews and the major radio and TV networks; they are already seventy percent full.

"In fact, for the first time at any of these encounters I've had to turn people down for accreditation," said Bristow. His criterion had been pretty straightforward: people specifically assigned for the flyby got preference for accreditation. "I hate it, it really pains me to do that. A lot of these people were here before, for the Jupiter and Saturn encounters. But there just isn't any room for them now. They understand, of course, but still, it's painful."

The workload was increasing for everyone, of course, and that included Bristow. He and the others would be working through the weekend of the 18th and on through near encounter and post-encounter. Every eventuality would be covered, every need of the press met as best as possible. "To give you one small example, we will make four hundred copies of each photograph from Voyager 2," said Bristow. "And there has to be a caption taped to the back of each copy of each picture, so Jurrie Van der Woude is marshaling a small army of people to carry out that job."

Bristow was proud of the work done by his office so far, and he made a point of singling out the secretaries. "They are *gold*," he exclaimed. "We simply could not function without their efforts." He also noted the arrival of some valuable temporary help for Wood, Murrill, Fuhrmann, O'Donnell, and the others. "Several people who used to work here, but have retired or gone to other jobs, have actually come back to work here just for this encounter." They included Deborah McCourtney, a Southern California grade school teacher who had gotten a leave of absence from her school district to come back and help out at JPL. Not only would she be present during a historic moment, but her students would have a teacher who could talk with real authority about the space program.

The problem at earlier encounters with VIPs and others who mingled about in the press area had been neatly solved by NASA's arrangements for science fiction writers, politicians, former JPL officials, and other "guests." They'd stay in six conference rooms in different parts of the lab. Bristow was more than satisfied with the arrangement. The SF writers and other space groupies would get to see the latest and newest images from the encounter, and would not be underfoot in Von Karman.

. . .

"Well, there was no rain in Spain or in Australia," Dan Finnerty reported on Friday morning, the 17th, "but last night we had about a 30-minute outage at Station 63 in Spain, and again this morning while we were uplinking the B723 computer load to the spacecraft. However, the load did get into the computer!" B723 was the second far encounter program for Voyager 2's CCS computer. It was now in the spacecraft and would begin running at 11:23 p.m. Pacific Time.

Murmurs of relief passed through the crowded room. Yesterday's turnout for the "MacNeil/Lehrer" filming had not been a one-time thing. The SCORE meetings would continue to be packed to the walls through the rest of the encounter. Scientists other than the PIs and the experiment reps were coming to the SCORE meetings. Carl Sagan, Hal Masursky, Robert Brown, Torrence Johnson, and other imaging scientists often sat in the audience, and sometimes on the floor when all the chairs were occupied. People from areas other than the Flight Science Office also sat in now, anxious to hear the latest from the scientists. This was what the project was all about; this was what their work had been supporting.

Some of the scientists in the audience contributed to the reports of the PIs and ERs. That morning, for example, Johnson remarked during the imaging team's report that "the Uranian satellites are now showing up as distinct bodies. Large areas of some of them now are seen to have blotches on them. My own feeling," he added, "is that they are more varied in their appearance at this resolution than were the Saturnian satellites at this same resolution." The moons of Uranus might turn out to be even more bizarre-looking than some of the moons of Saturn. But what could be more weird than hockey-puck-shaped Hyperion, or Mimas the "Death Star"? The next eight days would provide the astonishing answer.

The news from radio science was not so mysterious,

171

and less than happy. The masers at the Australian station were still down, but the problem would be resolved by Sunday. The other problem, with crosstalk between antennas 42 and 43, was also proving resistant to solution. It might indeed become necessary to uncouple the data from the two dishes in order to solve it.

Fred Scarf reported that the plasma-wave instrument (PWS) might have found evidence for a huge cometlike hydrogen cloud around Uranus. "This *could* cause the one-kilohertz emissions we have seen," he added.

But Jim Warwick's PRA, the planetary radio astronomy instrument, was still seeing nothing. "We have looked at data from the 15th and the 16th," he said, "and still see no signals coming from Uranus. However, we do know that the sun is active. The instrument detected two Type Three solar bursts. So at least we know the instrument is working."

One of the DSN antennas at Goldstone was having problems with a false alarm from an oil bearing. The bearing was a thin film of oil in the turning mechanism for the antenna. It was under high pressure and kept two huge rings of metal from grinding against each other as the antenna turned. If the oil-film height dropped too low, the two pieces would get dangerously close to touching. DSN had had two false alarms from one of two sensors, causing the antenna to stop turning. The antenna had lost its "lock" on the signals from Voyager 2, and that caused a loss of fifteen to twenty minutes of data each time.

The faulty sensor had been disabled, but the project could not continue to worry about false alarms causing loss of data. In the mission director's meeting on Friday the 17th, Marv Traxler of JPL tracking and data acquisition and his associates proposed a drastic "fix" to the problem. Dick Laeser called it the "damn the torpedos" solution. "We want to 'battleshort' antenna 14," said Traxler. The term came from a navy expression that referred to putting pennies in a fuse box during a battle. "We will simply ignore any alarms about a loss of oil height in those bearings. We will assume that all such alarms are false and go for broke. If it really *does* seize up, well, so it goes." The antenna, of course, would grind to a halt and be totally disabled for the rest of the encounter. The proposal was discussed for about fifteen minutes, with the proposal for antenna 14 finally being voted down. Goldstone's antennas were not vital enough to the encounter to justify millions of dollars' worth of damage. However, the group *did* tentatively decide to battleshort the Australian DSN antennas from the 24th through the 26th, the three most important days for data return at closest encounter.

A couple of days later the Voyager management talked it over again, and changed their minds about battleshorting the Australian antennas. Said Laeser afterward: "We decided it was just too potentially damaging to the other projects that would be using DSN's antennas later in the year. If we battleshorted an antenna, and the oil bearing *did* go out, then we'd have totally disabled that antenna for the Halley probes, for the Galileo launch later in the year, for Ulysses. . . . We decided it wasn't worth taking the chance." Better to risk losing a short period of Voyager data, in other words, than to risk sacrificing other projects in the pipeline.

On Friday afternoon, Voyager management held another meeting on TCM B-14. The navigational data were incredible. It seemed the spacecraft trajectory was drifting right toward the very aimpoint the scientists had wanted all along. McLaughlin, Laeser, and Don Gray shook their heads in amazement at the latest navigation reports. The spacecraft would be within 200 kilometers of its ideal aimpoint. The encounter had been remarkably trouble-free so far, and now it looked as if they were going to get an incredibly great break. A cancellation of the burn would have two positive side effects. One was immediate: it meant there would be no command moratorium on January 19 and 20. That in turn meant the navigators would get two more days of accurate ranging data. This would make it possible to get more information about the spacecraft's position for the late stored update, and to get it sooner than expected.

Navigation head Don Gray said, "I would recommend that we cancel TCM B-14." Everyone looked at George Textor, the mission director.

Textor, a burly man with a pleasant face who spoke in a deceptively soft tone, looked at the people gathered around the table. "Right," he said. "We cancel the burn."

On Saturday evening, January 18, the first—and, as it turned out, only—major problem of the encounter cropped up. Funny black and white lines began appearing on the images coming back from Voyager 2. Dan Finnerty, the SIS team's resident computer expert, later summed up the problem. "At first we thought it was related to the playback coming back from Voyager's tape recorder. Maybe there was something wrong there. Then people started looking through all the real-time data from MIPL, the Multimission Image Processing Lab. Those folks had just put a software patch into MIPL's computers to stop some flickering on the TV monitors that showed the images. So we thought it was due to the patch." There had also been a brief MIPL computer failure, Finnerty added, and some people thought the dropped lines in the images were due to that. But when a second, identical computer *also* started producing images with the dropped lines, "that took care of that guess."

174

Suspicion now shifted, albeit reluctantly, to Voyager 2 itself, and specifically to the backup flight data subsystem (FDS) computer. That was the one converted to do image data compression. On Saturday evening the spacecraft team sent up an FDS readout test, essentially ordering the computer to tell them just what the memory inside it really contained. The results came down early Sunday morning. When they looked at the readout, said Finnerty, the problem "stood out like a sore thumb. It was a stuck or flipped bit in the computer." In other words, one memory location in the backup FDS had spontaneously set itself at 0 rather than 1—or vice versa; no one was quite sure yet. In either case it was causing extraneous lines to appear on the images. Fortunately, said Finnerty, there were ways to detour around the stuck bit in the FDS, and FDS experts were working on those schemes at that very minute.

Finnerty, though, was amazed at how relatively *little* damage had resulted from the FDS glitch. "We'd always thought that if we had an FDS data-compression failure it would be catastrophic," said Finnerty. "We'd lose completely our ability to do image data compression on the images." That in turn would have meant a drastic reduction in the number of pictures Voyagers would have been able to send back to Earth—from 300 per day down to fifty or a hundred a day. "But it turns out to be a relatively simple problem with a simple fix," he continued. "Furthermore, the data we have gotten back, the pictures with the lines in them, can probably be reconstructed. MIPL engineers can fix them up. It'll take a lot of work, but they can probably do it." The fix on the FDS itself, Finnerty added, would be finished and beamed up to the spacecraft by about 6:30 Monday evening.

Said Finnerty, smiling broadly: "What can I tell ya? The goddam spacecraft has outsmarted us."

Chapter 8
FLYBY

One of the last major hurdles before encounter was the final torque margin test (or TMT) of Voyager 2's scan platform. The project personnel were, they said, unworried. Four years of work had assured everyone that the scan platform had completely recovered from the 1981 near-disaster at Saturn. The final TMT would be the "amen" to all the work, the confirmation of all the protestations of confidence. Were the gears functioning? Yes. Had the lubrication started migrating away from them again? Certainly not! Would the scan platform work, and point its cluster of instruments in the correct direction? You bet it would. Early Monday morning, everyone found out. The scan platform passed the TMT with flying colors. The people on the spacecraft team let loose with a collective sigh of relief.

The successful TMT was one bright note in the SCORE meeting on January 20. Not so bright was the news from Rudy Hanel that the IRIS neon signal oscillation had shown up again on Sunday. Fortunately, it didn't seem to affect the quality of the data. Lyle Broadfoot, the principal investigator for the ultraviolet spectrometer (UVS), had more interesting news to announce. "We are indeed seeing ultraviolet emissions from the planet," he said. The emissions were a type called Lyman alpha, produced by hydrogen surrounding the planet. In addition, Broadfoot said, they were seeing another kind of hydrogen emission called H2 emission. "However, we have not seen the type of aurora emissions we'd thought might occur."

"Anything from the plasma-wave instrument?" Peter Doms asked.

Fred Scarf stood up. "Let me show you something," he said, with a smile just short of a triumphant smirk. He turned on the overhead projector and placed a transparency on it. A series of squiggles traced out signals from the different channels in the plasma-wave detector (PWS). "I am happy to report radio emissions from Uranus," he announced. Applause and sighs of relief rippled through the room, and Scarf explained the squiggles and why he felt they supported his announcement. "This means that Uranus does have a magnetic field, and it is a very weak one, maybe only one-sixth the strength of Earth's."

Jim Warwick followed Scarf, and he immediately cooled the audience's ardor. "We are seeing signals at thirty-nine kilohertz and perhaps at about fifty-eight kilohertz," he said, "and they're about twenty-five decibels above the noise in the signal. The individual events last about six seconds each. However," he said, "as best we can tell these signals are local in nature. They *don't* come from Uranus but from the spacecraft itself." A hush descended in the room. "I'm sorry," Warwick said. "I'd like to see a signal as much as anyone else. But *we* cannot in good faith say that *we* see one yet."

Later that day, Bill McLaughlin put the previous

week's one-bit failure in Voyager 2's backup flight data subsystem (FDS) computer in historical perspective. It was the first hardware failure on Voyager 2 since the scan-platform problem in 1981—but not the first *computer* failure. In fact, the flight data subsystem computers were turning out to be the weak link on both Voyager spacecraft. Four FDS memory failures had taken place on both spacecraft since their launches in 1977. Voyager 1 had suffered a one-bit failure in one FDS right after launch, and had lost its entire backup FDS before the Saturn encounter. Voyager 2's backup FDS, in turn, had lost 256 bits before its Saturn flyby in 1981, and now had suffered a one-bit loss. Said McLaughlin, "We'll have to plan very carefully our use of Voyager 2's FDS computers for Neptune in 1989."

It still appeared it would be very difficult to salvage the three days of pictures damaged by the FDS's flipped bit. They might never be completely salvaged. The good news was that the FDS glitch had been fixed, as Finnerty predicted, by Monday evening. FDS programmer Dick Rice, from Mike Urban's Advanced Software Development Group, was the principal architect of the solution. The key was a software patch that essentially "detoured" the image data compression program around the flipped bit. Efforts to flip the bit from 0 back to 1 failed, but that was a minor defeat. The victory overshadowed it. A potentially disastrous problem had cropped up at the last minute—and the Voyager team had come through once again.

The first near encounter computer load, B751, was sent to Voyager 2 the morning of Tuesday the 21st. Voyager 2 was now just three days from encounter, 3.75 million kilometers (2.5 million miles) from Uranus and closing in on the turquoise planet at a rate of over 50,000 kilometers per hour. The images of the planet and its rings were growing almost visibly larger by the hour. At that morning's SCORE meeting Lonne Lane reported that "the readout of the FDS memory to find the image-compression problem essentially destroyed our data from a scan across the rings. This is really frustrating," he said, "especially when you consider all the work people put in to get us this scan. And now to have it all lost. . . ." Lane looked as exasperated as he felt.

The images received since the FDS had been fixed were excellent. "We are seeing a wealth of new features in all areas," exclaimed Larry Soderblom. "And we are seeing some rather tantalizing things in the rings," he added, but refused to elaborate further. He wanted to wait until the press conference on Wednesday before formally saying anything. He allowed, though, that there was "a complex structure" to the rings that he and others had not expected. "And we'll have more to say later about the moons, too."

The assembled principal investigators and some of their associates were now having daily afternoon meetings. It was a chance for them all to report on the latest results from their experiments to the others, and share conclusions, guesses, and outright speculations. For example, said Ed Stone, during the Tuesday science discussion some significant findings from imaging, PWS, and PRA were shared.

Richard Terrile reported that the imaging team had discovered two shepherding satellites for the epsilon ring. That brought the total number of Uranian satellites to fourteen, and increased confidence that still more of the shepherding satellites would be found. "There could be ten to eighteen of these types of moons," said Stone, "depending on whether or not some shepherds are shared by adjoining rings." The satellite discoveries would be announced in the first press conference the next morning.

The PRA and PWS instruments were also seeing

179

something: radio bursts. Fred Scarf was sure that his PWS readings were of radio bursts coming from the planet. Jim Warwick now agreed that there were bursts from the planet, but he would still not commit to saying they were from a possible magnetic field. "However, it is really hard to make a model for these bursts without a magnetic field around Uranus," said Stone.

"Jim Warwick did have a comment that I found interesting." Stone added. "He pointed out that the one really big radio burst his instrument detected was so large that if it had happened earlier, his instrument could have seen it as early as November. That tells me that these large bursts are quite rare, maybe happening only once every few months or so."

At 9:27 p.m. Tuesday evening, the B751 computer load began running Voyager 2. Near encounter had formally begun.

At the Wednesday-morning SCORE meeting, Brad Smith passed around the pictures to be released at the opening press conference later in the morning: the two ring shepherds, three of the seven satellites discovered earlier in the month, the family portrait of the classical moons, and a four-image picture of the atmospheric cloud features. "Now, is this one Umbriel, or is it Ariel?" asked Ed Stone, momentarily confused as he looked at the family portrait.

"What's the matter, can't you tell the difference?" Torrence Johnson joked.

It also now appeared the pictures damaged by the FDS glitch could indeed be fixed. In fact, a "quick fix" had been developed that would make it possible to actually do some scientific interpretation of the FDS-damaged images. In addition, said Soderblom, "We are beginning to see surface contrast on Miranda. Which is nice, since it's our primary satellite target. Ariel is also showing contrast at the terminator [the sunrise-sunset line], and that suggests there are elevated features of some kind on it." Umbriel, on the other hand, Soderblom described as "dark and bland." Not everyone was unhappy about that, though. "That could mean Umbriel will be pretty interesting when we get closer," said Torrence Johnson. "Maybe it's dark and bland because there are very few craters on it."

The IRIS was performing well, and Rudy Hanel's people had gotten their first temperature profile of the planet. The atmosphere measured a cool 50 degrees above absolute zero at the highest levels, said Hanel, and the temperature curve increased with depth.

"Has the oscillation come back?" Stone asked.

"No," Hanel replied. "It seems to have a period of about seventy hours okay, and thirty hours of flicker."

"So when might we expect it to act up again?"

"Right before closest approach," Rudy replied dryly.

The PPS was performing superbly, said Lonne Lane. The radio science team, said Len Tyler, was "practicing patience." There was nothing more they could do until Friday.

In the Von Karman news media area, the space science press corps had finally arrived en masse. In fact, a large media contingent had been at their assigned desks and using their phones and typewriters by Monday afternoon. For many the Uranus encounter was like a class reunion. The old hands of science reporting clustered together to trade greetings and war stories. Who had and who had not applied for NASA's Journalist in Space flight on the shuttle was a big topic of gossip. Several TV crews wandered into the area and shot film— a case of the media covering the media. It was much like the Jupiter encounters of 1979 and the Saturn flybys of 1980 and 1981, but with one interesting high-tech difference: fully half of the writers were sitting behind the keyboards of lap computers. Four years earlier, Jerry

Pournelle's brand-new Osborne transportable computer had been the center of great attention. In 1986 there was one old-version Osborne in sight. And there were many Radio Shack 100s and 200s, NEC PC-8201As, and Epson portables. Mike Mecham of Gannett News Service was writing stories on a "100" and dumping them over the phone lines to Washington, D.C. *Astronomy* magazine editor Richard Berry worked with an NEC and off-loaded the results via Sprint to his offices in Milwaukee. The reporters for AP and UPI wire services were also using tiny computers. High technology had come to the space press.

At the first press conference of the Uranus encounter, Ed Stone gave a historical overview of humanity's exploration of Uranus with ground-based instruments. Dick Laeser followed with a look at the engineering aspects of the flyby, beginning with a summary of the scan-platform problem at Saturn and how it was fixed. Then he explained the late ephemeris and late stored updates.

Brad Smith then began the picture show. Of the heavily computer-enhanced Uranus images showing the polar haze he said: "I don't know why I get the feeling that Uranus is looking back at us." And of the satellite family portrait he commented: "I expect over the next several days Larry Soderblom will be up here explaining what all those fuzzy things mean."

The two best questions came from Roy Neal of NBC and John Noble Wilford of the *New York Times*. Neal asked what was on everyone's mind, but unspoken until that moment: "Dr. Stone, could you tell us exactly what is the correct pronunciation of the planet's name?" Visions of Uranus pun jokes danced through everyone's head. Stone calmly replied that the official pronunciation, approved by the International Astronomical Union, was "YOU-ruh-nus." Wilford also asked Smith if the differences in darkness between the older-known moons and the rings and new moons implied two separate periods of creation for the Uranian system. Replied Smith, "We haven't the foggiest idea. Why, we didn't even know yet what *makes* 'em dark."

That afternoon, sitting in the cafeteria patio, Randii Wessen talked about the beginning of the late stored update activities. The sky was cloudy and the temperature had dropped considerably from the week before. A breeze blew tiny pink petals off a nearby tree.

The Voyager navigators, Wessen explained, first determined as precisely as possible the positions of the planet, its moons, and the spacecraft itself. That was the late ephemeris update, or LEU. Those data were essential for making the final little adjustments to the B752, the final aiming "tweaks" for the cameras and other instruments. It had not, said Wessen, gone as smoothly as hoped. "We ran about an hour-and-a-half late," he said. "The problem was with a ground-computer file called the maneuvering file, which supplies information for the image motion compensation slews for the Miranda pictures."

The LSU would not have the slop in its schedule that the LEU had. "No padding," said Wessen. "It's got to work the first time, with no significant delays. This is for all the gonzo beans."

At 2:30 p.m. the final meeting on the B752 load took place. Bobby Brooks oversaw the meeting. About a dozen key players on the project met to go over the sequence page by page, section by section. They included Flight Engineering Office chief McLaughlin; Flight Operations Office chief Griffith; Flight Science Office head de Vries; Finnerty, Doms, and Wessen from Science Investigation Support (SIS); spacecraft team chief Marderness; sequence team chief Ray Morris (Brooks's boss); Mission Director George Textor; and several others.

The atmosphere was relaxed and jovial. Few problems cropped up; the most serious was with the sequence of highest-resolution pictures of Ariel. It was too late to fix it in the B752 load to be sent to Voyager, but it could be corrected in the late stored update. The meeting went smoothly; thirty-five minutes after it began, Brooks said, "Aha! The *last page!* Here we go. Miranda opnav converted to NEWSAT"—a reference to the conversion of an optical-navigation image of Miranda into a picture of the first new moon found by Voyager, 1985U1. "Any problems?" There were none. "All right," Brooks said exultantly. His baby, *his* B752 sequence, was clean. "That's it, then. Shall we fly it?"

At 5:57 a.m. Pacific Time Thursday morning, the B752 computer load began its 164-minute journey to the spacecraft.

Brad Smith reported to the January 23 SCORE meeting that MIPL's computers were not doing a good job of processing the images coming down from Voyager. Part of it was a software problem, and part of it was inexperienced computer users. Despite the setbacks, Smith planned on showing new images of the moons Ariel and Oberon at that morning's press conference. "Larry doesn't want to talk about moons yet, though," he added.

"Miranda is beginning to show some surface details," Smith continued, and passed a photo around the room. "This is not for release," he warned. The image was somewhat fuzzy—Voyager was not yet close enough to resolve tiny details of its surface—but there were markings on it. The one truly visible detail looked a bit like a white V on a dark background.

Lyle Broadfoot noted his puzzlement with data from the ultraviolet spectrometer: a strong signal from the edge of Uranus. "It implies that there is a large hydrogen cloud standing off the surface," he said.

Rudy Hanel's IRIS was acting up again; the neon signal was oscillating. Lonne Lane's PPS was also experiencing some minor problems with the filter wheel, but Lane was now confident of good results. The first of the two stellar occultations by the rings began late that evening. It was an occultation of the star Sigma Sagittarius, also known as Nunke, but usually abbreviated by the science people to Sigma Sag, pronounced "Saj."

Scarf's plasma-wave instrument continued to see strong signals. Furthermore, they were polarized, which meant that they were coming from a place with a magnetic field. The strong implication was: Uranus.

"Planetary radio astronomy?" asked Flight Science Office chief Pieter de Vries, who was chairing the SCORE meeting that morning. Jim Warwick smiled.

"I think we may have something," he said. "Michael Kaiser of our group has been looking carefully at the data on this, so I will turn this presentation over to him."

According to Kaiser, the planetary radio astronomy instrument was now picking up radio bursts with a period of sixteen to seventeen hours. Kaiser urged caution at drawing conclusions—but it was true that the periodic signal strongly implied a magnetic field, a field that was rotating with the planet. It also suggested that Uranus, like Earth, Jupiter, and Saturn, would have a bow shock —an area in space where the solar wind from the sun slammed into the planet's magnetic field. When a spacecraft crossed the bow shock it could well and truly be said to have passed into the influence of the planet. "Is there gonna be a bow-shock party?" someone asked. No one answered; of course there'd be a bow-shock party.

Later in the day Warwick amplified a bit on the discovery of the PRA signals. "It turns out that we were actually receiving the planet's 'signature' all along," he said, "but we couldn't see the forest for the trees" of other signals. Warwick was not overly upset by the oversight, though. In fact, he was quite animated about the discovery. "The last couple days have really been *fantastic*," he said. His eyes gleamed with the wonder of it all, and the floppy blue fishing hat sat jauntily on his head. For Warwick, science was more than a job: it was pure and simple fun.

The Thursday press conference featured the report on the radio emissions and Uranus's possible magnetic field, and the latest pictures of Uranus and the moons. The images included a picture of Uranus showing four faint clouds, and color shots of Miranda and Ariel. A black-and-white image of Ariel showed several bright spots. Smith referred to them as "bright white things." "Don't worry," he added. "Larry Soderblom will be up here in a day or two and will explain them to you." Everyone laughed. During the questions that followed, *Sky & Telescope's* J. Kelly Beatty asked Smith about material in the rings. Smith replied that "at the limits of resolution we think we see some matter in the space between the rings, yes." Smith also confirmed that water ice had indeed been detected on the surfaces of some of the large moons.

The first navigation meeting for the LSU had taken place at 5:00 a.m., and the numbers had been very good. The canceled TCM B-14 had paid off with two extra days of optical navigation photos and other ranging data from the spacecraft. Voyager 2 seemed to be very close to the trajectory the navigators had originally estimated. Miranda was close to where they had earlier expected it to be, and the figures for its mass and diameter hadn't changed appreciably.

A second meeting, held Thursday afternoon, was even better. "Sorry we don't have anything dramatic for you," said Bill McLaughlin dryly to Laeser and Mission director George Textor. It was a bit of an understatement. After a journey of nearly eight and a half years and more than 4 billion kilometers, Voyager 2 would arrive at Uranus half a second early and about 4 kilometers off-target. It was an extraordinary achievement. The frosting on the cake was pronounced by navigation team chief Don Gray: "We are exceeding the requirements for the best possible images of Miranda—by a factor of two!"

Late Thursday evening, Flight Operations Office chief Doug Griffith was still at his desk. For FOO, these were the most critical hours of the encounter. The vital B752 computer program would be sent to Voyager; then the late stored update would be fitted into it as the program was running in Voyager's command and control subsystem (CCS) computer. Griffith seemed surprisingly relaxed. Lonne Lane was pleading for a last-minute change to commands for his photopolarimeter (PPS). He hoped to avoid potential data loss from possible rain at the Spanish DSN station. But even this tempest didn't bother Griffith. "Hey," he said to Dan Finnerty at one point, "I don't care what you folks do. It's just one lousy real-time command. Maybe your guess about weather in Spain will be right, maybe it'll be wrong. You pays your money"—his Southern accent getting as thick as the scent of magnolias on a summer night—"and you takes your choice!"

A little later the hallway outside his office quieted down. "Actually, things are going fine," said Griffith. "They're going very well indeed." And the Deep Space Network's Mark IV-A system, the bane of Griffith's existence for the last year? "It's gonna work," he proclaimed. "It will take a lot of handholding, but it's gonna work. The only thing that could get us now is something we can't prepare for."

By now the spacecraft had told the people back home that B752 had successfully taken up residence in its CCS computer. At 10:27 that evening it began running the spacecraft. Uranus flyby was twelve hours away. Project Voyager, like its spacecraft, was racing toward its goal. The years had turned into months, the months into weeks, the weeks into days, and now the days into hours. Bob Brooks and the other sequence engineers had worked on the LSU since 8:00 a.m. Thursday. Everyone knew what to do, how to do it, and when to do it. The LSU commands ran through JPL's mainframe computer simulators like Brooks's goose excrement. At 1:00 a.m. on Friday morning the commands were beamed up to the spacecraft. Two brief outages at the Spanish DSN antennas did not interfere. Voyager 2 heard and obeyed, and the LSU modified the still-running B752 load about six hours before close encounter. The late stored update that was for "all the gonzo beans" came off without a hitch.

At 7:10 a.m. Pacific Time on January 24, Voyager 2 passed within 365,200 kilometers of the Uranian moon Titania. About twenty minutes later (Earth time), in an office on the seventh floor of Building 264, the PPS experimenters were gathered around a group of whining printers and silent computer displays. Lonne Lane was eating a breakfast from the nearby Chez McDonald's and watching numbers on the computer screen. "Umm, look at dat," he said, pointing with a plastic fork. The data from the Sigma Sagittarius ring occultation were pouring in, and Lane was clearly elated. "Yeah, 'Saj' worked just great, no problems at all," he said. Linda Horn, who was taking a break from her IRIS duties to work with the PPS group, called Lane over to a printer. A tracing of a small part of the epsilon ring had just come off it. "Wow," someone exclaimed, "look at that detail." "See that?" "Jesus!" "That's incredible!" (Not present in the office, but working with Lane and his associates, was James Elliot. Nearly nine years after his discovery of the rings, Elliot was on hand to help in the latest ring revelations.)

188

Lane ducked out briefly, then reappeared with a sleeping bag draped over one arm. Along with Horn and several others, he had camped out in the offices, waiting for the occultation data to begin coming back. "Okay," he said, "the SCORE meeting's in just a few minutes. I would like *this*"—pointing to a chart tracing from the printer—"and *this* and *this* turned into transparencies, so I can show it to those people. And I need to be left alone for a few minutes so I can get my thoughts together about them." People scrambled. A plastic plate of eggs sat next to a terminal, forgotten. . . .

Hal Masursky led off the Encounter Day SCORE meeting with gloomy news. "The stuff we are getting from MIPL is catastrophic." The computers at the Multimission Image Processing Laboratory were producing garbage instead of pictures, he said. Brad Smith and Larry Soderblom had been in the MIPL area for several hours already, presumably trying to figure out ways to salvage the images.

Lonne Lane's news was much better. His people had produced the transparencies for him, and he dazzled his audience with his report on the epsilon ring. "There's a complicated structure here," he said, pointing to the sharp spikes in the tracing. There was no evidence of rings outside the epsilon ring, at least to a resolution of 25 meters. However, he did have an indication of a ring inside the delta ring.

More surprising was the report from Tom Krimigis, principal investigator for the low-energy charged particle experiment. The LECP instrument, he said, showed that Uranus was surrounded by a powerful and deadly radiation belt, much like that around Saturn. Excited murmurs filled the meeting room. That meant not only that Uranus did indeed have a magnetic field, but that—contradicting Scarf's earlier guess—the field was quite powerful.

The most startling announcement, though, came

189

from Dick Laeser. "The Giotto spacecraft has had an emergency," he told the SCORE meeting, and the Voyager team had been asked for help. Earlier that morning, he explained, the European Space Agency antenna in West Germany that was tracking the Halley-bound space probe had suddenly lost almost all contact with it. They could barely hear the signal from the spacecraft, and were asking NASA if the larger and more powerful DSN antennas in Spain and California could be pointed at Giotto. Perhaps then they could get enough data from the probe to determine what had gone wrong.

Laeser and the Giotto project manager (who happened to be in California that morning) had quickly gotten together on the phone. Fortunately, the Voyager Project could do without Spain and Goldstone for a while. Contact with Voyager would soon pass to the Australian stations, freeing up the other two DSN antennas for use with Giotto. Laeser had given the go-ahead.

As the SCORE meeting was in session, Voyager 2 had made its closest approach to the moon Oberon at 8:13 a.m., at a distance of 470,600 kilometers. It came within 127,000 kilometers of Ariel at 8:22 a.m. The spacecraft swiveled about, aimed its cameras at Miranda, and began shooting the close-approach mosaic of that tiny moon. Brooks's LSU-modified B752 load was running flawlessly. The probe flashed past Miranda at 9:04 a.m., missing its icy surface by a mere 29,000 kilometers. Voyager was now fifty-five and one-half minutes from Uranus closest approach.

One hour later, Ed Stone led off the press conference with the announcement: "Just a few minutes ago, at approximately nine fifty-nine a.m., Voyager 2 made its closest approach to the planet Uranus." The auditorium erupted in applause. The spacecraft had come within 81,500 kilometers of the planet's cloudtops. Voyager 2 was 2.9 billion kilometers away from Von Karman Auditorium, now rushing *away* from Uranus at 79,200 kilometers per hour. Stone then recited a short history of Herschel's discovery of the planet. He also read a letter from the mayor of Bath, England, congratulating JPL and NASA on the achievement. Laeser then told the press corps about the Giotto emergency and what JPL was doing.

Then the scientists on the dais reported in. Norm Ness announced bow-shock crossing and the information that "the magnetic field is substantial in magnitude and appreciable in extent and influence." The field was at least as strong as Saturn's. Almost certainly this meant that the planet had a conducting fluid deep below the atmosphere which was producing the field. Ness added that he was sure that Uranus had an intense radiation belt.

Brad Smith, having returned from his battle with MIPL, reported the discovery of structure in the rings. Two images flashed on the screen showed variations in brightness and thickness in both the epsilon and eta rings. The episilon ring's shepherd moons were as dark as lumps of coal, he continued, while the moon Titania was somewhat bland in color "with lots of rays and impact-looking structures. We are also seeing evidence of impact craters on Umbriel—and another feature as well. We don't know what it is.

"And then there is this curious feature on Miranda," he concluded, showing a fuzzy image of the moon. Nearly in the middle of the dark moon was the V that Smith had shown at the SCORE meeting the day before on an earlier picture. Smith referred to it as a "chevron." "Don't tell Standard Oil about this," someone whispered loudly.

Voyager 2 sped farther and farther away from the seventh planet. At 10:26 a.m. the ring occultation of

191

Algol had begun and Lane's PPS began measuring the star's flickering through the rings. At 11:44 the rings began blocking the radio signals from Voyager itself, as seen from Earth. At 12:36 p.m. the radio science experiment began in earnest as Voyager 2 started passing behind Uranus itself. As commanded by B752, the spacecraft had turned off all data broadcasts to Earth. Now it began beaming its two pure carrier waves through Uranus's atmosphere. Len Tyler's long-awaited and agonized-over radio science experiment had begun. One hour and fifty-nine minutes later, Voyager 2 reappeared on the other side of the planet as seen from Earth. The rings then partly occulted the radio signal one more time. The months of anger and frustration with the Deep Space Network melted away. The experiment had worked after all.

As morning turned to afternoon, and afternoon to night, the excitement and anticipation in the press room waned a bit. Most of the data were being stored on Voyager's tape recorder for broadcast to JPL the next day. The silly season set in. Someone devised a list of Voyager acronyms and some possible meanings. MIPL, for example, was not just Multimission Image Processing Laboratory but also Multiple Images Produced by Liquids (perhaps coffee or whiskey or both). UPHOCC, which scientists thought stood for a stellar occultation of the planet studied by the UVS instrument, might also stand for Unhappy Publisher Hacks Off Carl's Corduroys. JPL didn't just mean Jet Propulsion Laboratory. It could also stand for Juggling of Polar Labels, Jedi's Pajamas are Lost, or (perhaps most truthfully) Jerks Pestering Laeser.

In much the same vein was the anonymously produced "Puckish Dictionary," redefining some planetary-flyby terms:

DENSITY: The ratio of the quantity of equipment toted around by a journalist to his/her brain mass.

EXOSPHERE: The press-room smoke haze.

NAVIGATION: Maneuvering your way into the press room past the coffee klatch in the foyer.

MAGNETIC POLE: A very handsome East European.

PLASMA SCIENCE: Trying to find a method of direct injection of caffeine into the bloodstream.

STELLAR OCCULTATION: Standing between a TV journalist and his/her camera crew.

Dick Laeser began the January 25 press conference by reporting that "the spacecraft is performing flawlessly. At six thirty-two we began getting real-time telemetry again from Voyager. You'll all be pleased to know the data show that there was no scan-platform problem *this* time!" Laeser did announce a problem with antenna 43 in Australia, and the unfortunate loss of the playback of the image of moon 1985U1. "However," he added, "we are going to try and do a second playback of that image, either tomorrow afternoon or tomorrow night." The part of the tape with the 1985U1 image would not be written over by other data until early Monday morning, so it was still possible to play the singular image back to Earth. Finally, the Giotto problem was cleared up: the comet probe was fine—the controllers had mispointed their ground antenna.

Rudy Hanel announced that data from IRIS gave a temperature of Uranus's upper atmosphere of about 50 to 60 degrees Kelvin, or −370 degrees Fahrenheit. Other data clearly showed the helium content of the atmosphere was no more than 10 to 15 percent. "And it could well be less than that," Hanel added. The great debate over the 40 percent helium figure suggested by Glenn Orton was now over. Orton's indirect data were wrong. The standard model of solar system evolution was safe for another day.

Magnetometer PI Norm Ness reported the dramatic

193

discovery that the planet's magnetic pole was positioned 55 degrees from its rotational pole. It was the largest such tilt in the solar system, appropriate to a planet with the largest rotational axis tilt. Further, said Ness, the field's strength was at least as great as Earth's, and the magnetic pole facing the sun was a *north* magnetic pole.

Then Lyle Broadfoot dropped *his* bombshell. The UVS instrument had detected a new kind of emission from Uranus. It was not an aurora (no aurora was ever spotted near either the sunside or south rotational pole or the sunside north magnetic pole), and it wasn't airglow. "This is so different that we have given it a new name," said Broadfoot. "We are calling it electroglow. It is generated by the collision of electrons with molecules of hydrogen in a vast hydrogen cloud surrounding Uranus." The electroglow emission extended 200 to 400 kilometers above the Uranian cloudtops.

Brad Smith then announced the discovery of still another moon, 1986U9, about 50 kilometers in diameter and orbiting Uranus between the outer shepherd satellite and the innermost tiny moon previously seen. Smith also reported the discovery of the tenth Uranian ring, lying between the epsilon and delta rings. It would be tentatively called 1986U1R. Larry Soderblom then (at last) discussed the latest moon images from Voyager 2, dating from late January 23 and early January 24. The images from Voyager's closest approach to the major moons would not start arriving until later that afternoon. He talked about Umbriel being "the real enigma of the system so far," with its extremely dark color and lack of any visible features. Titania, he said, showed ridgelike features. Oberon had craters filled with dark material. And on its horizon, he pointed out, was a tiny pimple that was actually a huge mountain. The press contingent gasped as it saw the image.

Concluded Ed Stone: "As you can see, we have had some surprises."

Norm Ness's tilted magnetic field was the focus of most of the questions. Reporters kept pestering Ness about north versus south, and Ness and the others on the dais kept trying to explain it. Uranus was like Earth: the north magnetic pole was in the same hemisphere as the south rotational pole, and vice versa. The reporters didn't get it. A widespread and somewhat embarrassing ignorance had been exposed. Practically nobody knew that Earth's north magnetic pole is really a south magnetic pole. Now Jupiter's and Saturn's north magnetic poles were indeed north magnetic poles, Ness noted. But that just confused things even more.

Rudy Baum of *Chemical and Engineering News* asked why Uranus's magnetic field was so radically tilted in respect to Earth. Ness responded, "Maybe Earth isn't normal." He raised his eyebrows and smiled faintly at Baum. "That's a very, ah, *geocentric* question." Ness's statement put the entire encounter in perspective. Those were alien worlds out there. They were not like Earth at all, at all. We humans, confined to the postage-stamp-sized surface of a minor planet circling a dull main-sequence star in a fairly average galaxy, had always assumed that we were the norm, the standard, the yardstick against which the rest of the cosmos was to be measured. We were not. Perhaps Earth wasn't normal. Perhaps bizarre Uranus, with its rotational poles askew and its magnetic fields radically tilted, with its deep blue atmosphere of hydrogen and helium and methane and acetylene, with its cloud of hydrogen and its electroglow, with its girdle of coal-black rings and strange little moons—maybe *Uranus* was normal.

At 2:26 p.m. the first picture of the Miranda closest-approach mosaic began flickering across the monitors in the press room and throughout the rest of the lab. The picture was extraordinary. A huge notch seemed to be cut out of Miranda. People talked excitedly. Writer and astronomical artist Jon Lomberg was walking around with a brilliant smile on his face. Another image of Miranda flashed up on the screen. Gasps erupted in the press area.

"A myriad of swirling patterns, intersecting and transecting one another," said Larry Soderblom, who was talking on the JPL TV channel, and visible on the screen of a second monitor. "They might be fault patterns of some kind, the way they turn. Turning corners in such smooth bends is remarkable." The "Von Karman imaging team" also swung into action. "Those look like butterscotch swirls," said one writer. "It resembles some parts of Ganymede," added someone else. A few minutes later still another image from the Miranda mosaic came up. "Doesn't that look like Phobos, the Martian moon?" said another reporter.

"Terrain after terrain after terrain," said Soderblom, as he gazed in wonder at the new Miranda images. "Variety after variety. This is incredible. For a body this small to have this much variety is simply incredible. Some very complex process of geology has gone on here." He continued trying to explain the terrain, and someone in the press room coined a new word to describe the instant science being done by Soderblom and the Von Karman imaging team: "swag-ing," or "scientific wild-ass guessing."

The image motion compensation (IMC) technique had worked. The spacecraft had swung around as the camera shutter was open for each exposure. With Voyager moving at 79,000 kilometers per hour and passing Miranda at a distance of less than 29,000 kilometers, IMC was essential to get Miranda images with resolution of less than a kilometer. The work by the spacecraft team, by Candy Hansen and the imaging team, by Bob Cesarone and the navigators, and especially by Bob Brooks and the sequence engineers had paid off with images beyond even Larry Soderblom's wildest hopes.

"Voyager really has threaded the needle," he exclaimed. "We couldn't hope for this to be better."

Hansen had done her share of work under circumstances more stressful than most of the Voyager people knew. She was pregnant. Few people on the project had known about her condition, and Hansen wanted it that way. "I just didn't want people to get all worried and upset about me," she said. "I was okay." So she had told Brad Smith and Larry Soderblom, and practically no one else.

"Okay" wasn't an entirely accurate assessment: Candy Hansen had a problem pregnancy. "I have a real problem with high blood pressure," she said several months after the encounter. "And my doctor was not at all happy about me working during the flyby." Hansen was naturally concerned about the health of the unborn child, but anxious to stay with the flyby as long as she could. She and her doctor worked out a medically acceptable compromise. Right after the flyby Hansen had progressively cut down her hours of work, giving herself time to rest and keeping her blood pressure low. Her infant daughter was eventually born two months premature and in precarious health. The baby, though, was as tough as her mother, and slowly gained weight and strength in the months following.

By 5:30 p.m. the press room was winding down. More and more desks lay abandoned, scattered about with paper, headphones, empty plastic coffee cups, and overflowing ashtrays. The TV monitors never rested, though. The images continued arriving. In Building 264 a tired Bill McLaughlin philosophized. "I think that with this encounter we had two flybys of the Uranian system," he said. McLaughlin was not being literal, of course, but trying to explain the somewhat disjointed nature of this particular encounter. "We had one yesterday, the real

197

one. That was the one where we wanted to see that the spacecraft was functioning and didn't do anything awful, at least from my point of view. Everything went just beautifully.

"And there was one real cliffhanger, too. We had a cycle error early in the morning. A cycle error is what happens when the AACS computer in Voyager 2 gets too busy. The AACS essentially says, 'Master, you have given me too many tasks, I can't do them all.' So it doesn't do something. Usually it's very trivial stuff, but what *could* happen if you got too many cycle errors is what's called an FCP swap. And an FCP swap"—McLaughlin paused and dropped his voice dramatically—"is . . . *bad*. It's kiss it off, it's dead city. You don't get *anything*. Now, that wasn't very likely. But we monitored it closely all day. And it went very well indeed. We all sat around here about eight p.m. last night and felt very relieved. The harvest had been reaped, we were reasonably certain on this 'first pass' through the Uranian system, and now the question is, the quality of the harvest.

"And we made our 'second pass' through the system today, when the data stored on the tape recorder from yesterday began coming back. And it turned out the quality of the harvest was excellent!"

The temporary outage at DSN antenna 43 in Australia, which had wiped out the picture of moon 1985U1, was actually a minor thing, said Donna Wolff. DSN had performed absolutely magnificently. "The outage was just bad luck," she added. "We're gonna make it up. We'll get the picture of the rock back from the tape recorder." For Wolff, the highlight of the day had been the receipt of the Miranda images. "I was really excited by those closeups, when they came in. We all worked so hard to get those."

"Yeah," McLaughlin added, "Miranda was in some way the pivot of what we tried to do.

198

"And let me say this for the record," he continued. "The flight team on this encounter is the strongest one I've ever been associated with. The people are just amazing. Whenever we had a problem, somebody could always run up and they'd have the answer and bang! It'd be solved.

"This has been a mission of superlatives. And it's so nice to get it safely tucked away. Now it's there for analysis, and civilization can add another jewel to the crown. Someday the NASA Special Publications will come out, and your book will come out, and we will begin incorporating all this into the way we view the world. It's a good feeling. It emboldens you to go out and try it again."

The sky was covered with clouds and dinnertime was approaching. Dick Laeser was sitting on a stone bench in front of Von Karman. The dark hollows under his eyes spoke volumes; so did the pleasure in his voice. "This is the stuff that counts, the payoff!" he said. "It's a combination of exhaustion . . . and I probably look like I'm playing the roll. And I've just gotten over a real high after seeing the Miranda mosaic. God! I was jumping all over the place. That was the stuff I was really looking forward to. All the stuff we worked so hard on, it came in great."

University of Hawaii astronomer David Morrison walked past as we were talking. "Congratulations and thank you!" he shouted to Laeser. "Miranda couldn't be better!"

"Isn't it great?"

"It's fantastic!!" Morrison replied as he walked past. He was practically floating above the concrete.

"It all worked great," Laeser continued. "I have to pay the project members their proper compliments. I hope they can hang in there and operate close to the level they've been operating at for just a few more days.

"You know what? There's *nothing* that didn't work."

Up in "Disneyland," Bob Brooks leaned back in his chair, a relieved smile on his face. "I'm happy as hell. And still a little nervous. But seeing pictures like Miranda —oh, man, that makes it all worth it. It was worth all the work and sweat and bullshit and anxiety.

"I tried to keep busy with things, and looking at the images as they came in, so I could keep out of my mind the fact that the load that was running was my load. But my real fear was during occultation of the spacecraft by the planet. What if something went wrong while it was out of sight? Like the scan-platform thing. And all that fear started welling up from inside.

"But it sure does feel good now, doesn't it?"

At the press conference on Sunday, January 26, Larry Soderblom struggled to find words to describe the Miranda pictures. "If you can imagine taking all the bizarre geological formations found on other objects in the solar system, and putting them on one object, you've got it here," he said, as image after image flashed onto the screen at the front of the auditorium. He spoke of "stacked pancakes—or better yet, crepes," referring to the mysterious grooved ovals on the Mirandan surface. He also called them "racetracks" and "circi maximi." One journalist later speculated—tongue firmly in cheek —that the formations were really gargantuan debris piles left by an alien methane-ice-mining operation.

The moons of Uranus had once been points of light on photographic plates. Now they were real, but still shrouded in mystery and conjecture. For all the astonishing scenes the Voyager photos might show, it was still a fact that the scientists had only seen, at most, one side of each of the moons. As Hal Masursky quipped later that day: "The other half of Umbriel probably looks just like Miranda!" Masursky could very well be correct. The unseen half of Umbriel could be home to an alien outpost, a 2-kilometer-high black monolith, and a McDonald's—and no one would know.

That afternoon, Peter Doms sat in his office and smiled a smile of relief and happiness. "The images of Miranda were just . . . *outrageous.* That was one of the things that made all the extra work worthwhile. Another thing was watching the radio occultation data come in. That was just incredible." For Doms, who had worked with the radio science team during the Jupiter flybys, the success of Tyler's experiment was especially sweet.

Down the hall, the imaging team was having a giant party. "Outsiders" were allowed in "by invitation only"; it wasn't long before several science writers were wandering through, plastic glasses in hand. Brad Smith started the formal festivities by opening a bottle of five-year-old champagne, "the only one that escaped us at the last Saturn flyby," he said. He and Soderblom toasted the success of the Uranus encounter and tipped cups. The stuff was flat. "Oh, well, we can save the rest of this for a salad," said Smith.

The corks started popping on other champagne bottles and bouncing off the ceiling in the imaging team area. Bob Brooks had popped in for a glass of bubbly. Brad Smith asked him to stand up, and toasted him and the rest of the sequence team. Brooks was visibly embarrassed by the huzzahs, and visibly pleased as well. Other toasts were made: to Candy Hansen and Dave Bliss, the imaging team's two experiment reps; to Brad Smith—"the biggest billy goat gruff"—from Soderblom; and to Soderblom—"the little billy goat gruff"—from Smith; to Voyager 2, from science writer/astronomer Patrick Moore; to Uranus. And someone finally called for a toast "to William Herschel, for starting the whole thing."

Even during the party, the science went on. Just before the champagne was poured, an astounding image came up on the monitors. It was a ninety-six-second exposure, looking back at the rings as the light of the distant sun shone through them. The rings were backlit —and there, spread out between ring after ring, was a fine disk of tiny particles. None of the other backlit time exposures showed it. The extra-long exposure—the only one done in the entire encounter—was just enough to see the dust disk. The effect, called forward-scattering, was similar to that encountered when one is driving and the sun is shining through the windshield. Tiny dust particles on the glass that are otherwise invisible show up with blinding clarity. How far down does that disk of fine dust go? a writer asked Brad Smith. All the way to the Uranian atmosphere? "I haven't the faintest notion," Smith said, shaking his head.

Before the January 27 press conference began, Acting NASA Administrator William Graham was to make a televised thank-you to JPL. The press was slightly exasperated with the bureaucratic back-patting, but waited patiently. Halfway through his speech, the sound in Von Karman began echoing, and the picture on the giant screen began freeze-framing and then went completely out. The room erupted in raucous, sarcastic laughter and applause. A public affairs officer from NASA headquarters came back to the podium and nervously apologized. The irony was lost on no one: we can get pictures from a space probe nearly 2 billion miles away, but a Comsat link to Washington, D.C., 2,000 miles away, craps out. Frank Bristow then took over and masterfully covered the glitch. He thanked Graham on the part of JPL for his kind words, assured the press that "a full transcript of Dr. Graham's remarks will be released later in the day," and announced that the main press conference would begin in ten minutes.

The true story of the incident came out months later. The same communications satellite channel that was carrying Graham's speech, the NASA "Select" channel, was also used to monitor and transmit TV broadcasts of the space shuttle to NASA facilities. That channel was controlled by someone sitting at a console at the Johnson Space Center in Houston. Apparently the controller decided—at that very moment—that he wanted to take a look at some live shuttle-related TV transmissions. So he literally pulled the plug on the acting NASA administrator.

The press conference at 10:00 a.m. went more smoothly. Jim Warwick led off with a figure for the rotation period of Uranus. Data from the PRA on radio emissions indicated a rotation period of about 16.8 hours, plus or minus 18 minutes. Explained Warwick: "It's like determining the rate of rotation of a lawn sprinkler by noting the times the water jet hits you, instead of reading numbers off a tachometer attached to the metal shaft of the sprinkler." Warwick also thought that the PRA could track Uranian radio emissions from the planet's darkside for the next several months.

Imaging team member Andy Ingersoll announced seeing features such as cloud systems at a pressure depth of about 1 to 2 bars. He interpreted that as evidence of positive wind shears, as existed on Earth. But that meant that the poles had to be *cooler* than the equator, and the IRIS instrument clearly said they were not. The atmospheric temperatures, he said, "reflect a complex and unknown dynamic internal process" on Uranus.

Lyle Broadfoot's big announcement was the discovery of an aurora around the planet's "south" magnetic pole. That was the one 55 degrees from Uranus's north *rotational* pole—by definition, the rotational pole just above the planet's orbital plane around the sun. Groans rose from the media as they stepped again into the quagmire of north versus south on a planet that essentially rolled around the sun.

203

Len Tyler followed Broadfoot to the dais. The radio science occultation experiment had been a nearly unqualified success. They saw all nine previously known rings, he said. The particles in the beta ring were centimeter-sized and larger. But astonishingly enough, there were very few particles in the outermost epsilon ring between 6 and 13 centimeters wide. Most, said Tyler, were probably at least a meter or more wide—nearly a yard in diameter. No one had ever expected the epsilon ring to be made of such relatively large particles. Once again, the scientists had been lulled to sleep by their preconceptions and previous experience. Small moons are probably geologically inactive . . . only Saturn has rings . . . Saturn's narrow rings are made of tiny particles, so Uranus's rings must be, too. . . .

Larry Soderblom followed with pictures and comments on the moons and rings. In particular, he showed the one and only closeup of 1985U1. Again, the work of Marderness's spacecraft team had paid off. Voyager had finally returned the image of the tiny moonlet. It was about 160 by 170 kilometers, crater-pocked, with an albedo of only 5 to 10 percent. And the rings! The superring picture was astonishing. It showed all of the nine known rings, but also "many more features," said Soderblom, and a "very diffuse and sparse material filling much of the space between the rings, but filling it at a very low density."

Ed Stone summed up the reports: "I hope you are half as surprised as I am. Each day it gets better and better." Later he said, "The Uranian system is totally different from anything ever seen before. We have never, for example, seen a magnetic field which turns and twists like this one."

It was pretty apparent that the scientists, at least, were getting tired. Many of them had gotten by with very little sleep over the last several days. At one point, in answer to a question, Stone's exhaustion betrayed itself.

"After all these press conferences are over," he said, "we will all dissipate—uh, disap*pear*—to our various universities to work on the data." There were some chuckles over the slip, but it revealed some truth. Many of the people on the project were feeling ready to "dissipate." Or at least they'd like to *get* dissipated.

"We were really dodging bullets during the radio occultation experiment," said Len Tyler. It was lunch, and sunny, and he and FSO chief Pieter de Vries sat in the cafeteria patio. "I was up on the fifth floor of Building 264 talking with Australia. Between the time we got the Miranda data and we began occulting the rings, the receiver on one of the Australian radio antennas went out. Then we started losing the spacecraft lock on the second dish and our signal started dropping. We weren't using the third dish at all. Well, the second dish went out completely about thirty minutes after the end of the occultation!" Successful, yes—but by the skin of their teeth.

He sighed. "Today I'm beginning to feel human again. For a while I was just trying to get through each day and do it right. I either had a touch of the flu or I was overstressed." He smiled his slight smile. "But on Friday the 24th I had a very good time. It was fun! We got it going, we knew what we were doing, it was pretty clear that it was going to work. We made a lot of good decisions and did the right thing and got a great data set. But it was pretty stressful on either side of that!"

The radio occultation of Uranus was indeed successful. The radio beam from Voyager was bent completely around the planet as the spacecraft moved behind it. The experiment detected subtle structure in the Uranian atmosphere. Tyler's team might even be able to get a global average for the chemistry of the atmosphere. In addition, the radio occultation would theoretically allow the experimenters to measure the mass of Uranus and its major moons with extreme accuracy. "We have the mass of Uranus itself," said Tyler. "But the measurement of Miranda's mass—well, we had a problem at a station, and we don't have all the data that we should have. We will have to go back through the handwritten logs at the station to find out what happened. But the Miranda data's probably recoverable. But we lost all our opportunities for mass measurements of the other moons. So we will not be able to contribute to determination of the mass of the other major moons."

The amount of data was immense. But Tyler felt confident that "we'll have the major data reduction, the process of manipulating the data and putting it in a form in which it can be analyzed, finished in a few months. We'll be ninety percent finished in a few months. And we'll be completely finished in six to nine months. Then it's probably worthy of a year or two of thinking about, preparing for Neptune."

And the Deep Space Network? "Hey, DSN really pulled through. They did a great job. They did the best they possibly could. And it was good."

Chapter 9
ENDINGS AND RETURNS

Tuesday morning, January 28, 8:35 a.m. The last formal press conference of the Uranus encounter was scheduled for 10:00 a.m. The science operations report (SCORE) meeting had been primarily concerned with picking which scientists would report which scientific findings to the media. Now it had broken up, and most of the people had returned to their offices. About two dozen remained in the room, including SIS chief Peter Doms and Jim Warwick, principal investigator for the planetary radio astronomy experiment. They were watching one of the monitors in the conference room. It was tuned to the NASA "Select" channel and carrying a live NASA broadcast of the launch of space shuttle mission 51-L—*Challenger.* The crew included commander Dick Scobee, pilot Michael Smith, mission specialists Ellison Onizuka, Ron McNair, and Judy Resnik, and payload specialist Gregory Jarvis.

And one other. "Isn't this the one with the teacher?" someone in the room asked.

207

"Yeah, Christa McAuliffe," I answered. Doms was to my right. We were standing in front of the monitor, but not so close that the view of others was blocked. Warwick was sitting at a table behind us and to the left.

"This is great," a man standing to my left said. "They oughta launch two or three teachers a year. What a boost it would be for the program! What an inspiration!"

I looked at the man: older, graying hair, an excited smile. "And McAuliffe is such a great kid," he added.

"You know her?" I asked, surprised. I hadn't expected to find too many people connected with the shuttle in the middle of the Voyager Project.

"Oh, yes," the man replied proudly. "I was on the committee that picked her."

The countdown continued; the three main engines on the shuttle ignited. Gargantuan clamps held the straining machine to the pad until the zero count, and the solid rocket boosters, the SRBs, ignited with a rush of smoke and bright flame. With a full-throated roar, *Challenger* lifted off the pad. Medium-range cameras caught the space shuttle clearing the top of the launch pad's tower. The ship began its roll onto its back, tilted slightly, and arrowed into the blue cold sky.

Shouts and cheers rose in the room. "Go! Go!" "Awright!" "Look at that sucker go!"

I turned to Doms and remarked, "The first two minutes are the most dangerous. If something goes wrong now they're in deep yogurt." The ship trailed a beautiful white stream of smoke as it climbed for orbit. The room quieted down slightly, but in the background I could hear voices, feel the tension. All that fuel. . . .

One minute, ten seconds post-launch. *Challenger* was still clearly visible on the TV monitor, though small. It had reached nearly 15,000 meters altitude—over 47,000 feet, more than 8 miles high and about the same distance downrange from the Kennedy Space Center. The chatter between the space shuttle and Ground Control at Houston came clearly through the monitor. *"Challenger,* go for throttle up." The shuttle was now moving at a velocity of 1,800 feet per second, twice the speed of sound.

"Roger, go at throttle up," came Dick Scobee's reply at seventy-two seconds post-launch. A second later, unheard by the watching millions, Michael Smith spoke his last recorded words:

"Uh-oh."

On the television screen, *Challenger* became an orange-white chrysanthemum. A tower of flame streaked out of the top. For three heartbeats I wondered if the SRBs had burned out and were now being jettisoned. But I'd watched launches before; it was much too early for SRB ejection. The solids came careening out of the firebloom, still burning.

I already knew. Part of me knew at the moment of the chrysanthemum. "Oh, fuck," I said out loud. "Shit. Shit. It's blown up. The fucking shuttle's blown up." I turned to Doms. "It blew up," I said again. Doms said nothing. He *knew.*

Pieces of shuttle were flying out of the fireball, trailing wisps of smoke. One of them, unknown to us at the time, was the crew cabin, blown free from the rest of the vehicle by the explosion. The cabin and its seven occupants—all almost certainly still alive and at least three of them still conscious—kept lofting into the heavens. But no rocket exhaust powered it into orbit now. Gravity ruled. Twenty-five seconds after the explosion it reached an altitude of 65,000 feet and then began its 12-mile freefall to the Atlantic Ocean. Two minutes and forty-five seconds later, at a speed of 207 miles per hour, it smashed into the surface of the sea.

The room was incredibly quiet. It was the quiet of a mortuary I remembered from my childhood. It was the quiet of a sudden death, the quiet of death witnessed live-on-TV. It was the quiet of death not yet believed.

I began backing away from the TV screen. Behind

209

me, Jim Warwick said, "What's going on?" I looked around. Warwick was sitting at the table, funny fishing hat on his head, dressed in sky-blue sweatpants and a white pullover. He was smiling, but it was a puzzled, anxious smile. "What's the matter? Is there something wrong?"

"It blew up, Jim," I said him. "The shuttle just blew up. They're all dead."

I looked back at the monitor. The bloom began to dissipate; tiny fragments trailing smoke rained down into the ocean. The rain seemed to go on forever. I walked away from the screen. Not until later did I realize that the man to my left had already disappeared; left the room. The man who helped pick McAuliffe for the crew.

As I rounded the table I noticed Warwick. He was slumped over the table, head in his arms, shoulders shaking. I felt as if I were looking at everything through a thick pane of clear glass. I could hear sounds, voices, expressions of horror, dismay, but they were somehow muted. Belatedly I realized that the sound was sobbing. Warwick was crying, uncontrollably.

Much later, I realized that Warwick's open grief had put everything in perspective. Everything. At that moment the Voyager 2 spacecraft was sailing out of the solar system at more than 70,000 kilometers per hour, headed for a rendezvous with Neptune in August 1989. The spacecraft and its human handlers had just pulled off an incredible scientific feat, unprecedented in the history of the human race. Jim Warwick had played a key role in that triumph. New knowledge of the universe is beyond price. More precious still is human life. The triumph had turned to ashes.

I tried to console Warwick. He seemed not to notice. "I have to go," I said out loud. "I have to get to the press room, Jim. I can't stay here." I left the room and dashed down three flights of stairs to the first floor, leaping two and three steps at a time. My curses echoed in the stairwell. I ran into the hallway and out the front doors of Building 264; then dashed past two of the press trailers, across the patio and its fountain, its green plants and shrubs, up the steps, and into Von Karman Auditorium.

The press area was a chaotic madhouse. Phones were ringing like crazy. The ones not ringing were already in use. Journalists were calling in stories, answering questions from editors. I grabbed my chair, sat down, and pulled out my list of phone numbers. It was time to work . . . or go crazy. The radio station in Seattle I had done Voyager reports for the week before would want live reports. So would my local newspaper. On the four TV monitors I could see (two to my right, two to my left) were two scenes: a crescent image of Uranus from Voyager 2, and an orange-white chrysanthemum. It bloomed again. And again. And again. And again.

"Christ, that's sick," a print journalist said. "Why don't they stop showing that."

Hours after the shuttle explosion, the mood in the press area was still one of stunned sadness. Everyone looked *bruised*, as if someone had kicked him in the face. But there was also an atmosphere of professionalism. There was work to be done, and people were doing it. Voyager was on hold; reporters were calling their radio stations and newspapers and filing reports on the reaction of JPL scientists to the disaster. But the work was done with aching hearts. This particular group of reporters and journalists was a special one. They were as objective as possible in their work, especially since their beat was science and technology. Objectivity and accuracy were paramount in that line of reportage. But at the same time they were a tiny, tight band of colleagues with a fierce commitment to the space program.

211

The impact of the *Challenger* disaster was especially hard. There was disbelief, horror, great anger, sadness. And a lot of reddened eyes.

The "Von Karman imaging team" was gone, replaced by a press-room-sized group of reporters trying to figure out for themselves what had gone wrong. People clustered around different TV monitors, watching the various taped replays of the explosion. For long minutes, all that was visible on the monitors was a scene of an empty sea—the splashdown point east of the launch site, where an attempted recovery operation was going on. There were only tiny fragments of *Challenger* visible: almost nothing to recover. Network camera crews walked through the press area, filming the reporters watching the monitors. It was a bizarre replay of a similar scene a week earlier, when the press area had first officially opened. Everyone studiously ignored the cameras and kept watching, occasionally talking. Free-lance writer John Graham told a strange story. He had been on the San Diego Freeway, driving in to JPL, when he heard the awful news on his car radio. "At that moment," he said, *"all the cars on the freeway slowed down at once."*

The press scrambled to get information on the disaster, but NASA wasn't cooperating. Within minutes of the explosion the word had gone out from Space Agency headquarters: "No one talks to the press. Keep your mouths shut. Period." The men and women of JPL were for the most part quite upset about the directive, but almost everyone clammed up. The media were left with nothing to report but rumors, scraps of information passed from person to person, and perhaps a few whispered conversations over the phone. NASA's public relations handling of the *Challenger* disaster served only to sour a twenty-five-year history of friendly media relations.

Charlie Kohlhase was in his office, like everyone

else watching the grim scenes on the TV monitors. NASA had already spread the word that no one was to talk to the press about the explosion, or attempt to offer any comments on either its cause or its effects on the space program. Kohlhase talked anyway, but admittedly had little concrete to say. "No one in the Voyager Project has any firm idea at this point of what went wrong," he said. What speculation there was centered on the space shuttle's main engines. "If a turbine blade fractured in a main engine, it could easily cause them to explode. But that is total speculation," he added. "We don't know any more than anyone else." Kohlhase's speculation turned out to be wrong. It was a solid rocket booster, an SRB, and not a main engine that had malfunctioned and caused the explosion.

Later in the afternoon, Hal Masurky explained the cancellation of the day's press conference from the scientists' point of view. "No one was willing to do the press conference after that," he said in a quick phone call. For Masursky in particular, the death of the seven astronauts was especially painful. He had trained some of the Apollo astronauts in geology, so they could do good science on the moon missions. And while he didn't know many of the new breed of shuttle astronauts, "all of them, all the astronauts, are fine, fine people. They are the best."

The next morning, during a special press conference, NASA officials at the Johnson Space Center in Houston were asked if the *Challenger* disaster meant they would officially cancel or postpone the planned May shuttle launches of the Galileo Jupiter probe, and the Ulysses under-the-sun spacecraft. The officials said no, they were not canceling those launches. Despite the denial, most of the journalists at JPL agreed that the space shuttle would not be ready to fly again in time to

213

meet the deadlines for those two launches. At least four major unmanned space projects, in fact, were in danger of long postponement:

- Ulysses, the under-the-solar-pole mission—May 1986.
- Galileo, the new mission to Jupiter—May 1986.
- The Hubble Space Telescope—October 1986.
- Magellan, a new probe to orbit Venus—April 1988.

Ulysses and Galileo would almost certainly be postponed at least thirteen months. The next possible time to launch them was June 1987. The Space Telescope would also probably be postponed, but no one knew for how long. Unlike Galileo and Ulysses, the ST had no specific launch window. However, it would almost certainly not be able to provide the Voyager Project with images of Neptune before April 1987. That was the cutoff date for final selection of Voyager's Neptune flyby trajectory. Magellan might be postponed if, when the shuttle schedule was started again, it received lower priority than other projects. The Department of Defense was already making it clear that its payloads would have priority on the three remaining space shuttles. Next, everyone was sure, would be commercial missions. They made NASA some money. At the bottom of the totem pole: scientific payloads.

The media speculation turned out to be mostly correct. The Galileo and Ulysses shuttle launches were indeed canceled, within weeks of the original denial. The Space Telescope was to be one of the first launches of the shuttle after it was back in service. That would probably not be until mid-1988 at the earliest. The replacement for *Challenger*, which would take six years to build and launch, would be based at Vandenberg Air Force Base in California for the nearly exclusive use of the military. One surprising move, however, was the decision by the president that NASA would begin phas-

214

ing out launching of commercial satellites on the shuttle. That would open the door for the development of privately owned space-launch companies.

Later on the morning of January 29, Von Karman Auditorium filled up for the final Voyager press conference. It began with a short and somber opening statement by JPL director Lew Allen. Said Allen, "There will be inevitable delays in the missions to follow. But we will proceed on the basis that we will meet our launch schedules in the coming months." But he admitted that "the loss of *Challenger* puts a major crimp in that plan." And despite the *Challenger* disaster, and the looming specter of budget cuts from the Gramm-Rudman Act, Allen declared that "NASA's firmly committed to its plan to support Voyager" for its encounter with Neptune in August 1989.

Len Tyler led off the science presentations by explaining some of the results of the radio science occultation. Among other things, he reported evidence that the Uranian atmosphere was primarily 88 percent hydrogen and 12 percent helium. It was the final nail in the coffin for the 40 percent helium theory. Lonne Lane and Larry Esposito of the PPS experiment reported on various aspects of their work. Lane discussed the photopolarimeter observations of the satellite surfaces, and Esposito concentrated on the data from the two successful ring occultations. Jeff Cuzzi of the imaging team followed with a report on the pictures of the rings. Among other things he reported the discovery of an eleventh ring, a thin, broad dust ring inside the previously known innermost 6 ring.

Larry Soderblom then stepped to the podium and led the press corps through a long but fascinating look at the five major Uranian moons. He showed preliminary maps of Oberon, Ariel, and Titania and graphs of crater counts for the moons and how they compared with counts for several other moons in the solar system, and

215

he offered possible explanations for the very dark color of the Uranian moons and rings.

Then Soderblom got to the meat of his presentation: bizarre Miranda. He presented an explanation for the creation of Miranda and the presence of the three "circi maximi" or "racetrack" ovals. According to this science-fiction-like scenario, the Miranda we see today may not be the original Miranda.

In the beginning, said Soderblom, Miranda formed from the accretion of chunks of ice and rock, gradually growing to several hundred kilometers in diameter. The ice included water ice and perhaps methane ice. The rocks were mostly silicate, with small but significant traces of heavier radioactive elements. Over time, the more massive rock components sank to the center of the moon, forming a rocky core surrounded by a thick crust of ices. However, said Soderblom, the accretion phase was not quite over. Still orbiting Uranus were other large chunks of rock and ice. One of them smashed into Miranda. Unlike the Saturnian moon Mimas, which barely survived a similar impact, Miranda was shattered. Most of the pieces stayed in orbit around Uranus, following the same path as the original moon. Eventually they reaccreted, coming together to finally form a new Miranda: a patchwork Miranda of rock and ice chunks stuck together. As the radioactive elements in the rocks decayed, they heated the surrounding ice. The melting ice welled up to the surface, beginning the formation of the racetrack formations.

Ed Stone then stepped to the podium. Fred Scarf had already left, so Stone played his "Sounds of Uranus" tape for the media. There were three separate sections. The first sounded like whales singing, the second like the *Twilight Zone* theme, and the third like nothing anyone had heard before.

Stone then summarized the encounter. "Here are some of the questions we were asking last week, when we first met here," he said, "and some of the answers.

"Does Uranus have a magnetic field? Yes, and it's strong and has a major tilt, larger than any other in the solar system.

"What is the rotation period of Uranus? It now looks to be about seventeen hours.

"Is the atmosphere composed of forty percent helium? No.

"What are weather patterns like on Uranus? Not too strange, or all that different from Earth—but we just plain don't understand how it works.

"We have discovered a new phenomenon called electroglow.

"The ring system—we've found new rings, ringlets, structure in the rings, diffuse material within the ring plane, two ring shepherd moons, and that the rings are made of *big* particles.

"We've found at least ten new satellites.

"We know that the major moons are about half ice and rock, and are very active and unusual."

On Monday, February 3, ten days after the flyby, Lonne Lane was still deep into Uranus science. "The photopolarimeter is performing well," he said. "And we have some star calibrations coming up about a week from now." These major, long-range star calibrations were post-occultation measurements of Sigma Sagittarius and Beta Persei which would be compared with the actual occultation data.

"We are also beginning to look at stars for the Neptune occultations," Lane added. "There are five or six candidates, and we want to look at as many of them as possible while we still have time to think about them. That'll happen in the next couple of months."

Other than that, said Lane, he and his colleagues still had to go back and find all the holes in the data from the occultations and the other PPS observations. "We have to go for completeness. Of the data supposedly transmitted by the spacecraft, what percentage do we really have? Are there areas that we must get replayed? Can we find the ground tapes and replay them? All that will take the better part of a month and a half."

Voyager 2 had begun its epic journey in 1977. It would fly past Neptune in 1989, nearly twelve years to the day since its launch. In early 1986, following the Uranus encounter, it was already the most successful space probe ever built by human beings, if not the longest-lived. Many of its builders and directors had been with the project since its inception, others since the spacecraft's launch. Some would stay on for the Neptune encounter. Others were already planning on moving on.

Bob Brooks was quite certain about where he'd be. He was leaving Voyager, and relatively soon. "Yeah, I'll be going to the Mars Observer Project," he reported. The MO Project would put a spacecraft in orbit around Mars in the late 1980s or early 1990s. The Observer would monitor the Red Planet's weather, and carefully examine the Martian surface for different minerals and for signs of underground water. Brooks would be finishing up some work for Voyager over the next several months, and would then eventually move to the Mars Observer Project to work his programming wizardry.

Charlie Kohlhase, too, was looking for something new. It seemed time for him, he thought, to move on. In particular, he was very interested in Cassini, an unmanned mission to orbit Saturn and drop a probe onto its bizarre moon Titan. However, the position he wanted—science and mission design manager—wouldn't be available for three years. Kohlhase's second choice was a planned probe to an asteroid and a comet in the early 1990s, the so-called CRAF mission, Comet Rendezvous/Asteroid Flyby. And, of course, he hoped to see some nice pocket money from the still-selling Wilderness Survival computer game.

Dick Laeser, on the other hand, planned to stay. "Hey, I'm not going to miss out on the rest of it," he said. Ed Stone, the chief scientist, also fully expected to be on hand in August 1989 for Neptune.

Bill McLaughlin refused to be totally pinned down. "You never know what new or interesting challenge may pop up," he said one afternoon. "But as far as I know *now*, I plan on being here for Neptune."

Donna Wolff was more definite than her boss. "Yes. I will be involved with it."

The space gypsies, the journalists, would be back too. As Carl Sagan had said at one point in the encounter, "It isn't often that one knows exactly where one will be at a particular moment in the future." The space journalists knew where they would be the week of August 20, 1989. The "Von Karman imaging team" would meet again, this time to examine the latest and greatest images of Neptune and its mysterious giant moon Triton.

Voyager 2 coasted out from the sun, leaving Uranus behind. Would a probe ever return there? NASA associate administrator Burt Edelson had predicted, right after the encounter, that it would be at least two hundred years before any space probe returned to Uranus. At the January 29 press conference, Larry Soderblom had politely disagreed. "I hope it's not two hundred years," he said. "I'd look to an ion propulsion system for a space probe to get us back earlier than that. I think there are near-term possibilities for a return, surely within a few tens of years."

Voyager 2's mission of exploration was far from over. Forty-two months and another 1.6 billion kilometers away lay Neptune. And Neptune, said Bill McLaughlin, would be as exciting as the Uranus flyby had been, and maybe even more. "Neptune itself is one of the strangest planets in the solar system. It probably has an internal energy source like Jupiter and Saturn, and now we've found a ring system. A weird ring system. It may be just an arc, a part of a ring. Neptune may be the grand finale. And Triton, its giant moon, is about the size of the planet Mercury! And we go by Triton right after Neptune. So we have Neptune, its ring, and Triton."

Nearly six months after Voyager 2's flyby of Uranus, the July 4, 1986, issue of *Science* magazine carried the first detailed reports of the spacecraft's discoveries. In early August, a few weeks after the articles appeared, the Voyager principal investigators gathered at JPL for a day-long Science Steering Group (SSG) meeting. It centered mostly on the 1989 Neptune encounter, but people were still talking about Uranus.

Chief scientist Ed Stone remarked on how the findings reported in *Science* differed little from the "instant science" reports the Voyager scientists had made at the daily press briefings during the week of near encounter. "It's really quite interesting how well the investigators managed to get the first-order answers out during the encounter," he said. "A few important things have been found out since then, but many of the things concluded during the encounter have been more carefully quantified, not qualitatively changed."

Stone felt that the most startling—and, at times, puzzling—findings by Voyager 2 centered on Uranus's magnetic field and associated magnetosphere; its rings; its moons, especially Miranda; and the weather patterns in the planet's atmosphere.

"That tilted, offset magnetic field is a very important discovery," Stone commented. "It affects not only our understanding of the interior of the planet, but also provides us with a magnetosphere where the flow of material through the magnetic field is different from anything seen before."

At the "surface" of the planet, a location defined

as 26,500 kilometers from Uranus's center, the magnetic field is 0.33 to 1.8 times the strength of Earth's magnetic field. But the first real surprise for Norm Ness and his colleagues was the field's extreme tilt: 60 degrees (not the 55 degrees first reported in the press conferences) from Uranus's axis of rotation. Earth's magnetic field, by comparison, is tilted about 11.4 degrees from the axis of rotation.

Even more surprisingly, the center of the magnetic field is offset from the center of the planet. If Uranus's magnetic field were caused by some gargantuan bar magnet deep in the planet (which it is not), the centerpoint of that bar magnet would lie 8,530 kilometers from the center of Uranus. "This is the largest such offset in the solar system, by a factor of four or five," Norm Ness later said in a telephone conversation.

As for "north" versus "south" magnetic poles and rotational poles, Ness gamely tried to resolve the confusion. "Physicists define a north *rotational* pole as the pole that has a positive angle of rotation," said Ness. A north *magnetic* pole, on the other hand, is the magnetic pole from which the magnetic lines of force emanate. The *south* magnetic pole is the pole where the lines of force come back in. With these definitions in mind, continued Ness, Earth's *south* magnetic pole is the one located near its *north* rotational pole.

And Uranus? Ness paused a moment. "Well, here we have a problem with definitions. The International Astronomical Union, the IAU, defines a north rotational pole as the rotational pole that lies *above the planet's orbital plane*. We physicists don't like that definition. While the IAU calls Uranus's dayside rotational pole its south pole, we consider it the planet's north rotational pole." What Ness and his colleagues found, using physics definitions of rotational and magnetic poles, is that Uranus's north *magnetic* pole lies in the same hemisphere as the planet's north *rotational* pole.

The high tilt, plus the huge offset from Uranus's

221

center, means that the Uranian north magnetic pole lies about 15.2 degrees from the planet's equator. Its south magnetic pole (which is in the darkside hemisphere of Uranus, the same hemisphere as Ness's south rotational pole) is 44.2 degrees from the planet's equator. If Earth's magnetic field were tilted and offset the way Uranus's is, our south magnetic pole would not be somewhere near Bathurst Island in the frozen Arctic, but in the Pacific Ocean about 250 kilometers south of Acapulco. The north magnetic field would not be just offshore of Anarctica's Piner Bay, but halfway between New Zealand and Chile.

The magnetic field has a rotation period of 17.29 hours, plus or minus 6 minutes, which is presumably the rotation period of Uranus's interior, where the magnetic field originates. It adds up to the astonishing image of the Uranian magnetic field and its associated magnetosphere and magnetic tail wiggling and wagging in space every seventeen hours like jets of water from a spinning lawn sprinkler. Some researchers think the tilted field—like the tilted planet itself—suggests that Uranus was hit by an Earth-sized object early in its history. Others have suggested that the tilted field is evidence that it is flipping its polarity, magnetic south to north and magnetic north to south. Earth's magnetic field has done this many times in the past. Is it possible Voyager 2 flew by Uranus right in the middle of its own magnetic field flip? Whether or not that is the case, the tilt, offset, and strength of the field offer clues to the mechanism that actually generates the magnetic field. The best guess, six months after the encounter, is that a huge, hot ocean of water and ammonia lies beneath the Uranian clouds and atmosphere. Currents in that ocean, presumably like similar currents in Earth's molten mantle, generate Uranus's magnetic field.

Uranus's magnetosphere has trapped within it regions of charged subatomic particles. Uranus has radiation belts, and those belts are rather powerful. The moons and rings of Uranus also lie within the planet's magnetosphere and, because of the field's large tilt, they regularly "sweep up" particles trapped in the radiation belts. That has the effect of lessening the strength of the Uranian radiation belts. It also has still-uncertain effects on the surfaces of the moons and the ring particles. It may, for example, be the cause of the darkness of the rings and of several of the moons.

Uranus also has auroras near the magnetic poles. But those auroral zones lie far from the rotation-axis poles. A darkside aurora was not seen until after Voyager 2 had flown past Uranus and looked back.

The rings of Uranus also revealed some surprises to Voyager scientists. Said Stone: "Perhaps the most interesting new thing about the rings was the discovery of a different distribution of particle sizes compared to Saturn's rings. There are a lot of large particles and much less small dust material and marble-sized material. And the material is not uniformly distributed in longitude through the rings," he added. "Those are very important data that will tell us something about the lifetime and dynamics of the rings." What Stone was implying, and other scientists were saying out loud, was that Uranus's rings may be very young, much younger than the planet itself. Such a suggestion is almost heretical. The standard theory has always held that planetary rings are as old as the planets and the solar system itself. Voyager 2's data from Uranus would seem to throw that into serious doubt, at least as far as Uranus is concerned.

Other ring discoveries were equally interesting. Voyager 2's cameras detected two new rings in addition to the nine discovered in 1977 by Jim Elliot and others. Ring 1986U1R lies between the outermost epsilon ring and the delta ring, 50,040 kilometers from the center of Uranus. It is narrow, about 1 to 2 kilometers wide, like most of the other previously known Uranian rings. Ring 1986U2R is a very broad, diffuse ring, looking somewhat like the inner D or "crepe" ring of Saturn. With a width of about 2,500 kilometers, it is totally unlike the other Uranian rings. It is the innermost known ring of Uranus, lying 37,000 to 39,500 kilometers from the planet's center. Other instruments detected evidence of still more Uranian rings. Lonne Lane's stellar occultation data from the photopolarimeter revealed the presence of hundreds of rings, ring arcs, and other ringlike features within the region of the nine major rings.

The edges of the epsilon and gamma rings are quite sharp. The outer edge of the epsilon ring, for example, goes from empty space to its full thickness in less than 40 meters. The epsilon ring is at most 150 meters thick at the outer edge. The ring itself is 22 to 93 kilometers wide. All the rings seem to have complex internal structure, much like the rings of Saturn. The eta ring, for example, has two parts to it, and the inner part may actually be a ring arc rather than a full ring. Much of the internal structure of the rings may be caused by the gravitational influence of Uranus's major moons.

Six months after the encounter, the images of the moon Miranda still stood out as the most spectacular of the flyby. "It's clear when you look at the satellites that Miranda is particularly interesting in terms of the degree and nature of geologic activity. It is certainly one of the highlights of the moons," said Stone.

Miranda is about half covered with old cratered terrain. The rest of it, however, is utterly bizarre: three large regions, somewhat oval in shape, with intricate arrays of parallel ridges and grooves. Brad Smith and the imaging team informally dubbed them "the banded ovoid," "the ridged ovoid," and "the trapezoid." The trapezoid contains within it a feature that looks like a bright V or L. Miranda also sports a huge super Grand Canyon which is part of a fault system wrapping partway around the moon.

But Miranda was not the entire show. Oberon and Umbriel were found to have heavily cratered surfaces that resembled the Jovian moon Callisto or the ancient cratered highlands of our own moon. Umbriel is almost completely covered with dark material, suggesting some ongoing process. Umbriel also sports a mysterious bright ring of some material, perhaps fresh ice. One possibility is that a large meteor or small asteroid recently hit Umbriel, exposing bright subsurface ice and in the process blanketing the moon with dark asteroidal dust.

Titania and Ariel, however, have populations and patterns of cratering that are different from those on Oberon and Umbriel. Their craters may well have been caused by impacts from debris in their own orbits. Both moons are also covered with many surface cracks. Geologists have identified them as extensional faults, caused by the expansion of the moons' surfaces. Ariel seems to be covered in places with material that has welled up from its interior.

Voyager 2 also discovered ten new, small satellites to go with the five previously known large moons. They range in size from 40 to 165 kilometers (25 to 102 miles) in diameter. Nine orbit Uranus between Miranda and the outer epsilon ring. The tenth lies between the epsilon ring and ring 1986U1R. That moon (1986U7) and moon 1986U8 may be shepherd satellites for the epsilon ring. However, no other shepherd satellites were detected in the Voyager images. All ten of the newly found moons are extremely dark in color, as dark as the rings themselves.

Finally, Uranus itself both yielded some answers and offered up new puzzles, Stone said. "Getting the rotation period was important. But our whole understanding of the transport of heat from the pole to the equator needs to be worked on." Data from Rudy Hanel's IRIS instrument and from the TV cameras, among others, revealed that Uranus has a very odd weather system. That was expected, of course: a planet whose rotational poles point at the sun continuously for forty years at a time ought to have weird weather. But Uranus's weather patterns were odd in still another way. Explained Stone: "It's clear that Uranus's equator is *not* colder than the pole, and that is a surprise. Also, the winds in the atmosphere don't seem to blow in the direction we expected, given the known temperature gradient. These are fundamental issues that have been exposed by the detailed measurements"—and for which the Voyager scientists still have no explanations.

By August 1986 some of the faces had changed on the Voyager team. Bill McLaughlin had left his position as chief of the Flight Engineering Office to lead a new JPL section, the Mission Profile and Sequencing Section. Donna Wolff had gone with him from Voyager and was also in the new section. Doug Griffith had left the mind-crushing job of Flight Operations Office chief and moved into a position in JPL's Space Flight Operations Center. Also gone was Bob Brooks, who was working for the Mars Observer Project. Brooks's old boss of the sequence team, Ray Morris, had also left; in his place was Marie Deutsch—the first female team chief in the fourteen-year history of Project Voyager.

Few significant personnel changes had taken place in the Flight Science Office, according to Peter Doms. The chief of Voyager's Science Investigation Support (SIS) team was sitting in his office looking relaxed and excited at the same time. "We've seen very few changes in the Science Office," he explained. "We've kept most of our core group. No team chiefs are leaving. Ellis Miner, Pieter de Vries, and Ed Stone are all staying—thank heavens Ed is staying! I don't think it would work without him! We've had a few of the assistant experiment representatives leave, partly because of staffing reductions, partly because some of them desired to go on to other things. But basically, we have held on to enough good people so that we're in good shape."

Doms himself planned on staying with Voyager through the Neptune encounter in 1989. However, he had also taken a second position at JPL, working as group supervisor for the Project Science Support Group, in Bill McLaughlin's section. "So far we're having a great time of it," said Doms. "The role of my group will be to provide some kind of support that the science support team here on Voyager provides, for all the upcoming projects. It's a lot of work learning the ropes and doing two jobs at once, but I enjoy it."

Meanwhile, work continued on the Voyager's 1989 Neptune encounter. Much of the preparation, Doms explained, involved training new people in FSO procedures and cleaning up all the documentation for those procedures. The really fun part was what Doms called "the brainwork. It's the application of imagination to what it is we're going to do at Neptune." Doms was grinning with anticipation. "We're starting with a clean canvas again. We're having a great time with that. We are working on new targeting strategies, for example, and on new spacecraft capabilities."

One such new capability was called nodding image motion compensation, or nodding IMC. Others called it real-time IMC. When Voyager 2 got to Neptune and its big moon Triton, the project didn't want to load Voyager's tape recorder with nothing but images. They needed to preserve some space for other data. "That means," said Doms, "sending more pictures back to Earth in real time. The spacecraft's antenna has to keep pointing toward Earth for real-time return of this data.

"So what we're doing is designing some tiny little spacecraft maneuvers. While Voyager is making its flyby of Triton, it will actually 'drift' with Triton, the cameras constantly pointing at the moon and getting a long un-blurred exposure. This will pull the antenna just a *little*

227

bit off its lineup with Earth, but not enough to break the radio contact with us here at home. Then as soon as we finish that one picture frame, the spacecraft goes back to full Earth lock. Then it will start to drift again. So you can imagine this nodding motion of the spacecraft.

"Now, for highest-resolution images of Triton we won't do that. Probably we'll use the regular image motion technique we used at Uranus, store the images on the tape recorder, and then send them back to Earth later."

Imaging Triton would not be the only major technological feat of the Neptune encounter. Just surviving the flyby of the planet itself might be a bit tricky. Voyager had discovered a huge extended cloud of hydrogen surrounding Uranus, and it was possible Neptune might have the same thing. When project scientists used Uranus-like models of an extended hydrogen atmosphere for Neptune, they discovered that Voyager might just wind up flying through a hydrogen atmosphere. "Now, I'm talking about a very upper atmosphere, mind you," Doms explained, "but there might be enough drag to, say, slow Voyager down a bit, perhaps challenge the attitude-control thrusters, possibly even cause some electrical arcing in the instruments.

"The big joke around here is that we have to get a model of Voyager and do a wind-tunnel test!"

"Naw, we won't need any wind-tunnel tests," laughed Dick Laeser. One floor below Peter Doms's office, the Voyager project manager was delightedly trying out what he jokingly called his "new toy," a Macintosh personal computer. He finally—reluctantly, it seemed—tore himself away from his computer's mouse to talk about the past and future of Voyager 2.

"Well, I'm gonna see it through!" he said. "There

228

has been one attempt to get me to transfer to another area, which I have rebuffed. I mean, when one has the opportunity to have fun and do neat stuff and make good money doing it, you don't wanna turn that down."

Earlier in the day, Laeser had told the SSG meeting that Voyager's funding was "precarious" and that they would have to mount a "vigilant defense" against "torpedos which are sometimes unknowingly aimed at us by our friends at NASA headquarters." Now he backpedaled a bit on the precariousness of the situation. "It's all a consequence of the shuttle fallout. There isn't anyone in Washington, D.C., who thinks we shouldn't have what we need to get our job done. What I worry about are second-order effects, if you will. But there are so many of them you have to have eyes in the back of your head and stay awake at night."

Despite the *Challenger* tragedy and the subsequent disarray in the U.S. space program, Laeser felt that morale was high among the Voyager people. He was amazed at how quickly people wanted to get on to Neptune. "Hey, they're chomping at the bit," he joked. "But seriously, compared to other places in the lab or NASA, we are in great shape. Voyager is a very desirable place to be. We're doing something constructive and not going through what-if exercises or—worse—sitting on our thumbs. That awareness has helped us a lot with people who were tired. They looked around and saw that this really was the best place to be."

Laeser also talked a bit about the awards ceremony scheduled for September 1986. New NASA Administrator James Fletcher was to come out to JPL and give various citations to people on the Voyager Project for a job well done at Uranus. "Yeah, Fletcher's gonna sign the citations and show up in person to pin the medals," said Laeser. "I've been told he's already got a speechwriter working on it. It'll be a big event. They're going to do it on blue carpet out on the mall, where the foun-

229

tains are. There'll be a band." Laeser paused and smiled a very sly smile. "But, you know, I just couldn't convince them to have a skydiver deliver *my* medal." He started laughing. "I asked for a naked skydiver."

"Neptune will be a *great* encounter," exclaimed Candy Hansen, sitting in her crowded office in the imaging team's area. "Unlike Uranus, we expect to image a lot of activity in the Neptunian atmosphere. The light levels will be very low, of course, but we are already planning what to do to pick up subtle details. And Triton! If we can keep our miss distance to thirty thousand kilometers, the images will be great."

Like Dick Laeser, Hansen planned on being around for Neptune. "I mean, it's hard to imagine *not* being a part of this. However, what I would like to do during the three-year cruise is participate quarter-time or half-time in something else. I plan on keeping my eyes open to see what comes along. Maybe I'll go back to school," she mused. "I've thought about that, too.

"A lot depends on how things go with Christina." Nearly five months after her daughter's birth, the infant was still in the hospital. Hansen's voice dropped a bit. "That's kind of scary, you know. Babies as small as she was are given only a fifty-fifty chance of survival. I go to the hospital and visit every night. . . . She's been on the brink for four-and-a-half months now. . . ."

Bob Brooks still occupied his old space in the Voyager sequencing area, but only because his new office in JPL's new Multimission Building was not finished. By August 1986 he had been working with the Mars Observer Project full-time for three weeks as the sequence team chief. Six months after the Uranus encounter, though, Brooks still remembered the Miranda images.

"There's no question in my mind," he exclaimed, "that that was the real show-stealer. For me personally it was the most satisfying because we busted our asses for it. And I know for the sequence team as a whole it was just the big thing. Watching the pictures coming back was just *dumbfounding*. The entire effort was worth just those pictures. I mean, Miranda's an *entirely new place*. Before Voyager these places were just tiny dots of light. Now you can look at it and say, 'That's Miranda —I *know* that's Miranda, that looks like somebody went at it with a hatchet.'"

As enthusiastic as he was about the Voyager flyby of Uranus, Brooks seemed downbeat about the near-term future of the space program. "I think it bothers people here at JPL that the *Challenger* disaster is having such a devastating effect on the unmanned effort," he said. "We have projects being canceled or outrageously delayed. Lonne Lane has pointed out that we are farther away from the Galileo encounter with Jupiter *now* than when the project first started back in the 1970s! That's sad. We had so many missions! Ulysses to the pole of the sun; Magellan to Venus; Galileo doing all that great Jupiter science; a possible Cassini mission to Saturn— who knows if that will ever get approved?

"And CRAF, the mission to a comet and asteroid— which I'm hearing may be canceled. None of us on Voyager were ever afraid that we'd lose our mission, since we knew that it was the only thing flying, and up there. NASA wasn't gonna cut that off. But it bothers people on Voyager that other projects are getting screwed. It doesn't seem fair.

"Please understand me. The manned effort has its place, it's good. But the unmanned effort is at least as important, and in some ways it's better to use robots to do things. We'll never send people to Jupiter, for example. Those powerful radiation belts mean that they'd end up looking like sizzled bacon. But you can build a

robot that can stand it." Unspoken was the fact that the
same was true of Uranus.

"Oh, I *like* my new job. I think it's fun; I enjoy it."
Bill McLaughlin, the new head of JPL's Mission Profile
and Sequencing Section, was sitting in his brand-new
corner office in a brand-new building on the JPL
grounds. The smell of fresh paint from the corridors
outside wafted in. Somewhere else in the building was
an unfinished office waiting for Bob Brooks. But Mc-
Laughlin was already comfortably settled in his new
digs. "Of course, I liked Voyager so much—it was a
tough decision to leave. But the long cruise probably
decided it for me. Basically I'd be sitting for three years
marking time. And it's hard to resist doing something
new! In this job I get my fingers in a lot of pies, in different projects and activities. I mean, we have some
artificial intelligence research going on, for example."

McLaughlin still followed the fortunes of Voyager,
in part because he was making speeches about it: the
National Air and Space Museum in early September;
Brighton, England, for the British Interplanetary Society; the Naval Postgraduate School in Monterey, California, in October. He was also writing his regular column for the British magazine *Spaceflight*, as well as a
philosophy paper that had been published in *Vistas in
Astronomy* entitled "Kantian Epistemology as an Alternative to Heroic Astronomy." He laughed. "A lovely
title!"

However, McLaughlin was mostly focused on the
future of the U.S. effort in space. As usual, he was optimistic in his outlook. "Oh, I guess we could do a
'Fortress America' thing, but I really doubt it. That's a
very low probability. I think people look now at space
as a reasonable activity—as something a nation does.
And we're gonna be doing it.

"Look at JPL's menu," McLaughlin continued. "We have quite a few projects. There's Voyager, of course, and Galileo to Jupiter, Magellan to Venus, Mars Observer, and Ulysses with the Europeans."

Nor did McLaughlin think the *Challenger* disaster and the cancellation of the shuttle-Centaur upper stage would seriously set back the U.S. space effort. He was much more optimistic than Bob Brooks. "I'd be very surprised if Galileo is delayed ten years," he confided. "Maybe five. The loss of the Centaur is serious. But we could fly Galileo with a two-stage version of Boeing's inertial upper stage, the IUS. It's really all a question of politics. Let me put it this way: if the United States government *wants* to launch Galileo in 1989, it could do it. But even if they mothball it to 1991 or 1992, Mars Observer will go in 1990. And I'd bet that if Galileo *doesn't* go in 1989, Magellan will."

"The signs of recovery are in sight," McLaughlin concluded. "And I don't think I'm being overly optimistic. As for the international space scene—well, space exploration is just starting to really *break out!*"

Charlie Kohlhase was in fine shape. His health was good; the computer game was still doing reasonably well in sales, and the IBM version was coming out; and the Mission Planning Office was rolling along with its work on Voyager's Neptune encounter and beyond. Kohlhase was uncertain where he would be in 1989, when Voyager encountered the eighth planet. The proposed Cassini mission to Saturn and the CRAF comet/asteroid rendezvous mission, both of which Kohlhase was interested in, were in serious danger of being completely canceled. For the time being, he was content staying with Project Voyager.

Also in fine shape, as of August 1986, was Voyager 2. A torque margin test done a few weeks after the

Uranus flyby showed the scan platform was working perfectly. A post-Uranus trajectory-change maneuver was not needed and so it was canceled. The spacecraft team ran a diagnostics test on Voyager 2's backup flight data subsystem computer, which had had the one-bit chip failure just before encounter. Except for the permanently flipped bit, the FDS was fine. A few of the spacecraft instruments had experienced minor glitches, but nothing serious. Besides the "nodding IMC" capability, the spacecraft team was refining the Uranus "anti-smear campaign" to a point where picture smear at Neptune from Voyager's natural wobble would be half of that at Uranus.

Neptune was waiting, and after Neptune, deep space. The Voyager Mission Planning Office was already developing several options for a Voyager Interstellar Mission or VIM. The mission options would be in their final form by mid-1987. For the most part VIM would be a "fields and particles" mission, with those instruments continuously sampling the space beyond Neptune and periodically reporting back on the strength of magnetic fields, speed and direction of the solar wind, and data on charged particles. The ultraviolet spectrometer would also play a role in the VIM. The one on Voyager 1 was already being used to examine various stars. The UVS in Voyager 2 would be set a similar task.

Another experiment would not involve anything more than Voyager's radio transmitter. JPL scientist John Anderson was using the two Voyagers and Pioneers 10 and 11 as "gravitational antennas." By carefully tracking the four spacecraft and their radio transmissions, he hoped to detect tiny changes in their trajectories. Such discrepancies in position might be caused by giant unseen objects near the outer edges of the solar system: a tenth planet, for example, or a brown dwarf star companion to the sun. Some astronomers believed such a star (which they dubbed Nemesis) might be responsible for periodic "comet showers" in the inner solar system. Such cometary bombardments, every 28 to 33 million years, would have been responsible for the extinction of the dinosaurs 65 million years ago. It was a slightly bizarre thought: using interplanetary spacecraft to learn more about the dinosaurs.

One important observation by Voyager 1 might come early in the interstellar mission. It would have another encounter, with the heliopause. That could occur as soon as the early 1990s. The heliopause is the region in space where the sun's wind of charged particles impacts the particles and magnetic fields that fill the space between the stars. Voyager 1 had already been hearing radio emissions coming from the heliopause. It would still be a few years before either spacecraft actually reached that region.

Meanwhile, the two probes would continue sending data back to Earth. Both spacecraft would probably stay alive until 2005 or 2010, barring something wretched happening to them. When power supplies from their radioisotope generators dropped so low they couldn't run the scientific instruments anymore, then their missions would be over. But until then, there was plenty on the menu.

In truth, the term "interstellar mission" was a bit misleading. The two Voyagers would likely send information back to Earth from beyond the heliopause, but the solar system's boundary extends far beyond that point. Orbiting the sun in the vast blackness, half a light-year and more distant, are giant agglomerations of ice and rock: protocomets, trillions of them, still tied to the sun by the bonds of gravity. This is called the Oort Cloud. Voyager would fall silent many centuries before it reached the realm of the protocomets.

But Voyager could reach it. And beyond. Voyager navigators Bob Cesarone and Andrey Sergeyevsky had run a careful plot of Voyager 2's path into interstellar space after the Neptune encounter. They had projected it far into the future, and taken into account the continual movements of the stars nearest the sun as they—and the sun as well—moved about the center of the Milky Way galaxy. Their purpose was to find out if Voyager would make any close encounters of other *stars*. Shortly after the Uranus encounter, Cesarone had rechecked the data and rerun the calculations for their work.

Voyager 2 would not come within a light-year of any other star besides the sun in the next 328,326 years. In 8,554 years the probe would come within 4.057 light-years of Barnard's Star. Voyager 2 would make a 3.186-light-year encounter with Proxima Centauri in 20,703 years. In 275,724 years the spacecraft would come within 3.5 light-years of Sirius, the "dog star." Voyager 2's closest stellar approach would be a relatively close 1.562 light-years to the obscure star Ross 248. That would happen 40,457 years after the 1989 Neptune encounter.

"But do you really want to know what *I* think?" Cesarone asked one morning, shortly after the Uranus encounter. "I don't think Voyager 2 will ever make it to the stars, or even the Oort Cloud." He smiled slightly. "We won't let it."

Long before Voyager 2 reaches interstellar space, someone will find it. Perhaps in a century or two, people from Earth will look up the navigational calculations of Bob Cesarone and his confreres. And out they will go, into the dark ocean of space beyond Neptune, out in ships not yet dreamed, out to find that ancient craft of history and legend.

One day, children and adults, elders and teens, will visit the Smithsonian National Air and Space Museum. They will go to see the historic machines of exploration.

And there—along with *The Spirit of St. Louis* and the X-15 and Freedom 7 and Apollo 11—there will be Voyager 2.

Home again.

JOEL DAVIS is a freelance science writer whose articles and news reports have appeared in nearly every major popular science magazine in America, including *Astronomy, OMNI, Science Digest,* and *Science News.* He has been a longtime enthusiast and supporter of the U.S. space program, and has reported on the Voyager 1 and 2 missions since 1980. His previous popular science book, *Endorphins: New Waves in Brain Chemistry,* was published in 1984. He lives in Olympia, Washington, with his wife, Marie Celestre.